Sacred Dread

Sacred
DREAD

Raïssa Maritain, the Allure of Suffering,
and the French Catholic Revival
(1905–1944)

BRENNA MOORE

University of Notre Dame Press
Notre Dame, Indiana

Manufactured in the United States of America

For quotations of the poetry of Raïssa Maritain, the author and publisher gratefully
acknowledge permission from the Cercle d'Études Jacques et Raïssa Maritain, Kolbsheim,
for *Oeuvres complètes de Jacques et Raïssa Maritain;* from *Commonweal;* and from New Directions
Publishing for Thomas Merton's translation. We also thank the former Stanbrook Abbey
Press, publisher of *Patriarch Tree/Arbre Patriarche.*

"The Prisoner," trans. Thomas Merton, from The Collected Poems of Thomas Merton,
copyright © 1977 by The Trustees of the Merton Legacy Trust.
Reprinted by permission of New Directions Publishing Corp.

Library of Congress Cataloging-in-Publication Data
Moore, Brenna.
  Sacred dread : Raïssa Maritain, the allure of suffering, and the French Catholic
revival (1905/1944) / Brenna Moore.
    pages ; cm
  Includes bibliographical references and index.
  ISBN 978-0-268-03529-7 (pbk. : alk. paper) — ISBN 0-268-03529-6 (pbk. : alk.
paper) — ISBN 978-0-268-08689-3 (e-book)
  1. Maritain, Raïssa. 2. Suffering—Religious aspects—Catholic Church. 3.
Catholic Church—France—History—20th century. 4. Authors, French—20th
century—Biography. 5. France—Intellectual life—20th
century. I. Title.
  PQ2625.A78739b Z76   2012
  282.092—dc23
                        2012037113

∞ *The paper in this book meets the guidelines for permanence and durability of the Committee
on Production Guidelines for Book Longevity of the Council on Library Resources.*

For John Seitz

CONTENTS

ACKNOWLEDGMENTS

It is a great pleasure to thank those whose generosity and care enabled this project, sharpened my thinking, and assisted me with support and encouragement every step of the way.

A project on Raïssa Maritain would not be possible without the assistance of René Mougel of the Cercle d'Études Jacques et Raïssa Maritain in Kolbsheim, France, and it is a privilege to thank M. Mougel here. Not only did he graciously guide me through the Maritain archives during my visits, but his measureless knowledge of the world of the Maritains—Raïssa in particular—was a tremendous resource he generously shared with me. I would also like to thank Noëlle Grunelius, granddaughter of the Maritains' dear friends Antoinette and Alexander Grunelius, for her thoughtful insights into this eclectic community of French thinkers.

Closer to home, Stephen Schloesser, S.J., brought my topic to life, and it is a pleasure to publicly thank him. His extraordinarily creative scholarship helped me know beyond a doubt that I wanted to learn more about the fascinating world of the *renouveau catholique*, and he showed me a way. For many years now, Steve has graciously introduced me to new resources and people, enriching my knowledge of French Catholicism immeasurably. The field is fortunate to have Steve blazing trails, and so am I.

I feel extraordinarily privileged that this book began as a dissertation at Harvard Divinity School, during a time of new and expansive thinking about religion and theology. It was a pleasure to work with a wonderful group of colleagues, friends, and faculty in the pursuit of new intellectual horizons. I am particularly grateful to my advisor, Amy Hollywood, who was the kind of mentor that a graduate student only hopes for. Her knowledge of Christianity, mysticism, women and gender, and French intellectual life sharpened my thinking inestimably, and I know many others agree with me when I say that her creative ways of studying religion inspired me to think more deeply and push myself throughout each stage of my work. Conversations with Amy always buoyed my spirits, and her kindness and sense of humor ushered me through each challenge that came my way. I am so appreciative of her early support and her continued friendship.

It is my privilege also to thank Francis Schüssler Fiorenza and Ronald Thiemann. Francis's excellent course on *la nouvelle théologie* first set me on my path by introducing me to the rich theological terrain of twentieth-century French Catholicism. Francis's advice has always been wise and generous with regard not only to this project but also to my preparation for the next stage of my professional life. Ron Thiemann has long been a deeply beloved teacher and mentor who has guided my thinking on many of the larger issues in the book, particularly around theology and culture, suffering, and European intellectuals in times of crisis. I will always remember and appreciate this. My teachers John W. O'Malley, S.J., and Robert A. Orsi both, in crucial moments, introduced me to new ways of thinking about Catholic piety and history that truly inspired me. I thank Bob especially for his tremendous commitment to the intellectual vibrancy of our field. The evening colloquia he organized at Harvard and his friendship energized my thinking as I began this project and in many ways still do. I am also grateful to Harvard's Minda de Gunzburg Center for European Studies and the Harvard Divinity School Dean's Office, whose resources made possible two research trips to France, and to the Jacques Maritain Center at Notre Dame, in particular Alice Osberger. And I (and many others) owe a debt of gratitude to Bernard Doering for his superb and prolific analyses and translations of all things Maritain. I am especially grateful to Bernard and his wife E. Jane Doering for their gracious hospitality in South Bend; I fondly remember our conversations there about Jacques and Raïssa.

Going back further, I am grateful for the very first community of scholars who introduced me to the study of religion, the wonderful religious studies department at the University of Colorado. I would like to acknowledge my mentor, Ira Chernus, whose teaching, creativity, and kindness catalyzed my earliest interest in the field.

Most recently, I have been incredibly fortunate to find an intellectual home in the theology department at Fordham University. I thank my colleagues whose terrific friendships have guided me to the ideas and resources that helped bring the book to completion: Terry Tilley, who exerted tireless leadership as our chair; Michael Lee and Natalia Imperatori Lee; Brad Hinze and Christine Firer Hinze; Ben Dunning; Telly Papanikolaou; George Demacopoulos; Maureen O'Connell; Tom Beaudoin and Martina Verba; Jim Fisher and Kristina Chew; and Elizabeth Johnson, C.S.J. Thank you also to Beth's community, the Sisters of St. Joseph in Brentwood, New York, and especially Lucy Blyskal, C.S.J., for enabling a week of solitude and writing. And I am grateful to Fordham's Ames Fund for Junior Faculty and to Deans Nancy Busch and John Harrington for their support through Fordham's Internal Funding for Faculty Research.

I am deeply indebted to my two good friends and fabulous colleagues Mara Willard and Mary Corley Dunn, both of whom read this manuscript in its entirety at very different stages and provided excellent feedback. They are so smart and generous that I can only hope they will be lifelong collaborators and friends. For the many good conversations about the issues I deal with in the book, my deep gratitude goes to Tamsin Jones Farmer, Carrie Fuller, Thomas Ryan (especially for his knowledge of Aquinas), Richard Crane and his excellent work on Jacques Maritain and Judaism, Tovis Page, Zack and Suzanne Matus, Mike and Karen Evans, Katherine Davies, and Toby Garfitt. I am grateful also to Charles Matthews and Kurtis Schaeffer and the excellent NEH Summer Seminar on Religion they hosted, which helped my thinking immeasurably. Heartfelt thanks also to Marian Ronan for her wonderful critical comments on an entire draft of the manuscript. And thank you to Christophe Perez, who helped me with French proofreading.

I thank the University of Notre Dame Press, especially Charles Van Hof, Harv Humphrey, Rebecca DeBoer, Wendy McMillen, and Elisabeth Magnus for her excellent work as copyeditor.

I am grateful for libraries and their staff near and far: the public libraries of Rockford and Grand Haven, Michigan; Thornton and Boulder,

Colorado; and Brooklyn and Hastings-on-Hudson, New York, as well as the private libraries of the Bibliothèque nationale et universitaire de Strasbourg; the Cardinal Stafford Library of the Archdiocese of Denver; and the university libraries of Harvard, Fordham, and Pratt. These institutions and the people that sustain them helped me track down documents and, most crucially, provided silence and solitude while my children were elsewhere.

On a personal note, I am endlessly grateful for the Moore, Seitz, and Palmer families. I thank my mom, Keasha Palmer, a lifelong reader, writer, and curious, passionate person who has been a role model for me in many ways. She and the wonderful Art Palmer have come to our rescue on countless occasions to help our family. I thank my dad, Tim Moore, for his sense of humor, support, generosity, and long-standing encouragement of creative and independent pathways. I am also grateful to Janel McArthur and my brother Jamie Moore for their humor, love, and friendship. Jamie inspires me so much. The love, friendship, and sense of humor of my two wonderful cousins, Emily Moore Brouillet and Sara Moore Karai, helped me immeasurably during the years I worked on this. I am grateful for the love and support from the wonderful Seitz family: Neal, Barbara, Chris, Jylene, Matt, and Anita, and their children. I thank my oldest friends, going on twenty-five years each, Francesca Owings and Kendra Kimmel. I also wish to express my gratitude to my Brooklyn mom friends: during a demanding time of life, their families bring immense joy to our own.

Deep thanks go to my daughter Tavia, who came into this world two weeks after I defended this in its dissertation form, and her brother Jonah, who arrived three years later, a month after the manuscript went to the press. It is life with these two tiny people that has given me something of a glimpse of life's ravishing intensity that these French Catholic writers describe so well. Jonah and Tavia enrich my life with the intensities of pleasure and amazement above all.

Finally, my deepest gratitude goes to John Seitz. I have benefited in every way from our shared appetites for thinking intensely together about religion, from our undergraduate days in the same classes up to the present, as we finish our first big projects and navigate life together as an academic family. This book came to life through talking with John at every single stage and learning from his precise, careful, and above all creative thinking. John has generously helped me with each chapter; the project is the fruit of our many conversations and has greatly benefited from his good editorial eye. I am privileged to keep learning from his ideas and experiences and to keep growing with him. It is with immeasurable gratitude, respect, and love that I dedicate this book to John.

Introduction

Vicarious Suffering, Its Interpretive Limits,
and Raïssa Maritain's Work

"Can there be a mystical life without death?"[1] Writing in 1931, the French Catholic intellectual Raïssa Maritain (1883–1960) named this the "question essentielle" in her private notebooks. She had raised this issue twenty-five years earlier, when she was baptized into the Catholic Church at the age of twenty-three. Even then, in 1906, she admired what she saw as Christianity's provocative way of acknowledging the reality of death and contending with human finitude and vulnerability. Describing her religious conversion, Maritain claimed that it is only when we affirm the realness of human mortality and suffering that we "discover an order more powerful than all that is human."[2] As she saw it, the ideological alternative to Catholicism in her day, scientific positivism, no longer "believes in" suffering and death, just as its advocates "no longer believe in God." She saw in the refusal to acknowledge death a sort of "strange blindness, a kind of madness" (un aveuglement étrange, une sorte de folie). But confronting finitude and suffering is no simple task, and Maritain would spend her entire intellectual career struggling to render them visible in the poetry, mysticism, theology, and philosophical aesthetics she authored.

1

Maritain was not, by any means, alone in this struggle. Upon her baptism in 1906, she entered a vast community of late nineteenth- and early twentieth-century French intellectuals who shared a fascination with Catholicism's focus on mortality and suffering. As Maritain and her fellow intellectuals puzzled over anguish and held it up as an object of analysis in their writings, they reveled in it, tapping into, deepening, and occasionally transforming the long-standing alliance in Christianity between holiness and affliction. Maritain's first mentor, Charles Péguy (1873–1914), wrote often about the power of *le suppliant* (the beggar, supplicant, imploring one) as the one "who is bent, *bowed under* misfortune, that absolute misfortune which marks the presence of force and of the gods." The *suppliant,* Péguy wrote, "whoever he may be, the beggar along the roads, the miserable blind man, and the man crushed," is the one who, despite appearances, "holds the upper hand, orders the course of the conversation, commands the situation."[3] Or consider one of Maritain's dear friends, Charles de Foucauld (1858–1916), the French priest who inspired Maritain with his solitary life as a mystic, hermit, and evangelist in the Sahara Desert. He drafted a rule for a new religious community of which he was the only member. Suffering and death were built into his "community": members must be "ready to have their heads cut off, to die of starvation and to obey him in spite of his worthlessness."[4] Or take, for instance, the writings of Maritain's younger acquaintance Simone Weil (1909–43), whose intensive reflections on what she called *malheur,* or affliction, occupied nearly all of her writings.[5] Likewise, the personalist philosopher Emmanuel Mounier (1905–50), Maritain's friend and colleague, admired Pascal for his claim that "the divine disquiet of souls, that is the only thing that counts!"[6] The writings of Léon Bloy (1846–1917), Catholic novelist and godfather to Maritain, offered the most riotously excessive paeans to pain: "*La douleur!* [Distress/sorrow/suffering!] Here is the key word! Here is the solution for every human life on earth! The springboard for all that is superior, the sieve for every merit, the infallible criterion for every moral beauty!"[7] In Bloy's theological vision, suffering and anguish are closely tied up with pleasure and joy: "It is commonly said," he wrote, "that Joy and Pain [la Joie et la Douleur] are opposites, incompatible! How can you understand that in some lofty souls, they are the same thing, assimilated with ease! . . . The joy of suffering! [La joie de souffrir!]."[8]

Indeed, the suffering-centered *imaginaire* saturates this moment in religious history, a moment also justly considered a "watershed" in the history of the Catholic Church and the golden age of French Catholicism.[9] In the years following France's Act of Separation in 1905, which enshrined laicism as a French national law and ended state funding of religion, through the Second World War, Roman Catholicism enjoyed an astounding and unanticipated resurgence in France.[10] Although the roots of the French Catholic revival can be traced to the 1880s, the early twentieth century marks the high point. It was in these years that novelists, artists, philosophers, and theologians forged the movement that became known as the *renouveau catholique*. The historian Stephen Schloesser, S.J., coined the phrase "Jazz Age Catholicism" to describe this period of incredible vitality in the church, which largely derived its energy from the creative output of the French Catholic laity. The French historian Frédéric Gugelot called the modern French attraction to Catholicism "an avant-garde cultural turn" that rejected the reigning positivist ideology and ended up "introducing new aesthetic and religious forms that offered an entirely new image of Catholicism."[11] In the revival, aesthetically powerful symbols and practices centered on *deuil* (mourning), *souffrance* (suffering), *douleur* (pain/sorrow), and *tristesse* (sadness) played a massive role in drawing these converts, atheists, and lapsed Catholics into the fold.

The central question of this book is: How did suffering and anguish achieve such a prominent presence in so many of the twentieth-century French Catholic revival works, and how can this fascination with suffering be understood?[12] I argue that one can answer this question by focusing on one prominent intellectual in this circuit, Raïssa Maritain, and making her life and writings both the central topic and the environment for inquiry into the historical and theological meanings of *souffrance* that dominate this intellectual milieu. Maritain and the world she inhabited—especially the friends, theologians, artists, and philosophers who deeply influenced her work—provide a key to understanding these discourses and practices. The themes in Maritain's works are undeniably dark, and she rarely, if ever, fully turns her attention away from the suffering of the cross, the affliction of the soul, and the Virgin Mary's sorrowful, wounded heart. In her writings, Maritain entertains an ecstatic, often vivid emphasis on death, blood, and the Crucifixion. But Maritain's life history, gender, and religious background as a Jewish convert gave her a unique perspective on these themes. *Sacred Dread* tracks the story of how Maritain made her way into—and ultimately transformed—this intellectual world and the Catholic idioms of suffering and grief. Exploring why a secular Jew would be drawn into this religious world, how this world could be remade as a result, and what would become of this suffering-saturated theology as it encountered the Holocaust, *Sacred Dread* enables a new understanding of the appeal of a radical kind of Catholic piety that curiously extended to other Jewish-born women in this cultural circuit, such as Maritain's acquaintances Simone Weil and Edith Stein.[13]

Readers have long noted this obsession with suffering in modern Catholicism's watershed moment and often see it as the most bizarre or even pathological of the movement's enduring legacies. For many in the English-speaking world in particular, French Catholic writers like Maritain and her colleagues are "irrational," their theological symbols merely a "vehicle for morbid hysteria" and "incipiently fascistic," demonstrating "sadomasochistic obsessiveness."[14] Because the roots of the revival can be traced to the late nineteenth century, we can detect alarm as early as 1872, when a writer in the *Nation* detected a "Roman Catholic revival in France" that exalted precisely those aspects of Christianity that disgusted Nietzsche: the author described the revival as "an eternal protest of weakness against strength. It is the deification, as it were, of the negative forces of mankind—a glorification of defeat, of suffering, of helplessness." The purpose of this exposé was to show "what a world of illusion France is mired in."[15]

This perception also reflects that of some theological interpreters closer to Maritain's own time. Maritain's dark preoccupations in her memoir *Les grandes amitiés* (published in two volumes in 1941 and 1944) prompted one reviewer, an Anglican minister, to suggest that she had offered an "unwitting exposure of the neurotic streak in French Catholicism," in which the "converts . . . are perpetually 'suffering' and being 'wounded.'" With confusion, sarcasm, and annoyance the reviewer complained that in Maritain's work

An inordinate amount of weeping goes on, for one reason or another reaching its climax in an illustration of "Celle qui pleure" (Notre

Dame de la Salette); and there is a perpetual recurrence of such words as "sufferings," "sadness," "grief," "anguish," "tribulation," which would evoke more sympathy if the victims were not so obviously luxuriating in their painful emotions. Possibly it was because Léon Bloy regarded the happenings at La Salette in 1846 as "the most extraordinary since the Pentecost," that for him union with God in the present life meant the "infinite distress of his heart." God moves in a mysterious way, and it is not for English Churchmen to sit in judgment on a piety so alien from their own; yet in the rarified atmosphere of these memoirs, perfumed with *la douleur* et *la souffrance* and watered by "the Gift of Tears," it is a little difficult to recognize the authentic note of the New Testament: "Rejoice in the Lord always, again I say rejoice!"[16]

This reviewer shows a certain habit of thought that is often built into an analysis of this moment in French Catholicism in general, and of Maritain in particular: the refusal to see why anyone would choose to seek out symbols and practices centered on *souffrance,* or even, as this reviewer points out, *luxuriate* in them.

Scholars have generally tended to frame the late modern French Catholic fascination with affliction within the doctrine of redemptive "vicarious suffering," which partly contributes to the widespread scholarly unease.[17] The excellent 1967 study by Richard Griffiths, *The Reactionary Revolution: The Catholic Revival in French Literature,* has exerted a significant influence on English-language scholarship. Griffiths argues that from 1870 through the end of World War I in France, vicarious suffering "assumed an importance out of all proportion to the other doctrines of the Church."[18] Revitalized in modern France, vicarious suffering has long and deep roots in Christian theology and piety, beginning with the scriptural interpretations of the death of Jesus. In 1 Peter 2:24 and Romans 3:25, Jesus's death is seen as the vicarious atonement for the sin of the entire human race. But crucially, Saint Paul says that this death is not complete: it is possible for the follower of Christ to become united with his passion—to "share in his sufferings"—and in doing so to then share in Christ's redemption and victory over sin (Rom. 8:17).[19] The doctrine of vicarious redemptive suffering takes this overarching theological claim and grounds it in Paul's statement to the Colossians, "Now I rejoice in my sufferings for your sake, and in my flesh I complete what is lacking in Christ's afflictions for the sake of his body, that is the Church" (Col. 1:24). The Christian, through his or her affliction and even death, can expiate the sins of others and participate in the salvation of all.[20]

A long-standing and orthodox part of Christian imagination, vicarious suffering moved from the margins of French Catholic piety closer to the center after the 1789 Revolution.[21] The doctrine of vicarious suffering in this more modern politicized key held that an individual's suffering could atone for the *political* sins of impious France that had begun with the revolution and had continued with the secularizing process of *laïcité*. In the nineteenth century, a range of Catholic devotional materials emphasized weeping, anguished figures framed within the doctrine vicarious redemptive suffering, also called *spiritualité victimale* or *réparation*. Here Christians were invited to suffer—spiritually, physically, mentally—on behalf of the sinners of France and to atone for their sins. One popular devotional image found in many nineteenth- and early twentieth-century pamphlets, prayers, iconography, and statuary depicted the infant Jesus ("le Petit Roi d'Amour") carrying a tiny basket of thorns and hammers, dreaming of the suffering he would endure as an adult, and summoning devotees to join him in his agony on account of a sinful, secular modern nation.[22] Other nineteenth-century devotional texts such as Antoine Blanc de Saint-Bonnet's *De la douleur* and Sylvain-Marie Giraud's *De l'esprit et de la vie de sacrifice dans l'état religieux* placed the doctrine of vicarious suffering even more prominently in the French Catholic mainstream.[23]

More recently, Richard Burton's 2002 text *Holy Tears, Holy Blood: Women, Catholicism, and the Culture of Suffering in France, 1840–1970* tracks the history and fate of the projection of vicarious suffering onto the lives of actual women in modern France. Burton identifies the doctrine's salience among dozens of French male writers, including Jacques Maritain and Léon Bloy. He argues that men like Jacques and Bloy relied upon the notion of vicarious suffering in order to reap the rewards of salvation through the painful lives of the women with whom they were close.[24] The suffering-centered theology here, according to Burton, amounted to a calculus in which an abject woman starves, weeps, bleeds, and someone else (an impious citizen, a confessor, a husband, a nation in sin) is redeemed.

Burton traces the stories of women such as Thérèse de Lisieux, Raïssa Maritain, and Simone Weil, all of whom he sees as entangled in the claustrophobic, grim fantasies of their husbands and confessors. For Burton, the theological world of *co-rédemption* encouraged French Catholic women to remain passive in the face of a steady onslaught of illnesses and disappointments that made up their deeply troubled lives.[25] With this analysis, Burton implicitly exiles these women into the ranks of the pathetic and bizarre.

Sacred Dread challenges this exile. The French Catholic fascination with suffering does raise an important set of ethical questions, which I discuss in the chapters that follow, but I argue that we need more tools to think about how these theologies and practices may have worked for people like Maritain who used them toward a range of complex ends. To be sure, the theology of vicarious suffering, a theology that insists that a disciple of Christ can suffer *for* and on *behalf of* someone else, has undoubtedly been a powerful force in modern French Catholicism. Raïssa Maritain occasionally drew on this doctrine herself. She once, for example, advised a friend devastated from the loss of her child to think of her pain as redemptive for others. She wrote to her in a letter, "God has suddenly plunged you both into the very heart of this ultimate reality: redemptive suffering [douleur rédemptrice]. And when one knows by faith the marvels he works on others with our suffering, with the substance of our crushed hearts, can one coldly refuse him?"[26] The theology of vicarious suffering undoubtedly has some crucial explanatory power in this religious world. But I have come to see that vicarious suffering on its own is too blunt an instrument to explain the complexity and malleability of *souffrance* in France's late nineteenth and early twentieth centuries. *Souffrance* and *douleur* were too unwieldy in the lives of those who engaged them to be channeled neatly into one abstract, cosmological doctrine. As the sole analytic framework, vicarious suffering can flatten the variegated ways in which symbols of affliction and grief functioned, how they changed as French culture and politics changed. My work demonstrates the risks of our tendency to write off these suffering-centered theologies as little more than examples of pathology. A closer, more patient look at these discourses humanizes the writers of the French Catholic revival like Maritain and, in the process, enhances our ability to understand the persistence of symbols of suffering and death in modern religious thought and practice—a persistence that certainly extends beyond the world of French Catholicism. Although it tends to be seen as central to the "medieval" imagination, even in modern societies, whose medical and technological advances have kept suffering and death at further abeyance, religions are animated by idioms of blood, agony, pain, and death. We need richer morphologies to think about this beyond the atavistic and pathological.

HOLY SUFFERING: THE SHAPING OF A DISCOURSE

In making sense of *souffrance*'s prominent presence in French Catholicism, *Sacred Dread* exposes a whole other network of theological, literary, and political determinants, sources that are key to understanding this moment in Christian history and Maritain. Far from a uniform repetition of received wisdom, suffering was a mobile category and trope. What shaped Catholics' idioms of affliction was less exclusively the doctrine of reparative vicarious suffering than a convergence of fin de siècle literary movements such as modernism, realism, decadence, and spiritual naturalism. These literary movements crossed currents with other forces that energized the fascination with abjection, such as the resurgence of interest in Christian mysticism in early twentieth-century France, where the annihilation of the will was understood as the surest pathway to the divine. For some writers of the *renouveau catholique* suffering became especially visible, and prominent in their reflections, as Europe descended into violence and chaos during the two world wars. Furthermore, late modern France's interest in imagination, dreams, and fantasy galvanized the widespread attraction to Christianity's most shocking, potent visual images, such as the abject Christ and weeping Virgin.

In terms of the literary fixation on *souffrance,* Charles Baudelaire (1821–67), for example, the founding figure of French modernism, reacted against some of the optimistic tendencies of romanticism and claimed that poets like himself "feel themselves irresistibly pulled towards whatever is weak, ruined, saddened, orphaned."[27] Realist author Émile Zola (1840–1902) used accounts of weakness, degeneracy, and suffering to rebel against what he saw as the optimistic naïveté of bourgeois modernity and highlighted the shadow side of secular republicanism. Prostitutes, the insane, and the sick were all graphically depicted in realist novels as a means to shock and challenge the putative optimism of modernity. Catholic authors such as Bloy and his once-friend J.-K. Huysmans linked this realism with Christian supernaturalism, claiming that the most vivid artistic representations of suffering and anguish, in their paradoxically repulsive and attractive allure, were powerful vehicles to point beyond themselves to the eternal.[28] One of the first Catholic figures to make this link was Jules Amédée Barbey d'Aurevilly (1808–89), whose popular novel *Les diaboliques* (1874) featured horrific acts of violence committed by women and instead of condemning them portrayed them as awe-inspiring and strangely powerful. Barbey d'Aurevilly's decadent reversals led Bloy to his conversion, and Bloy eventually too sought to shock the literary and Catholic middle class through the embrace of the grim underside of the modern world. Catholic decadence, modernism, and realism came together in a shared antipathy toward secular republican positivism, which was seen as overly optimistic in its assumptions about progress and human flourishing.

Maritain and many intellectuals in the late nineteenth and early twentieth centuries were deeply immersed not only in this prevalent French literary fascination with abjection but in classic Christian mystical materials. The themes of *souffrance* and especially *anéantissement* (abasement) were, in Maritain's work, often connected to the French school of spirituality, founded by Pierre de Bérulle (1575–1629), whose authors Maritain had long been reading in Paris even before her conversion.[29] The French school included mystical writers like Jean-Joseph Surin and Francis de Sales and overlapped with the doctrine of vicarious suffering and the decadent literary movement in its emphasis on suffering but had little to say about physical and emotional anguish.[30] For them, *souffrance* and *anéantissement* referred to interiorized spiritual suffering and annihilation of the will. Like the mystical tradition of the Spanish Carmelites, also beloved by many revivalists, the French school of spirituality emphasized interior debasement as a way to incorporate oneself into the inner life of the suffering Christ. Such texts encouraged readers to remake one's own interior in the image of God and to allow God to enter and alter one's self. From 1909 until she died in 1960, Raïssa Maritain committed herself to the practices promoted in these materials that could engender such transformations, engaging in the daily discipline of contemplative prayer founded on total withdrawal from sensory experience, or *recueillement*. Throughout these decades, Maritain sporadically recorded her progress in a notebook that was published posthumously as *Journal de Raïssa* (1963). The suffering recorded in these texts is Maritain at her most vivid and graphic, where she imagines herself becoming assimilated into, internalizing, the suffering Christ on the cross. Maritain's mystical notebooks left even her husband Jacques "bewildered" by their expression of pain, and Jacques's friend Thomas Merton cautioned Jacques that they would be "too searing" for American audiences to read and understand.[31] The graphic images here come from a mystical language of suffering that follows the purgation—annihilation—of the ego to make room for God in the soul. Throughout her depictions of suffering in these discourses, Maritain draws on the vivid, daring language of the literary movements she knew from her godfather but employs it metaphorically to explore her own interior processes.

Maritain's language of suffering was shaped not only by literary movements and mystical writings but also by political and historical forces. By the time she converted in 1906, she had multiple resources from experience to draw upon in thinking about agony and its meanings—beyond just the fantasies of the men around her. Born into a Jewish family in Russia in 1883, as a child Maritain had fled with her family from the Jewish pogroms, arriving in France when she was ten years old. As a young adult, Maritain, along with the rest of France, faced the reality of death in the First World War (1914–18). Nearly one and a half million men were killed in France, and the disfigured and maimed—those known as the *mutilés*—reached one million.[32] Maritain was more fortunate than many women who lost sons and husbands; Jacques was never drafted because of health issues. But by the end of the war, Maritain's three close mentors—Humbert Clérissac, Charles Péguy, and Léon Bloy—had died. Her two-year-old godson, Pieterke van der Meer de Walcheren, whom she "loved so much," died during the same month that Bloy did.

Two decades later, suffering and political violence came together again. In the mid-1930s Maritain's thoughts turned, wearily, toward the gathering darkness of anti-Semitism on France's horizon. By 1939, still a

Jew under Nazi law, Maritain, with her husband and sister, left France for North America, where she remained during the war as an exile. At this moment, along with the rest of Europe, Maritain was "sucked into politics as though with the force of a vacuum," in the famous words of Hannah Arendt.[33] Several of Maritain's friends were included in the six million massacred in the Shoah. In her wartime writings, Maritain again drew on symbols of pain, but this time to describe a "deluge of blood spread over the earth," namely "the cataclysm [that] . . . plunged Europe into Darkness [les Ténèbres] and covered the universe" when "four million Jews—and more . . . suffered death without consolation."[34] This vivid evocation drew from four decades of reflection, at the levels of practice, thought, and devotion, on suffering—even at its most graphic—and its meanings. Indeed, this training had prepared Maritain to articulate the trauma of the catastrophe *as it occurred*—an act of honesty and courage most could not or would not muster.[35] The French Catholic suffering-centered *imaginaire* must be understood against this backdrop. The bleakness of the twentieth-century European experience, especially for a Russian-Jewish Catholic woman like Maritain, had no counterpart in America. As Thomas Merton predicted, this is part of what makes modern European Catholic materials so difficult to grasp for American readers.

Yet the European descent into violence and chaos, like the doctrine of vicarious suffering, cannot entirely explain the widespread preoccupation with suffering among the French Catholics of this period. The suffering *imaginaire* attracted Maritain in the early twentieth century well before the wars, particularly through the decadent literary movement and the early modern mystics. It is crucial to see Maritain within the story of the first half of the twentieth century in Europe—its pathos and traumas but also its revitalized interest, at the turn of the century, in realism and mysticism.

In considering these diverse political, literary, and theological sources, I nonetheless aim to resist an exclusively determinist account of Maritain's thinking. As important as these political and cultural forces were, we must also leave room for the ways in which her work refuses a simple notion of cultural determination. As Michel de Certeau, Joan Wallach Scott, and others have argued, human beings are not always driven by rational calculation, nor are they fully determined by the external structures of history.[36] *Sacred Dread* identifies not only the forces that shaped Maritain's life and thought but also her own intellectual interventions, leaving room to understand the generativity of her own prayer life and writings. Like all subjects, she was a product of forces outside her control, but she also occasionally exerted creativity in ways that influenced those forces.

Furthermore, I resist an exclusive reliance on social and political historical causation because Maritain's written reflections on *souffrance* were often galvanized by intense, vivid, and occasionally graphic personal religious experiences of God, experiences that do not always map neatly on the political and social currents of the day.[37] For example, Maritain's first direct encounter with God came in 1907 when, in the midst of an illness, she dreamed she was covered in blood and awoke to a vision of two heavenly hands presenting her with the host. The dreams, visions, locutions, and direct experiences of the divine continued, sporadically, throughout her adult life. In 1933, she recalls during prayer hearing God ask her to "accept a living death," followed by a vision of Christ in which he told her, "I will espouse thee in blood. I am a bridegroom of blood. It is a terrible thing to fall into the hands of the living God."[38] Maritain's written corpus on suffering must be understood—though not exclusively—in relation to experiences of direct, immediate felt contact with the supernatural. As I explain in chapter 2, the imaginative space afforded by religious devotion cannot be fully encapsulated by the straightforward narratives of historical causation. Historical causation can elide the imaginative terrain that can exist between the forces of history and the inner life of the subject.[39] In addition to historical analysis, categories such as fantasy and devotion are useful analytic tools to help us attend to the rich terrain of ambiguity that can exist between social forces of history and the inner life of the subject.

GENDER AND JUDAISM: FEMINIZED SUFFERING AND SUFFERING JEWS

Whether in the context of the doctrine of vicarious suffering, fantasy, the world wars, mysticism, or literature, in the French Catholic revival the holiness of affliction was often, regardless of the source, communicated through symbols of femininity and Judaism. The predominance of these symbols reveals, even if only implicitly, Catholicism's capacities and limits for contending with real women and with real Jews and Judaism. Throughout her writings, Maritain engaged (sometimes resisting and at other moments contributing to) notions of feminized and/or Judaized abjection as uniquely holy and redemptive.

Many revivalists were deeply philo-Semitic, and for many of these writers, a hypostatized Jew embodied the afflicted ideal of inversion and marginalization. The symbol of the "suffering Jew" served as a powerful rejoinder to the stereotype of the wealthy Jewish capitalist, and for reasons I describe in chapters 1 and 3 it was effective in provoking a reimagining of the boundaries between Christianity and Judaism. If Nazi national socialism declared Jews to be unassimilable and unassimilating, for Maritain suffering Jews were uniquely assimilable to the agonized Catholicism she cherished. The revivalists' passionate writings reflected not only on the symbolic representation of the people of Israel in theology but also on the historical situation of persecuted Jews in the twentieth century, particularly during the Dreyfus affair (1894–1901), in the midst of the ascendancy of anti-Semitism in the 1930s and during the Shoah. Yet this symbol is one of the most obviously problematic and complicated legacies of the revival, trafficking in essentialism and stereotype, valorizing suffering instead of historicizing and analyzing it and working to eradicate it. It requires historically oppressed communities to bear the symbolic weight of human anxiety about finitude and suffering.

A similar dynamic pertained to these writers' use of femininity in the elaboration of suffering in France. The image of the suffering holy woman has a long-standing history in Christian thought, but for reasons I describe in chapter 2 it became especially prominent in late modern French Catholicism.[40] Léon Bloy, for example, described, in page after page, abject women and girls—prostitutes, impoverished widows, young girls accused of being insane—as sites of power and holiness. Paul Claudel's most famous play, *L'annonce faite à Marie* (1912), narrates the tale of a medieval French peasant woman whose life is one long journey of self-oblation: she willfully contracts leprosy and dies the death of the martyr. One of the most famous films of this period, Carl Theodor Dreyer's *La passion de Jeanne d'Arc* (1928), is a visual meditation on the last hours of Jeanne d'Arc. The film focuses almost exclusively on Jeanne's face, up close, tears streaming down, head shaved, during her trial, torture, and execution. The Virgin Mary was another important source of feminized suffering. When Maritain, along with her husband Jacques and sister Véra, dedicated herself to the Virgin Mary as her "slave" in 1909, she joined the likes of J.-K. Huysmans in devotion to the Marian apparition at the French village of La Salette. The Virgin had allegedly appeared there weeping, wearing a crown of thorns. To understand these powerful associations, *Sacred Dread* explores the Christian exegetical and theological traditions that align women with the suffering body and endow their suffering with holiness. This project also investigates how Maritain's life and work both strengthen and transform these associations.

I explore the complicated political and ethical issues involved in these associations, but I also show that the powerful, widespread symbolic associations between suffering, holiness, women, and Jews worked *for* Maritain and *through* her in a range of ways. For many in her community, including her husband, godfather, confessors, and her massive network of friends and godchildren, Raïssa Maritain herself was the embodied articulation of this abject ideal. As Jacques would write as early as 1908, Raïssa served as "an earthly intermediary" between himself and God. "*Everything*," Jacques emphasized, had come to him "through her, from her heart, from her reason, from her counsels, from her example, from her sufferings."[41] Chapters 2 and 3 explore the issue of how to read Maritain's own reflections on Jewish and female suffering against the backdrop of Jacques's and others' valorizations.

Raïssa Maritain was not unreflectively entangled within the doctrine of feminized and Judaized suffering; she was an intellectual who critically analyzed the doctrines that came her way, sometimes detaching from them and modifying them, and at other times embracing and even intensifying them. In her discipline and reflection, Maritain both absorbed and challenged the various traditions she inherited. But while I cannot see her as simply a victim caught in the web of the French Catholic male imagination, I also refuse an equally seductive exaggeration of her agency (to borrow Amanda Anderson's concept) or desire to transcend it.[42] I aim to see Maritain's attraction to and modification of feminized and Judaized suffering beyond the primary binary that tends to drive some feminist studies of Christian women, in which women either reproduce their own oppression or resist and subvert it.[43] I caution against assuming any straightforward relation between the norms and symbols of a community and the simple embodiment of or blatant resistance to those norms and symbols among the community's members. Maritain's engagement with these symbols and practices was far more complex. I see her as a conscious contributor to a narrative in which suffering was holy and redemptive, but also as one who exhibited a capacity for critique, using the resources at hand.

Raïssa Maritain understood in this way, as a situated thinker—an intellectual—has scarcely been recognized.[44] This omission is significant, considering she was one of very few women involved with the intellectual labors of the revival. The simple fact that she penetrated this exclusive club of Catholic *hommes de lettres* is noteworthy. Maritain had so many strikes against her: a woman in a male-dominated society, an immigrant whose native language was not French, and a convert from Judaism who lacked the religious *habitus* of those born into Catholicism. Her presence in that world is remarkable. Maritain's relative obscurity in the scholarly community can be explained, at least in part, by her early tendency to publish furtively and to channel, support, or reproduce the voices of others. Like many of her colleagues in this milieu, Maritain began her career translating and presenting portions of classic Christian texts in the new journals dedicated to mysticism and asceticism that proliferated in early twentieth-century France. But unlike most of her established male theological colleagues, she often did this work anonymously or under her initials "R.M." Very early in her career, she translated and presented portions of Thomas Aquinas, John of St. Thomas, and Teresa of Ávila to a community hungry for mystical texts.[45] Even when she was not translating others' texts, Maritain's voice tended to be absorbed by those of other Catholic luminaries, past and contemporary. In her early years as a scholar, for example, she researched, crafted arguments, and wrote essays that were later integrated into writings published under other names. (Her husband Jacques Maritain's first book, *La philosophie bergsonienne* [1913], and Henri Massis's essay "La vie d'Ernest Psichari" [1919] drew from her work and can be counted among these.) Her first theological work, *Le prince de ce monde* (1929), a major piece on the reality of the demonic in the world, also initially appeared under "R.M."[46] Slightly more visibly, she published in the 1920s as a coauthor with her famous husband Jacques Maritain.

It wasn't until 1931, in her late forties—twenty-five years after her conversion to Catholicism—that she published her first poem under the name "Raïssa Maritain." This elegiac lamentation poem (entitled "La couronne d'épines" [The Crown of Thorns]) was broadly appreciated, and Maritain's reputation as a writer grew in her own right. After this point, she became less intellectually deferential, which helped her become a widely praised writer and lecturer. Her productivity was also key to her reach: she published several books of poetry and multiple theological texts on contemplative prayer, intellectual life, mysticism, and aesthetics. As a Jewish convert, she wrote on the relationship between Judaism and Christianity. She lectured widely on aesthetics and religious experience in France and Latin America. Such successes invited backlash. Maritain was the object of Étienne Gilson's sardonic critiques; he described her as "l'ange courroucé" (the irate angel) and worried that she had driven a wedge between Jacques and his fellow Thomists with her theory of aesthetics.[47]

Maritain gained her greatest recognition, however, through the publication of a memoir entitled *Les grandes amitiés*. Published in two volumes in 1941 and 1944, this text returned to the early impulses of Maritain's scholarly career. As the title *Les grandes amitiés* suggests, it was not Maritain's name that immediately rose to the top but the names and voices of others. Yet the approach here was not necessarily one of deference; she chose the great friendships of her life as the vehicle for its retelling. Maritain's *grandes amitiés* were the leading figures of the *renaissance catholique*. As in her earlier turn to medieval and early modern mystics and doctors of the church, Maritain was engaging in a new kind of *ressourcement,* relying on friends and mentors of a more proximate but no less forsaken community in the past as a way to retrieve resources for the present. The relationships are the story, but she is the hub.

An analysis of Maritain's intellectual interventions complicates interpretations that would see her as a passive victim. *Sacred Dread* also aims to push back against the readings of her as the apolitical, silent partner of Jacques Maritain. Perhaps Jacques's fame makes it too easy to portray Raïssa as his opposite: if Jacques was public and philosophical, she was private, mystical, suffering, and isolated from history and politics. A typical assessment captures this tendency: "Jacques Maritain lived a vital, active life. Within this whirl of activity, Raïssa became a contemplative cloistered within her home, devoting long hours to prayer, meditation and her journal."[48] Widespread claims that she was a "saint," "wholly supernatural," "suffering and cloistered," and "holy" illustrate a hagiographic impulse accompanying this caricature. Raïssa, one commentator insisted, could not be "a model to emulate" because "she never involved herself with Jacques' extensive political work, nor addressed, at least in conventional terms, social problems."[49]

Although Raïssa's writings tend to be more mystical, more poetic, and certainly darker than those of Jacques, her works do not evade the political but access it from another angle, both responding to and shaping it.[50] Jacques's political work tended to focus on the juridical realm of state and international politics, a realm Raïssa only very rarely reflected upon as explicitly as Jacques. But her relation to politics must include the racialized state violence she experienced as a child with her family in Russia, and later as an adult in Europe in the late 1930s and through the war. Maritain's writings on questions about grief, imagination, and memory, though not juridical, can be usefully understood in relation to the political. Her wartime poems, such as "Deus excelsus terribilis" (1944) and "Aux morts désespérés" (1939), are among the very few powerful Catholic theological voices of lamentation during the Holocaust. Moreover, since all forms of politics require a particular kind of subject, one who is formed through a range of discourses and practices, we have to take a close look at Maritain's own lifelong disciplinary work centered on self-formation. For decades, her prayer life and religious practices centered on embodying Christ's suffering, praying, and inhabiting the norms of the revival community, what the anthropologist Charles Hirschkind has called the "formation of a sensorium."[51] These practices of formation should count as part of an expanded political imaginary that attends to the issues of subjectivity in the political sphere.[52]

PLAN OF THIS BOOK

In the first chapter, I ask the simple question: How did Raïssa Maritain move from committed atheism on the left to a conversion to Catholicism in 1906? I investigate Maritain's journey from an enthusiasm for atheistic positivism then prevalent at the Sorbonne to a desire she shared with many of her generation to find an alternative. In looking for new horizons, Maritain joined many in Paris who immersed themselves in Christian mystical texts of the medieval and early modern periods. These became widely available in early twentieth-century France, thanks in part to the members of religious orders who edited, translated, and published them in order to breathe life into a highly rationalized neoscholastic theology.[53] Her initial attraction to *souffrance* was linked in complex ways to a fascination with the premodern Christianity—an important marker of Catholic intellectual creativity in modern France.[54] In her first encounter with the work of her would-be godfather Léon Bloy, Maritain read of a lionized "Middle Ages" as "*the* great Christian period of mourning [deuil]."[55] Maritain's encounter with Bloy also provides an opportunity to explore Bloy's notions of the Jewishness of Christianity. His unusual but vivid claim that suffering and holiness come together around the figure of the Jew was crucial in fostering Maritain's conversion to Catholicism.

In the second chapter I move forward chronologically, continuing to explore the relationship between Bloy and Maritain but foregrounding issues of gender and feminized suffering. I begin with a broader historical analysis of the "feminization of Catholicism" in France. I give special attention to the theme of suffering femininity in Bloy's literary aesthetics and to Jacques's spiritualization of his wife's illnesses. Through an analysis of her *Journal*, correspondence, and early publications such as *De la vie d'oraison* (1924), I trace Maritain's investment in these gendered models of suffering and analyze her uses and modifications of them. I see her as partially critiquing the association between women and suffering from an embedded perspective, aided most notably by her appropriation of Thomas Aquinas.

In chapters 3, 4, and 5, I extend my analysis of Maritain's use of *souffrance* to include the social and political context of early to mid-twentieth-century France. Throughout the book I show how Maritain's multifaceted work emerged from a whole network of discourses and determinants, including political ones, but these three chapters provide a particular opportunity to see Maritain as a political thinker, engaging in the European catastrophes related to the rise of fascism, the escalation of anti-Semitism, and eventually the Shoah. I show in chapter 3 that Maritain was a leader in the interwar ecumenical efforts to forge a unity between Catholics and Jews. For Maritain this unity was rooted in the hope for a kind of internationalist, cosmopolitan Catholicism, in which conversions from Judaism into the Catholic Church would be celebrated as an inauguration of the "ecumenical dimensions" of a "new Christendom."[56] I show the multivalence of these interwar philo-Semitic projects, which entailed both outspokenly condemning anti-Semitism and, simultaneously, promoting and praying for Jewish conversions.[57] Maritain's thinking on Judaism and suffering illustrates the tensions and constraints at the heart of French Christian thinking on this issue. By paying close attention to her wartime poetry and a theological essay on Jewish-Christian relations entitled *Histoire d'Abraham* (1935, revised in 1942), I show Maritain both inheriting and transforming classic multivalent features of modern French Catholic philo-Semitism.

The fourth chapter extends the analysis of Maritain's politically inflected writings on suffering but explores the connections she and other Catholic revivalists had begun to make between politics, aesthetic theory, and poetry. I pay close attention to her essays "Le poète et son temps" (1936), "Du recueillement poétique" (1937), "Message aux poètes qui sont à la guerre" (1939), and "La poésie comme expérience spirituelle" (1942) to show the revival's transformations of suffering. Viewed alongside the gathering storm clouds of anti-Semitism and fascism in France, the *peine* that predominates in her poetry and theory of aesthetics was not merely a theological concept that could fit into a narrative of another's redemption. It gave voice to her experiences of personal betrayal and devastation as a Jewish Catholic in the context of escalating violence.

In the fifth and final chapter, I explore Maritain's wartime corpus—a small set of lamentation poems and her memoir *Les grandes amitiés*—written in New York, where she was an exile learning the news of the Holocaust as it came over from Europe, including the names of many friends who had died in the gas chambers. As Maritain's world crumbled around her with the collapse of the Catholic ideals of universalism and philo-Semitism during the Second World War, her wartime works were characterized by stunned disbelief. She took up the symbols of *souffrance* in radically new ways. For most of Maritain's life, suffering had been bound up with the promise of redemption and had pointed to the intimacy between mortal humanity and the God who suffered on the cross. Yet during the Holocaust her previous thinking on the redemptive power of anguish came to a halt. In the face of genocide the romance and allure of the Christian narrative of redemptive suffering faltered, even for its staunchest advocates and most creative theorizers. Yet I argue in this chapter that Maritain would not leave this defining concept behind altogether. In the midst of the war, suffering became a project of memory—a way of redeeming the past and her own life story as a sign of opposition to the tragedy of the war. It was the project of writing her memoirs that gave Maritain the chance to preserve redemptive suffering, if only by projecting it into the past. In these famous documents, Maritain told the stories of her own life and those of her friends just as the culture that had sustained them was disintegrating. Her memorial writings in 1940–44 are colored by the strange triumph and joy of the agonized existence she once called "sacred dread" (crainte sacrée). Understanding Maritain's turn to the past in the midst of present human cataclysm opens a view onto the complications faced by those who valorize suffering. This combination suggests a need to think more carefully about the relationships between the faculty of memory, the religious imagination, and grief.

These chapters together rest on the conviction that it is worth the effort to think through the *renouveau catholique*'s fascination with suffering with greater analytic precision for several reasons, beyond merely humanizing the strange. One reason is that the *renouveau catholique,* particularly the main protagonists I treat in *Sacred Dread,* laid the groundwork for some of the most richly creative thinking in late modern Catholicism. It was Charles Péguy who, in a 1904 essay, coined the term *ressourcement,* which would come to symbolize the hermeneutical principle for the changes inaugurated at the Second Vatican Council.[58] Many theologians associated with the movement known as *la nouvelle théologie,* among them Yves Congar and Henri de Lubac, specifically cite Péguy and other revivalists as crucial influences.[59] With regard to Raïssa Maritain's influence more specifically— and this is something I unpack more fully in the chapters that follow— the conciliar document *Nostra Aetate* draws directly from Jacques and Raïssa's rethinking of the relationship between Jews and Judaism that took place at least three decades before the Second Vatican Council. Moreover, Raïssa Maritain was a godmother, mentor, and direct influence to countless unexpected figures—the American poet Emily Snow, the literary critic Alan Tate, the Polish theater critic Jan Kott, and the Russian painter Marc Chagall, to name only a few. The most radical, even outrageous, of these thinkers, such as Léon Bloy, left a profound mark on the most enduring figures of twentieth-century Catholicism. In addition to Jacques and Raïssa Maritain, Julien Green, Thomas Merton, Flannery O'Connor, Graham Greene, Dorothy Day, and Georges Bernanos have all cited Bloy's ferocity as a source of inspiration for their own work.[60] It pays to seek a fuller, richer way to make sense of the dominant preoccupation of these writers.

In fact, the "Catholic" preoccupation with affliction that we see in the *renouveau catholique* figures has also exerted a real influence even on secular continental thought.[61] Figures as diverse as Walter Benjamin and Emmanuel Levinas drew inspiration from Léon Bloy.[62] Moreover, from Georges Bataille's fascination with suffering-centered mysticism to Julia Kristeva's most recent work, *The Severed Head* (2012), French theory remains fundamentally preoccupied with abjection.[63] The "Catholic" discourse on suffering explored in *Sacred Dread* intersects with themes in continental secular thought in ways that are not always fully acknowledged.

Furthermore, the story of *Sacred Dread* helps fill out the ongoing scholarly conversation about Catholicism and modernity.[64] Scholars have now revised the old narrative that sees religion in modern European history as a gradual process of disenchantment that began in the Protestant Reformation, accelerated during the Enlightenment, and then predictably faded until religion nearly disappeared. The old teleological narrative promoted the classic stereotype of modern Catholicism as a waning institution on the defensive, gasping for its last breath until the Second Vatican Council. Scholars instead now highlight a revised story of modern Europeans, popular and elite, who do not align easily along the old reiterated battle lines in which enlightened moderns are pitched against archaic believers, the church against the republican state, the supernaturalists against the positivists, and the Right against the Left. Similarly, the community I have come to know were not the last hostile relics of a dying world or right-wing defenders of the monarch but a group of thinkers—among them lapsed Catholics, Jews, atheists, émigrés—who actively sought out Catholic theologies and practices centered on suffering, in a range of ways, because they saw there something that was missing from the world of atheistic positivism.[65]

Their immersion in suffering before the two world wars enabled these artists and intellectuals to encounter and describe the suffering and tragedies of the twentieth century in a way they insisted others could not do or refused to do. Like many of her revivalist colleagues, Raïssa Maritain sought in her writings richer morphologies of affliction to describe what it meant to be human, how one could alter one's interior world and make room for God, and how to face the tragedies of history in new ways. By 1944, Maritain and many of her surviving colleagues had experienced unimaginable personal loss—the death of sons, friends, and godparents and, in many cases, the forced abandonment of their homes and communities. The Catholic *imaginaire,* so fixated on suffering, spoke to these experiences. These anguished symbols did not necessarily make the violence of the twentieth century "meaningful" (Maritain assigned the Holocaust to the anomalous category of "Ce qui ne peut se dire / Ce que l'esprit se refuse à porter" (What cannot be told / What the mind refuses to bear).[66] This imaginary enabled its advocates to describe suffering in the most vivid, graphic, almost unbearable detail. In many cases this work deepened rather than simply made meaningful the experience of anguish and affliction. Many found something oddly alluring about this.

Yet these symbols of *souffrance* did more than move French Catholic writers through the dreadfulness of war and exile. Part of what I found in *Sacred Dread* is that before the wars the "old story"—the utter antagonism between Catholicism and republicanism currently under revision by scholars, for good reason—*was,* on some level, true.[67] In a strange way this mutual hostility even partially enabled the revival. French *laïcité* is animated by a long-standing tradition in French social and political thought that identifies secular humanism as the only viable source of human unity and progress.[68] As Maritain came to see it, as early as 1906 the philosophy of secular positivism in France refused to believe in either death or God, in what was for her a sort of bizarre refusal to see reality. Because of this refusal, many rejected republican ideals as bourgeois and tepid and fled to republicanism's "other": What could be more "countercultural" to the *laïcité* than picking up the broken pieces of a tradition scorned and demonized by the mainstream, embracing its symbols of grief, crucifixion, and tears? Particularly in the early part of the revival, as writers tapped into Catholicism, they tapped into the Catholic Church's scorn for modern republicanism and, like most European Catholics, veered uneasily between the Right and the Left, holding within their community all positions on the political spectrum.

This kind of ambivalence is at the heart of the fascination with suffering in French Catholic revival. For this generation, the allure of Catholicism's suffering-centered *imaginaire* was a turn away from the liberal idea that suffering could and must be overcome, toward Catholic symbolism that channeled emotions of grief, mourning, and loss to acknowledge, consecrate, and deepen the reality of suffering and pain, and that did so in ambiguous ways that highlighted the suffering of women and Jews. This raises important ethical and political questions about the potentially problematic valorization of the suffering of those who are historically oppressed and the legacy of this mode of thinking for today.[69] It places before us perennial issues: Can graphic accounts of affliction ever act as a vehicle for social reform and transformation? Or do such accounts merely naturalize, sanctify, or otherwise further entrench historical suffering in their intense reiterations and re-elaborations? In light of the French Catholic revival's central preoccupations, what to make of Theodor Adorno's formidable criticism that representations of suffering and pain always contain, "however remotely, the power to elicit enjoyment out of it"?[70] Does the possibility of pleasure in reading about others' pain prevent other affective responses, such as compassion, empathy, or outrage?

A term often used by Maritain that captures the multivalence of this legacy is one made famous by Pascal: *l'abîme* (the abyss). She claimed that Catholic theologies of suffering enabled her to "lean over the abyss," to face death, suffering, and the tragedies of history in new ways. Yet proximity to the abyss, however conceived, is risky, always presenting a range of temptations at its edge—in this case, the temptations of sentimentality, the romanticizing or fetishizing of suffering that could otherwise be analyzed and eradicated, the view of suffering as the inevitable destiny of women and Jews, and the relinquishment of liberal modernity in its totality. *Sacred Dread* is an invitation to consider the risks and rewards of such a perilous posture, and to do so in the company of the forgotten presence of Raïssa Maritain.

CHAPTER 1

That "Strange Thing,
So Unknown to Us—Catholicism"

Steps to Conversion (1900–1906)

How did a Jewish atheist come to embrace Catholicism, to the point of converting, and go on to have a major impact on the intellectual and artistic revivals in French Catholicism, a world made up mainly of men? Consider where she started out, in 1902, as a young Sorbonne student and Russian-born Jew. That year, she wrote to her would-be-husband Jacques Maritain, describing her intellectual vision: "In order to be everything [pour être tout] it is necessary to be alone [être seuls]! I would like us detached from everything, free from every prejudice, *without any illusion* and without any weakness, to find in ourselves the strength to be, for the Beauty of being! To be alone [d'être seuls] and nevertheless strong!" She also disdainfully mentioned a friend who had given up on this quest for freedom, needing instead the crutches of faith in God: "Nothing of all that," she warned Jacques, "can exist for us."[1]

Within the span of three short years, she and Jacques had been captivated by "all that" and more, discovering through the novels of the Catholic writer Léon Bloy that "strange thing, so unknown to us—

25

Catholicism."[2] By 1906, at the age of twenty-three, Raïssa Maritain (as she was known after her 1904 marriage) was baptized into the Catholic Church along with her new husband and her sister, Véra. This shift demands explanation: Bloy's novels, filled with graphic depictions of suffering, valorized abjection and sorrow as models of Christian sanctity and seem to offer nothing of the heroism and independence she sought in 1902. Why the shift? Did she see in Bloy's vision an embodiment of a kind of detached strength—the ability to *être tout*—or had she given up on that dream, deciding, like the friends she scorned, to lean on God?

In this chapter, I aim to make sense of Maritain's improbable conversion as a first step in illuminating a broader attraction to Catholicism in Paris among individuals across the religious spectrum in the early twentieth century. Maritain's story focuses the issue on the appeal of Catholicism among Jewish intellectuals in particular, but as it would be with any Jewish man or woman, Maritain's relationship to her Jewish roots was complex, continually evolving, and constantly undergoing revision. The Judaism she reflects upon in the midst of her 1906 baptism (under consideration in this chapter) differs considerably from her interwar reflections on Judaism (explored in chapter 3), and even more from the rather astounding Jewish memories she excavates four decades later in 1940–45 (chapter 5). In each of these moments, Judaism was central to an *imaginaire* of Catholicism that was steeped in representations of suffering. Shifts in Maritain's thinking on this issue are crucial for understanding the evolution of her thinking and the complex mobility of representations of Judaism in the *renouveau catholique* more broadly.

Scholarly interpretations of both Raïssa's and Jacques's conversion to Catholicism tend to rely on Raïssa's vivid account detailed in the first volume of her 1941 memoir, *Les grandes amitiés*. Much of the material she recounts in these memoirs, including the details of her family's itinerary from Russia to France, the appeal of Henri Bergson, and the intense friendships of her earliest intellectual communities, *is* reliable as historical evidence, corroborated by countless other sources including her own diaries and those of her friends, her vast correspondence, and other contemporaneous writings from friends and mentors. Yet her evocation of Judaism in the conversion story of *Les grandes amitiés* stands out as odd; it markedly contrasts with her earlier writings. Written in the midst of the war, nearly forty years after her conversion, her 1941 and 1944 memoirs cannot be understood as a transparent retelling of her Jewish childhood or the theology of Jewish-Christian relations that led her to baptism. In relation to the issue of Judaism, *Les grandes amitiés* recalls memories under conditions of violence and exile—memories that were, at least in part, theological and political strategies to respond to immediate crises of 1940–44, rather than an objective account of "what happened" in 1906. Throughout this project, I use *Les grandes amitiés* critically, carefully, and selectively, and always in conversation with other supporting texts from this period. For the issue of her Jewish roots in relation to her baptism, safer sources are Maritain's writings closer to 1906, such as the handwritten essay "Récit de ma conversion" (1909), penned much closer to her actual conversion and printed posthumously for the first time in the 1983 issue of *Cahiers Jacques Maritain*.[3] This comparative reading of the 1909 essay, her journal, published and unpublished letters, the writings of her friends and mentors, and *Les grandes amitiés* reveals emotional and existential fissures that the formal finish of the memoir conceals.

But like all historical documents, even Maritain's 1909 essay on her conversion only obliquely gets at "what really happened" in these years. Composed three years after her conversion at the request of her Dominican spiritual director Humbert Clérissac, it describes the factors that led her to baptism. But strikingly, halfway through the essay, Jacques's handwriting takes over and the narrator's voice changes to the plural pronoun *nous*. Her essay becomes from this point forward a transcription penned by Jacques, modified to include him. Yet Raïssa's handwriting reappears throughout, crossing out the *nous* and correcting it in the margins back to the singular, *je*. The exchanges on the page illustrate complex exchanges between Maritain and the important men in her life that would both enable (it was Jacques and her confessor who urged her to write the essay in the first place) and alter her writing throughout her life. Maritain's thought was alternately authorized and circumscribed, encouraged and encroached upon.[4] Her voice always emerges from a complex field of pressures and opportunities, possibilities and constraints. Tracking Maritain's itinerary from the Sorbonne to Bloy and ultimately baptism not only requires sifting through these kinds of materials to find the voice made audible by the desires of so many others but also calls for a wider placement of Maritain within the larger chorus of the intellectual and cultural milieu to explain why Catholicism, particularly this mystical and suffering-centered kind of Catholicism, would have even been available to—not to mention attractive to—a young Jewish atheist at the Sorbonne.

Any analysis of the climate surrounding the late modern conversions to Catholicism draws from the pioneering work of the French historian of religion Frédéric Gugelot, whose masterful *La conversion des intellectuels au catholicisme en France, 1885–1935* provides a compendium of over one hundred stories of conversions that took place mostly in Paris between the years 1885 and 1935.[5] In this chapter, I draw from Gugelot's findings, but I also add a new perspective. Crucially, Gugelot argues just how central networks of "paternité spirituelle" were to those who found themselves drawn into the Catholic Church in this period.[6] Lines of spiritual paternity formed religious families that transmitted themselves through the generations. Converts in fin de siècle France became the godparents of those baptized in 1905, forming bonds of kinship that traversed the decades of the early twentieth century. The conversions, Gugelot argues, rebounded from one to another ("rebondissent de l'un à l'autre entremêlant amitiés et cheminements personnels"), animated by deep friendships that drew life from the vast number of intimate letters between godparents and children, friends, and mentors circulating every week of the French Catholic revival.[7] In-person visits, formal and informal meals, discussion groups, outings to museums and theaters, spiritual direction and conversation, and attendance at one another's baptisms and those of friends and children constituted the material out of which these deep bonds of affection were formed.[8] These were the bonds that led uninitiated friends to follow in friends' footsteps to baptism.

Consider this example: a few years after the Maritains' 1906 conversion, the Dutch novelist and artist Pieter van der Meer de Walcheren also came under the spell of Léon Bloy.[9] When Pieter confessed his need for a "spiritual father," Bloy agreed to fill the role, adding, "And I will give you a brother and two sisters, my godchildren, Jacques, Raïssa, and Véra."[10] Lifelong friendships soon formed among these young adults with their "unforgettable common godfather" at the center, bonds that continued well beyond Bloy's death in 1917. Years later, the Maritains became the godparents to van der Meer de Walcheren's own children (the horrible deaths of two of these children became the catalyst for some of Maritain's most moving, grief-stricken poems). Furthermore, in his memoir *Journal d'un converti* (1917), Pieter described his 1910 conversion and, most vividly, the intimacy and centrality of his relationships with the Maritains and Bloy.[11] This memoir was widely read in avant-garde circles in Paris and was a major source of inspiration for a "third wave" of conversions in the interwar period, sending even more seekers to the Maritains' salon in the outskirts of Paris in the 1920s and 1930s. Relationships that formed new kinship structures were the lifeblood of the late modern attraction to Catholicism.

In Maritain's network, relationships did not take precedence over ideas or people over doctrine; rather, they were linked. Ideas in the *renouveau catholique* were embodied in particular people (both living and dead) and carried out in relationships that were affectively, even erotically charged. Maritain once explained it this way: "Plotinus, Pascal, Péguy, Bergson, Léon Bloy bathed our souls with their spiritual influence. . . . It is said that Bloy ignored Bergson and Péguy, and they ignored him too, but we brought them together in ourselves by loving them."[12] An analysis of Maritain's conversion therefore requires an examination of her earliest understandings of Judaism and Christianity, but also of her friendship with her first mentor, Charles Péguy, and his own embodiment of his ideals, particularly the *mystique* he saw in medieval and early modern Christian saints' writings and his philo-Semitism in the wake of Dreyfus. It was about the captivating lectures of Henri Bergson, where she was introduced to Plotinus and found herself "on my knees before the book, covering the page I had just read with passionate kisses, and my heart on fire with love."[13] It was about the "luminous doctrine of Léon Bloy's life," particularly Bloy's intense and vivid ideas about Judaism and abjection. It was through Bloy, most of all, that Maritain encountered one of the most enduring legacies of the French Catholic revival: Christianity's debt to Judaism and the idealization of the suffering Jew. Through the image of the suffering, abject Jew, she came to see her own Jewish heritage— something she had only scarcely considered before—as fundamentally connected to the radical, antibourgeois Catholicism she discovered at the turn of the century.

MARITAIN'S INTELLECTUAL LIFE
IN CHILDHOOD AND ADOLESCENCE

Raïssa (Oumançoff) Maritain was born into a Jewish family in Russia in 1883 and immigrated with her parents to France in 1893. Maritain remembered that when she had been a small child in Russia, her family had rented an extra room to a teacher who used it to give private instruction there. Maritain often peeked in and was "filled with awe and desire for the mysterious things that were being taught there," perhaps an early indication of why she later was such a good student.[14] She wrote emphatically about how schoolwork, for her, had always generated emotions "of a religious character."[15] The seriousness that she showed toward her studies in part contributed to her parents' decision to immigrate: not only were the Jewish pogroms that had racked Russia since the mid-nineteenth century not decreasing, but opportunities were limited for young Jewish girls under Alexander III.

Maritain arrived in France with her family when she was ten years old, and they settled into a large and fairly well-established community of Russian Jews in Paris. Despite initial difficulties she felt upon her arrival, Maritain worked intensely "to pierce the tongue" of the French language. Intensive study meant overcoming loneliness and anguish in her new host country and enabled her to become reimmersed in the schoolwork she revered so deeply. She succeeded and within her first year found herself again at the head of her class, an achievement that reaffirmed for her that "the happiness of my life would be studies."[16] In her later adolescent years, Maritain received private tutoring from the Russian Marxist Charles Rappoport, who schooled her in the search for "*what is*" (ce qui est).[17] Her family's choice of a fairly well-known leftist like Rappoport to tutor their daughter suggests they shared the distinct educational and cultural norms of many Russian Jewish émigrés. Having lived under the Russian intelligentsia, these immigrants were less likely to be religiously observant and to speak Yiddish than other members of the Jewish immigrant communities. They were also more in touch with radical Russian politics and often came to France primarily with educational aspirations.[18] This seems to describe Maritain's family situation. She wrote in her 1909 essay that her childhood and adolescence lacked religious education, although she had "heard a lot about Jewish people" ("Enfant, j'entendis beaucoup parler du peuple juif, mais je ne reçus pour ainsi dire pas d'instruction religieuse").[19] More attuned to Russian and European political thought and the plight of the underclass (including Jews but also workers around the world), Maritain remembers Russian political refugees and students regularly debating social questions into the night in her parents' Paris apartment.

Maritain's nominal understanding of Judaism as a religious tradition during her childhood can be explained, not only by the particularities of the Russian Jewish émigré community, but by the pressures for assimilation in the French context. The term *laïcisme* is part of this story. First used in 1871, *laïcisme* meant the removal of religious staff and theological teachings from French schools, and programs of *laïcisme* peaked, famously, in the 1905 legislation on the separation of church and state. This law removed all religious workers from hospitals and state schools, declared all religious buildings to be the property of the state, denied government funding to religious employees, and eliminated all religious signs from public buildings (crucifixes in classrooms were the most contentious provision).[20] As Ruth Harris and others have shown, the philosophical underpinnings of French *laïcisme* were articulated in France well before the 1905 legislation and were long a part of French public discourse about religious particularity and citizenship. Included was a claim that secular humanism rather than religious particularity was the only viable source of human unity and progress.[21] Within the philosophical program of the *laïcité,* Jews were seen as "particular" and hence incapable of genuinely assimilating to universal citizenship. Many European Jews had subsequently become alienated from religion or were raised with only a nominal understanding of Judaism as a religious tradition.[22] It would make sense in this context that Maritain's leftist family of Jewish Russian émigrés would teach their daughters about the plight of Jewish people around the world and would sideline the particulars of ritual, practice, and sacred texts in the French assimilationist effort.

THE SORBONNE: GRAPPLING WITH "DEAD, DRY KNOWLEDGE"

At the age of fourteen, Maritain claimed, she considered herself to adhere to no religion but still yearned for philosophical truth: "An ardent desire to know the essential truth developed in my soul. This desire was in and of itself both a joy and a force for me."[23] Maritain enrolled at the Sorbonne at seventeen and immediately gravitated toward the sciences. "I believed that this science had arrived at the knowledge of that which is [de ce qui est]," she recalled in 1909. "This I called truth."[24] That a promising young student searching for truth would enroll in the sciences rather than philosophy was not surprising. The reign of science in a positivistic form in the late nineteenth-century and early twentieth-century French university system is well established.[25] Although he had died in 1857 and had never taught at the Sorbonne, Auguste Comte, who had emphasized experimental science as the only way to truth, continued to cast a shadow over the university. His famous formulation of the "law of the three states" was an evolutionary framework for the mind and society that claimed that every branch of knowledge must necessarily pass through three states: the theological or fictitious state, the metaphysical or abstract state, and the scientific or positive state.[26] In 1887 this framework helped spur the reformulation of the French university system, which aimed to modernize the school through an orientation toward the sciences.[27] By the time Maritain enrolled, the sciences were by far the most esteemed departments at the Sorbonne, and they housed the most popular scholars, including Marie and Pierre Curie.

In the fashion of many conversion narratives, Maritain's 1909 essay begins with a description of an early and illusory comfort in realms that would later appear to her as partial and limited. Maritain recalls that she initially internalized the Sorbonne's atmosphere of positivism: "I believed what was said around me: that ignorance, dark machinations [les machinations ténébreuses], and fanaticism were the share of religions, that light, moral good, the full blossom of reason were the share of science. . . . This Sorbonne, its scholars and their books, how I venerated them. What hope I had in them."[28] Yet when she began taking classes she felt that her real burning questions about truth and the absolute were unintelligible there: the Sorbonne scholars were preoccupied with various truths of experimental science but not with truth itself. She remembers her teachers told her, "You should erase from your mind any question of the origin and end of things, on God, the soul, the absolute [l'absolu]. All of that is unknowable and science only knows what is relative."[29] She recalls that such metaphysical and meaning-oriented questions went unrecognized and were dismissed by her professors as "mere mysticism." In 1909, Maritain mimics what she heard: "Man is only an accident, like any other in nature. . . . The mind may only be a manifestation of matter like electricity. . . . Conscience is only an epiphenomenon and free will is an illusion."[30] Maritain experienced the restriction of metaphysics to empiricism and historicism as stifling and distressing at the deepest levels of identity, and she wanted instead to engage in questions about "our very ability to grasp the real [saisir le réel]."[31] She became so despondent that her life, as she recalls it in her 1909 essay, was "miserable et désespérée."[32]

Within her first months at the Sorbonne, in the fall of 1900, she met her intellectual equal in Jacques Maritain, a fellow student who also was distressed at what he called the "mediocrity" and bourgeois complacency (a constant target of their contempt) of their academic community. Raïssa was struggling, frustrated at her and Jacques's inability to think their way beyond the cognition of sensible phenomena alone. She recalls that her spirit was in a pitiful state ("l'esprit se trouve alors dans un état si pitoyable") and claims she "took refuge in sadness," a sadness that deepened and intensified quickly over the next several months in 1901. "I did not know how to live anymore, since I wanted to live according to the truth but the truth seemed to be mixed up [se confondre] with disorder and nothingness."[33] In her 1940 memoirs, she describes a now-famous scene in the summer of 1901 when she and Jacques became so deeply distressed that they made a pact that they would commit suicide unless they found answers. Maritain makes no mention of the pact in her 1909 essay, but evidence from other primary sources from this period at the Sorbonne corroborates at least Maritain's claims that intense anguish in the face of positivism was widespread there. For example, in 1910, a few years after Maritain had enrolled at the Sorbonne, the young student Henri Massis, who would later become a conservative, royalist Catholic associated with Charles Maurras, wrote a series of articles under the pen name Agathon that were eventually collected in a volume *L'esprit de la nouvelle Sorbonne.* Agathon's claims echo many of Maritain's initial disappointments. He laments that Sorbonne students were expected to "inspect objectively, compile scientifically, and forbidden above all to think personally. . . . They have tried to reduce history, literature, and philosophy to I know not what

order of dead dry knowledge."[34] Massis writes that students went to the
Sorbonne with intellectual hopes but found instead "a vacuous science
[science vide] that does not take into account the needs of the intelligence,
a pedantic materialism, a skeptical, reductive viewpoint. Everything in
such an education obliges us to serve as inert slaves or to become exas-
perated rebels [à nous exaspérer en rebelles]."[35] Regardless of whether
this accurately describes positivist philosophy, the point here is the level
of exasperation, distress, and suffering so many young Sorbonne intellectuals claimed to have genuinely experienced in the face of it. Although
difficult to imagine, the story of Maritain's turn from secular positivism
and eventually toward Catholicism (and, I would add, the story of the
whole French Catholic revival) could not have unfolded the way it did
without that early experience of desperation and distress.[36] This story
starts with young intellectuals, from all sides of the ideological spectrum,
who saw themselves as pushed up against a wall.[37]

THE INFLUENCE OF CHARLES PÉGUY

In the spring of 1901, both Jacques and Raïssa, still enrolled at the Sorbonne, began to find relief through their friendship with one of the most
important critics of the Sorbonne's positivism and anticlericalism, Charles
Péguy (1873–1914). An elusive figure who defies categorization in the history of French thought, Péguy was a socialist, a Dreyfusard, and an atheist
who became a practicing Catholic. Péguy ran a socialist bookshop on rue
de la Sorbonne, in the Left Bank, just across the street from the Sorbonne.
There men and women gathered to work on his journal, *Cahiers de la Quinzaine,* and to participate in his weekly Thursday discussions. In the context
of Péguy's bookshop, Maritain joined a community of thinkers who began
to see organized religion—the religious particulars of both Judaism and
Christianity especially—differently than their elders, who had been nourished by the ideals of the *laïcité*.[38] Most of the older generation of leftists,
positivists, and republicans who had come of age in the 1890s were viru-
lently opposed to organized religion.[39] Péguy wrote in 1910 that "the same
people who had turned the country upside down in order that it should
not be said that in France a man had suffered on account of his race and
his religion [Dreyfus] were now expelling the teaching orders and declaring

war on everything religious."[40] Just as this came to pass, the younger generation began to see something in religion that the older generation had missed.

If positivism declared "tradition" and the premodern as immature and unevolved "mere mysticism," critics like Péguy and Maritain would look precisely to premodern mystical texts for viable alternatives. These texts spurred those critiquing positivism to develop broader critiques of modernity. As the modernity/tradition binary began to figure into Maritain's thinking, she reframed her intellectual struggles in temporal terms. Maritain mocked the voices of her teachers at the Sorbonne who denigrated the past in favor of the present: "More than anything," she remembers hearing, "get rid of the Middle Ages! There reason is the slave of theology. . . . We must put the past behind us. The former generations are certainly admirable, but like children with their grace and their naïveté, they hardly had anything of the scientific spirit."[41] In a reading group led by Péguy, Maritain read the *Catéchisme spirituel,* the early modern spiritual classic by Jean-Joseph Surin, and was profoundly affected. Surin's mystical treatise was suggested to Maritain by Georges Sorel (1847–1922), a fellow critic of scientific materialism and frequenter of Péguy's shop. Maritain recalled seeing something in Surin's text missing in the world of positivism: "When we grasped his charter of sanctity for the first time, it seemed to us, by its organic logic, to be the only one capable of dealing with the inner life, of awakening that life dormant in each of us, of making us really alive and human in our spirit as well as in all our acts."[42] The inner world was somehow malleable and could be worked on and tended to. Surin's "charter of sanctity" was the first among the many mystical books she encountered, each of which awakened the inner life that was unintelligible at the Sorbonne and crucially exhibited a willingness to articulate "the secret sufferings of the soul."[43]

In Péguy's bookshop Maritain joined a host of intellectuals in Paris who had immersed themselves in medieval and early modern mysticism looking for sources of critique and relief from positivism. Maritain read about the life of Anne Catherine Emmerich (1774–1824) and read works by St. John Vianney (1786–1859) and Catherine of Siena (1347–80). In reading the lives of Christian visionaries, mystics, and saints, she asked "how an erroneous doctrine, Catholicism, could create in the soul the wisdom and force, joy and peace [sagesse et force, joie et paix] that we see in every single saint? In their presence . . . we felt the force of reality."[44] The key words here—*force, joie, énergie*—are the same words she used to describe her adolescent searches for truth in intellectual work.

Along with Péguy's mentorship, Maritain's attraction to mysticism can be explained by the prominence, for this generation in Paris, of the Jewish philosopher Henri Bergson (1859–1941), who gave intellectual coherence to their distress. Bergson was a philosopher at the Collège de France, and according to Maritain the faculty at the Sorbonne "denigrated and dreaded" him. But for Maritain's generation, Bergson was *the* philosopher to hear.[45] It is difficult to overstate the impact of his public lectures on twentieth-century French intellectual life.[46] Starting in 1902, Maritain attended Bergson's lectures with Jacques, Charles Péguy, and Ernest Psichari, and there Maritain claimed to revive the pleasures associated with intellectual work she had known growing up. She noted the difference between Bergson's "genius" and the "saddest mediocrity" of her Sorbonne professors.[47]

The lectures Maritain attended from 1902 to 1905 were based largely on Bergson's earliest books, *Matière et mémoire (Matter and Memory)* and *Les données immédiates de la conscience (Time and Free Will),* where Bergson shows how the mechanism of science can describe the natural and inanimate worlds but not the inner regions of human consciousness and the most fundamental aspects of reality. What was crucial for Maritain was that this reality, in its fullness and depth, was recognizable and graspable by a *human faculty* that Bergson called intuition. According to Bergson, through the faculty of intuition it is possible to experience the flow of reality instead of breaking it apart into stable, discrete categories, as we typically do in the realm of ordinary activity and communication.[48] Maritain learned here that communion between the human mind and absolute reality could take place; she wrote in 1909, "I repeated after M. Bergson that 'by intuition we reach the absolute.' . . . The essential was the result: to reach the absolute."[49]

Bergson also insisted, unusually for the time, on the possibilities of genuine freedom; the self could be genuinely free and not wholly constrained by history and language, as the positivists and mechanists would have it. Scientific determinism, he argued, ignored the fundamental layer of self where imagination and creativity are located and where the roots of freedom reside. In her memoirs, Maritain liberally quotes passages from *Time and Free Will*. Freedom, she cites Bergson, "is the deep-seated self rushing up to the surface," the "sudden boiling over of feelings and ideas" that generates action, or enables one to think and feel in ways contrary to conventional thought. This is the "depths of the self" coming up into consciousness.[50] Bergson saw these acts as truly free.[51] For him, an act was free when the fundamental self reflected on all of its past experiences, pushed its way to the surface of consciousness, broke through the outer, superficial self of inherited ideas and expectations, and took decisive, creative action. Maritain used the Bergsonian concept to reflect on her own experiences at the Sorbonne. She took the notion of the deep self, *something* that rises up in resistance, as evidence of her own fundamental being that rebelled against the positivist climate. Her suffering, though it nearly drove her to total despair, was a kind of instinct of freedom irreducible to her surroundings that, as she put it, "protected her."[52] As she had come to understand it, her suffering at the Sorbonne was therefore an act of rebellion and a refusal to be wholly defined by the conventions of the academic culture there. Her thoughts—muddled, anguished, but certainly defiant—in their refusal to conform to positivism "testified" (témoignaient), as she put it, "on behalf of being" and freedom. She saw the suffering as evidence of this freedom in which her deep self, in anguish, rose up to break through the intellectual milieu in order to critique it and search for an alternative. As she elaborated years later in *Les grandes amitiés:* "What saved us then, what made our real despair a conditional despair was precisely our suffering" (Ce qui nous a sauvés alors, ce qui a fait de notre réel désespoir un désespoir encore conditionnel, c'est justement notre souffrance).[53] A new understanding of suffering recast as freedom became the foundation of her relief.

Bergson's lectures generated widespread interest in Paris and amplified the already-existing fascination with medieval and early modern mysticism. Bergson was interested in particular historical figures who exemplified the creativity of the "authentic" deep self, and often he saw religious figures, especially mystics and saints, as embodying this deep self in touch with the intuition. For Bergson, Péguy, and many others in Paris, no one presented more of a contrast with the stuffy rationalism of the Sorbonne than the mystics. Interests in Christian and Greek mysticism, esoteric religion, and the occult and spiritualism characterized the culture around Bergson in pre–World War I Paris.[54] Maritain participated in a reading group that Bergson led in 1903 on Greek metaphysical and mystical writers, especially Plotinus. Through Bergson, Plotinus, and later other Greek and Christian writers like Surin that she encountered through Péguy, Maritain revived the affective connections with reading and thinking that she had known as an adolescent. Maritain's description of reading the *Enneads* captures her typical exuberance and her affective, erotically inflected mode of intellectual work. "A wave of enthusiasm flooded my heart," she recalls, and she covered the book with kisses.[55] For Maritain, the capacity of this premodern material to expand the available intellectual options, to give rise to new emotive experiences, lent her rebellious suffering and distress clarity.

The revitalized interest in mysticism can be traced, not only to the interests and charisma of Péguy and Bergson, but to the earlier labors of several Catholic religious orders in France that mined ancient and medieval texts on spiritual life, monasticism, and liturgy with vigor and focus at the turn of the century.[56] Just as Bergson opposed scientific positivism, some French monks and priests opposed the theology of neoscholasticism that dominated European seminaries. Neoscholasticism shared in scientific positivism's intellectual style of rationalism and its sidelining of the inner life, leading these clergy to rebel against its highly rationalized and desiccated theology. The history triggering this turn-of-the-century revival had begun as early as 1841, when Catholic monastic and clerical efforts to make mystical texts available began with writers such as Dom Prosper Guéranger. This famous reformer of the Benedictine order restored and revitalized the Benedictine monastery at Solesmes and wrote a fifteen-volume study on liturgy, *L'année liturgique (The Liturgical Year)*. He also commissioned several studies of monasticism and spirituality in the ancient and medieval church.[57] This interest in premodern spirituality and liturgy can be detected also among lay Catholic philosophers and essayists such as Ernest Hello, whose 1868 French translation of Angela of Foligno's *Memorial* was widely acclaimed.[58] In 1901, a Jesuit scholar named Auguste Poulain published *Des grâces d'oraison (Graces of Interior Prayer)*, a book that brings together an enormous range of ancient and medieval teachings on affective prayer, the mystical graces, and mystical union.

Poulain drew on classical Christian mystical writers including Teresa of Ávila, John of the Cross, Dionysius, Catherine of Siena, Bonaventure, and Hildegard.[59] This compendium enjoyed wide acclaim throughout Paris in the early twentieth century, with Catholics and non-Catholics reading it in cafés, classrooms, and bookshops.[60] In a range of intellectual circles around Paris, from Péguy and Bergson to the Jesuits and Benedictines, reading groups were formed to discuss Teresa of Ávila's writings on prayer, Angela of Foligno's *Memorial,* and Catherine of Siena's *Dialogue.* These texts were translated into French and disseminated widely.[61] The French Philosophical Society held a panel on Teresa of Ávila in 1905.[62] Furthermore, the turn-of-the-century interest in mysticism built much of the foundations for the *nouvelle théologie* movement that would gain prominence in the years preceding the Second Vatican Council.[63]

When Maritain was at the Sorbonne, then, a shift was beginning to be felt in the overlapping circles of secular intellectuals and religious orders. Both found in these premodern writers something totally "other" to scientific positivism and neoscholastic, ultramontane Catholicism.[64] The focus on the inner life, what Bergson termed the "fundamental self" or "intensive psychic states," was perceived to be unintelligible both at the Sorbonne *and* in ultramontane Roman Catholicism.[65] The mystics proved able illustrations of intense focus on the inner life, particularly what Maritain identified as the "secret sufferings of the soul." As discussed above, Maritain had already begun to identify suffering as evidence that her Bergsonian "fundamental self" refused to conform to scientific positivism, testifying to the human capacity to transcend and critique its social surroundings. But suffering took a more distinct and directly Catholic and Jewish inflection in Péguy's bookshop in response to events in early 1905.

LES SUPPLIANTS: THE ROLE OF SUFFERING AND REVOLUTION

True to her upbringing, Raïssa Maritain, as a Sorbonne student and a young searching intellectual in Paris, stayed abreast of the news of worker movements around the world, particularly in Russia, so the 1905 events known as Bloody Sunday were especially important to her.[66] Bloody Sunday refers to January 22, 1905, when Russian peasants and workers delivered a supplication to the czar in St. Petersburg for food and better working conditions. Peasants were gunned down in front of the czar's palace. Thousands were killed and wounded. These workers were led by a Russian Orthodox priest, Georgi Gapón, a fact that fascinated those in Péguy's circle. A friend of Péguy, the historian Daniel Halévy, explained, "The double character of the event, religious and revolutionary, priestly and popular, had struck the imagination of a Europe grown unused to ritual and grown unused to bloodshed."[67] The response of Péguy and many in his community solidified the place of suffering in the *imaginaire* of the French Catholic revival.

After the news of Bloody Sunday reached Paris, Péguy dedicated an issue of his *Cahiers de la Quinzaine* to the event. Péguy reflected on the strange power of those whom he called *les suppliants,* a term that in this case meant the Russian workers but could also include, as he put it, "the wretched blind man [l'aveugle misérable], the outlaw, the exterminated, the citizen banished from the city, guilty or not guilty, the child expelled from his family, guilty or not guilty . . . the prisoner, the vanquished, the feeble old man, workers, and peasants."[68] Reflecting on an image of Russian workers on their knees gunned down at the czar's palace, Péguy saw supplication in religious terms. "Supplication," he explained, "is a prayer: the ancients gave it ritual form. The supplicant asks nothing, he has no voice, no strength. As the blind man shows his extinguished eyes, the cripple his stumps, the man with scurvy his sores, so the supplicant shows his destitution, and that is enough. Woe to the strong man who scorns him!"[69] In Péguy's understanding, the one who has been broken down commands religious attention because of his intimacy with fate, with the gods, and with those forces more powerful than human beings. The introduction of religious language after Bloody Sunday marked a shift in Péguy's thinking. Although he had been fascinated with mysticism, he had always proudly proclaimed himself an atheist.

This valorization of the cripple, the blind, the destitute, the thousands willing to die would speak directly to Maritain's early critiques of positivism: not only was the positivist horizon stifling, but it failed to recognize death and suffering. She had claimed that people within the positivist climate tended to be more at ease because of their "indifference concerning death."[70] Positivists, she claimed, have an idea that finitude does not "act upon them and does not affect them." She continued, "Only the consideration of death has us discover a reality absolutely undeniable and powerful, of an order superior to the power and knowledge of anything that is human, and the person who lives without worrying about this reality is completely crazy [fou]."[71] Péguy introduced her to an intellectual world that could render death and suffering visible and recast them in terms of a mystical power, a power denigrated by the scientism she was coming to abandon. But most crucially for Maritain, Péguy would tether the visibility of death and suffering to symbols of Jews and Judaism. Her would-be godfather Léon Bloy, whom she encountered later, would push this symbolic association to the extreme.

DRIPPING WITH THE WORD OF GOD: CHARLES PÉGUY'S *JUIFS*

For Péguy, long a Dreyfusard and friend of a handful of Jewish intellectuals in Paris, it was Jewish people who could most powerfully embody the abject ideals of *le suppliant* who suffers. Maritain, as a Russian and a Jew herself, would certainly have been affected by these ideas. Péguy's writings on Jews and Judaism are scattered throughout his vast corpus but are most fully developed in his famous essay "Notre jeunesse," published in 1910, a few years after Maritain had met him, though the ideas expressed there had long circulated among those who frequented his bookshop. This work is Péguy's nostalgic reminiscence of the early Dreyfus movement, when the Dreyfusards embodied *mystique*—charity and passionate commitment at no matter what physical and emotional cost—before the struggle denigrated into mere *politique*.[72] Much of the essay circles around a lengthy posthumous portrait of a Jewish friend, the writer Bernard Lazare, whom Péguy sees as the early movement's prophet. Péguy uses his reflections on Dreyfus and Lazare to include more general reflections on Jewish-Christian relations, introducing two of the most enduring themes of the philo-Semitic French Catholic imagination: the unity of Christians and Jews, and the Jew as the ideal sufferer. These would be the central philo-Semitic conceptual tools at hand that Raïssa Maritain would utilize and transform years later when she began her own writings on Judaism in the interwar period.

"Anti-Semites," Péguy writes in the essay, "speak of Jews. I warn you that I am about to say something shocking: **anti-Semites do not know the Jews** [bold in original]. They speak about them but they don't know them [ils ne les connaissent point]."[73] Through his portrait of Bernard Lazare and other Jews he has known for "twenty years," Péguy challenges long-standing Christian and secular stereotypes: against the cliché of the wealthy merchant who usurps France's financial assets, Péguy depicts Bernard Lazare as a destitute Jewish writer, raised in an impoverished ghetto—*le suppliant*—whose deep sense of solidarity and duty compelled him to dedicate his life to the well-being of the poor multitude of Jews living in the ghettos of Romania, Poland, Russia, and France. Péguy's text moves to make a general claim about the solidarity between Jews like Dreyfus and Lazare and Christians who are also abject and struggling in the modern world: "What I see," Péguy wrote, "is that Jews and Christians together, poor Jews and poor Christians, we make a living as best as we can, generally poorly, in this bitch of a life, in this bitch, this poor wretch of a modern society [nous gagnons notre vie comme nous pouvons, généralement mal, dans cette chienne de vie, dans cette chienne, dans cette gueuse de société moderne]."[74] The shared suffering of Jewish and Catholic men and women underwrites a kind of class solidarity, forged at the level of common humanity. Class difference overrides religious, racial, and cultural difference.

Péguy sees poor Jews and Christians as united in their capacity to suffer, and for him, though some Jews cower before danger like everyone else, no other community endures suffering as heroically. On the Jewish body, there is no place "upon which there is not an ancient pain, an old bruise, an old contusion, a dull pain, the memory of dull pain, a scar, a wound" (Il n'a pas sur la peau un point qui ne soit pas douloureux, où il n'y ait un ancien bleu, une ancienne contusion, une douleur sourde, la mémoire d'une douleur sourde).[75] For Péguy and other philo-Semitic revivalists, the Jew became the embodied articulation of the (abject) ideal of suffering and *mystique* that was gravitating to the center of Péguy's philosophical vision.

Péguy's valorization of suffering allowed him to assert the holiness even of secular, assimilated Jews like Lazare. In "Notre jeunesse," he imagines Lazare on his deathbed: "I still see him in his bed, that atheist dripping with the word of God. Even in death, the whole weight of his people bore down on his shoulders."[76] For Péguy, Lazare's suffering overrides his atheism to sanctify the man to God. The willingness to face suffering shown by Jews like Bernard Lazare unites them with Christians in *la mystique*. According to Péguy, Lazare died a martyr to his people from overwork on their behalf, but only a "handful of people" attended his funeral: "the same madmen, the same Jews and Christians. . . . For all those wretched, for all those persecuted people, he was still a flash of lightning, a rekindling of the torch that through all eternity will never be quenched."[77] Through this essay, Péguy (along with Léon Bloy, discussed below) planted the seeds for the most persistent, and obviously problematic, aspect of the revivalists' views on Jews and Judaism: the unity between Christians and Jews through the idiom of affliction ("the same Jews and Christians . . . wretched, persecuted").

Through this kind of *mystique*-centered philo-Semitic discourse, Péguy subverted the dominant prevailing narratives about Jews and Judaism, both secular and Catholic. If, as I have argued above, the secular discourses of republicanism saw Jewish particularity as the recalcitrant obstacle to citizenship and unity, the dominant rhetoric of the Catholic Church was just the opposite. From the Revolution onward, the church saw Jews as the instigators and elaborators of the universalism and cosmopolitanism of modernity, its rootlessness and violent opposition to religious (Catholic) particularity, tradition, stability, and morality.[78] In fact, in the same years that Maritain frequented Péguy's bookshop, acquaintances such as Massis and Sorel led efforts to harness Catholic symbolism to energize deeply anti-Semitic tirades against democracy and modernity, vilifying Jews because they were understood to have gained the most advantages from modern (read here as anticlerical, abhorrent) notions of citizenship.[79] Péguy here strikes out on a new path: he aims to unite Christians and Jews, as two distinct, religiously particular groups—he is interested in the differences between the two as religious traditions—around the shared theme of suffering and abjection, which renders them assimilable, not to the *laïcité,* but to the religiously inflected, suffering-centered realm of *mystique* and revolution. The same handful of fearless Jews and Christians of the *mystique* are equally alienated from their respective traditions (most Jews ignore the prophets, most Christians ignore the saints) but are united with one another.[80]

In some places, Péguy's vivid notion of a wounded Jewry remained stubbornly ahistorical, an essential aspect of Jewish identity rather than something that can be traced in time and analyzed politically. Yet for Péguy this symbol functioned paradoxically. Despite the allure of the symbol of Jews' suffering, Péguy worked tirelessly to improve their condition around the world. He was an ardent Dreyfusard, and it was not only the abjection of the Jews that attracted his interest: he wrote at length about the superiority of the Jewish tradition of literacy in comparison with that of Catholicism, and on the virtues of loyalty and commitment to friendship among the Jews he knew. And as his reflections of Bernard Lazare make clear, he did not want to erase the differences between Jews and Christians through either assimilation or conversion.[81]

Many Jews were attracted to Péguy for his interest in Jewish particularity, despite its flaws, and as many have noted, Péguy was unique in countering turn-of-the-century anti-Semitism with the affirmation of Jews *as Jews,* even as he trafficked in essentialism and ahistoricism. It is no surprise, therefore, that many of the Jewish intellectuals who came to his bookshop along with Maritain, like Péguy's good friend the writer Julien Benda, saw in Péguy's philo-Semitism an alternative to the secular assimilationist ideology of most leftist political thought. According to Annette Aronowicz, Péguy "rediscovered" in his Jewish friends "the Judaism they seemed to no longer remember."[82] He paved the way for young intellectuals like Raïssa Maritain to idealize the Judaism she claimed she knew little about at that point in her life. But for Maritain to go all the way to conversion, she would need the life and thought of Léon Bloy, who saw the suffering Jew as fundamentally unified, bonded, via *conversion,* with the Catholic Church. The "church" Maritain had been discovering was the church of mysticism and willingness to suffer.

LÉON BLOY, JEWISH SUFFERING, AND THE FINAL STEPS TO CONVERSION

All of this—the idealization of medieval mysticism, the philo-Semitic idealization of the abject Jew—would coalesce in Léon Bloy's life and thought. In light of Maritain's story so far it makes sense that she might be fascinated by this radical Catholic writer, whom she discovered in 1905, four years after meeting Péguy, three years after she started attending Bergson's lectures, and a year after her marriage to Jacques.[83]

In 1905, Maritain read Bloy's *La femme pauvre,* a novel valorizing medieval sanctity, something with which Maritain was by now familiar and to which she was deeply attracted. But rather than tethering sanctity to an ancient past, Bloy set his novels in contemporary Paris. As a person he *embodied* what she had been recently exploring. "Reading *La femme pauvre* we passed through the literary genius, as they say, we passed through the walls and went directly not to the author but to the man, the man of faith illuminated by the rays of that strange thing so unknown to us— Catholicism—and we identified with it, as they say."[84] Bloy's own life did indeed mirror his writings. He lived in total squalor in a cramped Montmartre apartment that he shared with his wife, Jeanne, and two young daughters. Bloy's poverty was no mere show. Before the Maritains met Bloy, his young son, André, died from hunger. In Bloy's house, she recalled, "our passage from his books to his life was without break. All here was as he said: true the poverty, true the Faith, true the heroic independence."[85]

In person, Bloy came across as a man of tenderness. Raïssa and Jacques wrote him a fan letter on June 20, 1905, and three days later a grateful Bloy responded with an invitation to his home. "You are awaited with love," he wrote.[86] They eagerly, if nervously, accepted. The Maritains visited Bloy and his wife, Jeanne, for the first time on June 25, 1905. "We were all of a sudden put in the presence of the complete Catholic doctrine," Raïssa recalled, "illustrated so to speak by the admirable spectacle of a very painful life, rejected, despised, and slandered by all [une vie très douloureuse, rejetée, méprisée et calomniée de tous]."[87] Here was Péguy's *suppliant* in the flesh.

From the flurry of correspondence between the Maritains and Bloy in the weeks that followed, what is striking is how *quickly* an intimate bond of friendship was forged. In particular, Bloy's immediate affection for Raïssa is apparent; he soon refers to her in his journals as "très-chère et très-bénie Raïssa," "la lumineuse Raïssa," "ma petite juive Raïssa," "ma petite amie Raïssa," and "douce Raïssa."[88] The nearly instantaneous friendship and affection are also evident in the style and intimacy of their correspondence. Extremely affectionate salutations always frame the letters and stress tender embraces, missing one another, carrying each other in the heart. Moreover, friendship itself was a topic of reflection and seen to be religiously significant. On August 12, less than two months after their initial encounter, Bloy told Raïssa: "You are among those who never arrive too late, my good friend. God knows what friendship does, and God held you for me for this moment in my very painful life—for this moment and not another. Oh what joy you will be paid to have had pity on [this] old Christian writer, Raïssa. . . . I am unable to do anything other than cry while thinking of it!"[89] This was not just a site of emotion, however. As an intellectual Maritain had to then consider the "principles, the sources, the motives of such a life. This time we were brought face to face with the question of God, both in all its power and in all its urgency."[90]

The essential ideas Maritain encountered in Bloy centered on the theme of holy suffering. This theme had been in circulation through Péguy and a revival of the writings of the medieval mystics, but Bloy took it to a new level: he once wrote to his fiancée, "The principal attraction that Christianity had for me was the immensity of the sufferings of Christ—the grandiose and transcending horror of the Passion."[91] For Bloy it was "unthinkably wonderful" and the most "sublime of all human conceptions" that the lover of God in Christianity was one who could ask for a "paradise of tortures."[92] This was precisely what Bloy thought had been erased in the modern world—especially among the rich: "They sympathize melodiously with the sufferings of Jesus, but his Cross fills them with horror—the *reality* of His Cross! They must have it in bright lights and gold, weightless and expensive!"[93]

Bloy's reflections resonated with Maritain's earliest accusations against positivism, that it concealed suffering and mortality. Bloy would speak to this critique directly, vividly: "It is always a good thing to see death," he once wrote, "and I am happy that this thought has filled you with the presence of God. Christians should constantly be leaning over the abyss."[94] It also solidified a notion that the medieval period—so scorned by the positivists and beloved by Péguy and Bloy—was the time in which these darker dimensions of the human condition were visible: in Bloy's novel *La femme pauvre,* a character identifies the medieval period as "*the* great period of Christian mourning [deuil]."[95] It makes sense that Maritain could begin to see, first in Péguy's *mystique* and now in Bloy's Catholicism, which placed death, suffering, and vulnerability at the center of life, a way of living "without any illusion and weakness," the vision she had articulated to Jacques in 1902.

While Maritain always insisted that Bloy's writings moved her in their vivid articulation of that which most people wanted to conceal, she also wrote in 1909 that it was ultimately his theology linking this radical suffering with Judaism that was the final catalyst for her conversion to Catholicism.[96] In 1905, when she met Bloy, Maritain had certainly been immersed in the philo-Semitic atmosphere of Péguy's bookshop, but recall that her 1909 essay opens with the claim, "As a child, I heard a lot about the Jewish people, but I didn't receive any religious instruction to speak of."[97] Yet just after meeting her, Bloy emphasized precisely Maritain's Jewish identity. "The young girl is a tiny Russian Jewess," he wrote in his journal just after meeting her, and he consistently linked her in their correspondence with the prophets and patriarchs of Israel.[98]

Throughout August 1905, two months after meeting him, Maritain was engrossed in Bloy's *Le salut par les juifs (Salvation by the Jews),* a book Bloy considered his most important, written in 1892 but out of print by 1895. After Maritain communicated her pleasure with the book to Bloy, he responded on August 25. "My chère Raïssa," he wrote, "It is certain that you are truly my sister, to have done me this charity. When one loves *Le salut,* one is not only my friend but something much greater. . . . For ten years I have suffered from hiding the most beautiful of my books, and I assure you that it is one of my greatest pains."[99] Bloy then asked her to consider helping him republish it. She and Jacques agreed, and for the next several months correspondence between Jacques and Bloy and between Raïssa and Bloy centered on new edits, publication costs, printing, and timing. Bloy wrote in his journal on December 9, 1905, "It is with as much pride as love that I dedicate it to my little Jewess Raïssa (Rachel), whom her *brother* Jesus will well know how to reward."[100] Five months later, on January 30, 1906, the new edition was ready for the public at five francs each. Even its inscription was an indication of her newfound identity as a Jew. It read: "To Raïssa Maritain: I dedicate these pages, written for the Catholic glory of the God of Abraham, Isaac, and Jacob." For several months preceding her conversion, Bloy referred to Raïssa affectionately as "la dédicataire."

Bloy's text exerted a profound influence on Maritain's decision to convert and furnished much of the conceptual and imaginative material out of which she would later formulate her own understanding of the relationship between Jews and Christians. But exactly what Bloy had in mind is difficult to discern; there is something deeply chaotic about *Le salut par les juifs*, which Maritain later insisted was a "great lyrical and scriptural poem" rather than philosophy or theology.[101] When Maritain published Bloy's writings for the first time in English many years after he died she pushed the chaos to its furthest limit, even exaggerating it by publishing scattered bits and pieces of *Le salut* among his other writings out of order. The frenzied style of Bloy's prose contributes to the lack of any scholarly consensus as to whether he was an anti-Semite or, like Péguy, an early, if imperfect, philo-Semite who aimed to dismantle the classic Christian contempt of Judaism.[102]

Bloy wrote the original text in 1892, two years before the Dreyfus affair, in a period when anti-Semitism was on the rise in France. *Le salut* begins with a polemic against the handbook of French anti-Semitism, Édouard Drumont's *La France juive*.[103] Bloy claims to "déclare la guerre" on Drumont's nightmarish ramblings, but in his effort to subvert prevailing anti-Semitic racism in terms of Christian eschatology he mimics Drumont's manic prose and re-energizes a set of powerful anti-Semitic tropes.[104] According to Bloy, the phrase *Le salut par les juifs* is a paraphrase of the "sublime eleventh chapter of the Jew Saint Paul to the Romans."[105] On Bloy's reading, Paul's chapter in Romans on the remnant of Israel is about the "grafting" of the Gentiles onto the Jewish stock for the salvation of both, underscored by the cryptic statement found in John 4:22: "*Salut ex Judaeis est.* Salvation is from the Jews! I do not recall that he [Drumont] quoted these simple and formidable words of our Lord Jesus Christ."[106]

To interpret Paul's notion, Bloy begins by excavating long-standing Christian and secular anxieties about Jews and reasserts them with vehemence: Jews are "wandering [errer sans vocation sur la terre]," homeless, "crawling," like vermin, "along the Danube, Poland, Russia, Germany, Holland, in France itself." They are the "Orphan People" (Peuple Orphelin), "condemned."[107] The Jews have "murdered the Word" (égorgé le Verbe fait chair). These myths of the Jews as a God-killing people and their fate of eternal wandering are old, anti-Jewish clichés. But the image of the wandering Jew in particular gained a new traction in the nineteenth century precisely because of nationalism and the notion that all real people belonged to a people and their land. Jews did not have a land: they were wanderers and hence never actually citizens.[108] For Bloy, the Jew in *Le salut* was the rejected embodiment of misery and homelessness, the lost stranger.

In his manic, vivid reiteration of these tropes, Bloy prepares his reader to assent to the claim that to "love [Jews] as such" (les aimer comme tels) would require a "miracle of the most transcendent holiness" or could only be "the illusion of a religious imbecile" (C'est le miraculeux de la sainteté la plus transcendante ou l'illusion d'une religiosité imbécile).[109] It is not clear if Bloy aims to deepen readers' putative repulsion toward Jews or to provide the reader a "transcendent" shock into "loving them." Perhaps both; by "flirting with the taboos of anti-Semitism" (to draw from the historian Samuel Moyn's useful concept here), he articulates a kind of bizarre Catholic philo-Semitism founded on a contradictory, twofold claim that the Christian Holy Spirit hovers within the suffering, wandering Jews precisely *because of* their abjection and that the redemption of human history is dependent upon Jewish conversion to Christianity.[110]

To support these two paradoxical claims, having established the marginalization of Jews, Bloy reminds readers that it was they who furnished Christianity with the prophets, the Apostles, the Virgin, early martyrs, even "our Savior himself, the Lion of Judah—an unspeakable Jew!"[111] It makes sense that out of such a scorned people could emerge Bloy's abject God on the cross: "the true King of abjection and pain" (un vrai Roi de l'abjection et de la douleur), "a leper king," "a Jewish orphan."[112] "The blood shed upon the Cross for the redemption of humankind . . . is naturally and supernaturally Jewish blood [sang naturellement et supernaturellement juif]."[113] Later, Bloy would claim that most Christians would do anything to deny this fact. From *Le salut* through his later publications, he believed that the recognition of the Jewishness of Christianity could subvert modern anti-Semitism: "That being the case, how is one to express the enormity of the outrage and of the blasphemy that consists in vilifying the Jewish Race?" he asked.[114] Although the assertion sounds implausible, Bloy was not so off the mark: in the years surrounding Bloy's writing on Judaism, the German philosopher Houston Stewart Chamberlain published *La genèse du XIX e siècle* (1899), which claims, "We do not perceive the least reason for admitting the relations of Jesus were of the Jewish race. . . . It is probable that Jesus did not have a drop of Jewish blood in his veins."[115] As later chapters will explore, some philo-Semitic Catholic intellectuals (Maritain included) during the Shoah would dispute Chamberlain's claims directly. Bloy can be counted here as an early, if deeply problematic, forerunner.

For Bloy, the emphasis on the Jewishness of Christianity is most importantly a way to render Christianity *itself* marginal and antibourgeois, like the abject, forsaken "Jews" at the root of the Christian religion. It is Jews and the Jewish Christ, the orphan and "leper king," from whom we learn that the markers of finitude and suffering are the marks of holiness itself: "The very abjectness of that Race," he writes, "is a divine Sign, the very manifest sign of the constant lingering of the Holy Spirit over these men so scorned by the world."[116] He names "à une sorte d'identité" between Israel and the Holy Spirit to illustrate the alliance between the people of Israel, rootless and cast aside, and God.[117] Even further, he endows the Holy Spirit with the classic markers of Jewish particularity: the Paraclete not only identifies with the wandering Jews but is *itself* wandering ("ce Paraclet errant").[118] In doing so, Bloy clearly draws from but significantly revises a long-standing theological and exegetical tradition in Christianity that supernaturalizes Jewish suffering in history. Since at least the fifth century, some Christian thinkers had seen Jewish marginalization and affliction as proof that Jews were no longer the recipients of God's providential care and had believed that because of this they should never be eradicated and should instead always remain on earth, with all their suffering laid bare for the world to see, as continued proof of Christianity's truth. Bloy similarly endows Jewish abjection with the aura of the divine but recasts it as an instantiation of the God who chooses the least and the lowest.

This way of sanctifying Jewish particularity follows from Bloy's doctrine of a God who is "lonely," "disfigured," at home with "the exiles" and "the dead, the dying, and the wounded" on earth, and at one with the protagonists of all of Bloy's books—the poor, the insane, widows, prostitutes, Jews, children.[119] Bloy's sanctification of the trope of the wandering, rootless Jew can also be illuminated by his critiques of modern nationalism: "The modern world, weary of the living God," he wrote in 1887, now "kneels before the nation." Patriotism, he claimed, was "the new national cult."[120] His critiques of nationalism as idolatry segue into the sanctification of those who are putatively landless, rootless (bracketing here, for a moment, Bloy's own extreme glorification of the French nation elsewhere).

Toward the end of *Le salut,* Bloy, to illustrate his point about the alliance between the Jewish community and the divine, vividly portrays the Holy Ghost as mysteriously dwelling with the lamentations of Israel itself. When this double voice of the Jew and the Holy Spirit speaks, Bloy switches to the future tense to describe in eschatological terms the depth and terror of its abjection: the Holy Spirit/Israel will have "no friends, and his wretchedness will make beggars look like emperors. . . . People will bend down to see the lowest term of Suffering and Abjection [de la Souffrance et de l'Abjection]. At his approach the sun will turn into darkness and the moon into blood."[121] "His" wretchedness, abjection, and suffering here refers to that of the Holy Ghost and of Israel and is seen in this passage as a frightening, overwhelming force, a force that could engender a kind of "sacred dread"—to use Raïssa Maritain's later phrase—and all the anxiety and fascination that this entails.

We can better appreciate the intensity of Bloy's language by situating him among the French decadents of the nineteenth century, like his one-time friend J.-K. Huysmans. In a move more aesthetically daring than Péguy's socialist *imaginaire* or Bergson's championing of intuition and mysticism, decadents mined Catholicism for its transgressive symbolism, its emphasis on death and sin. The decadent literary movement was a nineteenth-century offshoot of fin de siècle symbolism. Authors, like Bloy, affiliated with decadence rebelled against the seeming optimism of bourgeois modernity, highlighting and idealizing those cultural symbols most denigrated by the liberalism of the *laïcité*. For decadents, middle-class mentalities were tepid and mediocre but could also be relentlessly cruel. Decadents glorified and elicited in grisly detail the figures others shunned or ignored.[122] Prostitutes, Jews, the degenerate, the sick, and the female *hystérique* were all vividly depicted in decadent novels, in all of their lowliness and impropriety, as a means of subverting modern liberal ideals and making visible those typically cast aside. There was an ethical and political imperative to the decadent imagination: the readers of Bloy's texts encounter a brutal world in which the insane, the sick, orphans, prostitutes, the poor, children, and here, the Jews throw the underside of bourgeois modernity into sharp relief. In some of his writings Bloy gives voice to those traditionally voiceless figures (who tend to be the heroes and protagonists of his novels, though they all relish their abjection), just as the booming but utterly abject holy voice of Israel is the culmination of *Le salut.*

Bloy's deeply ambivalent reading of Judaism relied upon Jewish particularity—the Jews' terrifying suffering and dread—and reconciled it to an antibourgeois Christianity that placed the margins at a new center. In a way, this subverted the (at the time) prevailing anti-Semitic narrative of Catholics (in which Jews were too cosmopolitan, modern, and a threat to tradition) as well as that of the *laïcité* (in which Jewish particularism was something that had to be overcome and absorbed into universal citizenship). Although Péguy and Bloy both aimed to articulate the bonds between Jews and Christians through the idiom of suffering, Péguy crucially did *not* require Jewish conversion or assimilation. True Christianity, as Bloy described it, would renew contact with its abject Jewish roots, but true Judaism was ultimately destined for the church. He explained this in characteristic graphic, morbid language: Jesus's crucifixion was ongoing, not in the past ("Jesus always crucified, always bleeding"; "the Blood of Christ, still warm"). For Bloy this meant that Christ's agony would continue until he descended from the cross, which could not happen, according to his messianic imagination, until the Jews converted.[123] Although in some places, Bloy's "true Jews" accepted the "king of Abjection" even if they were not Christian in name. The combination of these contradictory claims—the recasting of anti-Semitic tropes as holy and the positing of the Jews' conversion as an eschatological requirement—animated the potential anti-Semitism and violence of Bloy's rhetoric.

Péguy and Bloy differed on more than just the issue of conversion. Unlike Péguy, Bloy, for all his outrage against modern anti-Semitism, had no faith in politics to ameliorate the situation of Jews or anyone else. Though his writings could ideally evoke readers' outrage, moral indignation, and sympathy with those who were persecuted, he saw Jewish suffering, not as politically, historically conditioned, but as *fundamental* to Jewish identity and salvation history. According to Bloy, humanitarians, such as most of the Dreyfusards, thought only "in terms of human means. All we hear about are leagues, congresses, elections, etc. . . . To my mind this is vain and profoundly stupid."[124] He believed in acts of charity and kindness, but his vivid, symbolic, detailed descriptions of the reality of Jewish suffering functioned primarily as an aesthetic invective to hurl at the bourgeoisie. Detachment from actual Jews enabled Bloy's recklessness and his willing redeployment of the ugly slanders that had established anti-Semitism as a default position in French Catholic circles. Jews appear in his text as vessels to communicate perversion and inversion, not as real people, and unlike Péguy he knew few actual Jewish men and women. The fascinating exception was, of course, his own goddaughter, Raïssa Maritain. Maritain's potential conversion was something Bloy had hoped for as early as July 25, 1905, just over a month after their first meeting. In his journal he describes her as a "dear little Samaritan" who can be "healed by the one" whom her "ancestors have crucified."[125]

"A CHRISTIAN SET ON FIRE": RAÏSSA MARITAIN AND LÉON BLOY

As a twenty-two-year-old woman and a Jew, Raïssa Maritain for Bloy was someone potentially *already* religiously powerful, "Christian even before her conversion." He wrote of her in his journal on July 29 as "the delightful [or delicious] little Jew, in whom we already see a Christian" (la délicieuse petite juive en qui nous voyons déjà une chrétienne).[126] He wrote to her in August 1905:

> "I am not a Christian," you say. "I can do nothing else in my deep sorrow but search." Why do you continue to search since *you have found* what you are looking for? How could you love what I write if you did not think and feel as I do? You are not just a Christian, Raïssa, you are a Christian set on fire, a daughter of the Beloved Father, a spouse of Jesus Christ at the foot of the Cross, a loving servant of the Mother of God in the waiting room of the Queen of all the world.[127]

Maritain might already be a "Christian of the heart" because Bloy linked her to the Pauline, Marian, and Christ-like Jews at the font of Christianity, or because his theology of inversion found something truly Christian in her lowliness. Maritain was not exactly abject and scorned, but Bloy did discern something powerful embodied in what he saw as her fragility: "In this charming and frail being," he wrote in his journal after meeting her, "there is a soul that would make an oak tree fall to its knees."[128]

It is difficult to formulate what exactly Maritain made of Bloy's views on Judaism when she encountered them in 1905, several months before her conversion. She made crystal clear that it was Bloy who removed the final obstacle to full conversion and that this obstacle was Judaism. She wrote in 1909 that, thanks to Bloy, "where I would have been afraid of finding struggles and opposition, I experienced with true joy only unity, continuity, and perfect harmony."[129] The union of the two testaments was key, but that union involved an evolution from Israel to the church. Bloy's supersessionism remained intact in Maritain's rationale for conversion: "We pass from one to another by means of Christ."[130] Her 1909 essay also suggests a reiteration of another of Bloy's doctrines, retrieved from the Pauline dichotomy between the false Jew who is material and literal and the true Jew who is spiritual (Rom. 2:28–29). For Bloy, the true Jew is not quite Jewish, since he is so blended with the abject, interiorized Christian. Maritain writes, "There are—as Pascal very well saw—throughout the history of the Hebrews, two types of Jews: carnal Jews and spiritual Jews, rebellious Jews and obedient Jews." Maritain's "spiritual Jews" are straight from Bloy and Péguy: they are "martyrs," "warlike saints," mystical "contemplatives," "prophetic"—these are the "real Israelites" who (and here she draws directly from Bloy) "are already Christians. Christians of desire . . . exspectans exspectavi," just as Bloy saw Maritain when he met her, "déjà une chrétienne."[131] This troubling distinction between true and false Jew, one spiritual ("déjà une chrétienne") and one carnal, circulated widely in French Catholic philo-Semitic circles. It was deployed even by Péguy in his portrait of Bernard Lazare, where Jews are described as either merchants or prophets.[132] For Maritain, Bloy's continual invocation of themes of suffering and abjection (which she claimed were avoided in positivism) and his emphasis on Jewish-Christian unity through the idiom of suffering were a potent combination that sufficed to dispel any misgivings she might have had about conversion. By the spring of 1906, on

April 5, Maritain communicated to Bloy that she was considering baptism. She and Jacques were baptized in Paris on June 11, 1906. Bloy was their godfather.

For Maritain, as for other assimilated Jews in Péguy's community, Péguy's and Bloy's ideas may have been among the few encounters with Judaism as a religious system. This was a Jewish woman in Paris whose family had long been pressured to assimilate; as a twenty-two-year-old, she knew almost nothing about Judaism and very little about Catholicism. The poverty of her conception of Judaism makes sense given that anti-Jewish violence had led her family to flee to France, where they encountered a strong assimilationist pull as a prelude to citizenship.[133] Bloy's contempt for all things bourgeois appealed to her leftist background, and his suffering-centered imagination consolidated what she had been exposed to through Bergson and Péguy. By centering holy suffering on the figure of the Jew, and emphasizing Maritain's Jewishness and holiness, Bloy personalized this valorization of suffering for Maritain and made it immediate to her. As I show in chapter 5, it would not be until the terrible years of 1940–44 that Maritain would herself draw from Bloy's vivid imagery about Jewish abjection and wounds.

Overall, throughout her life, Maritain emphasized that she could not read the chapters where Bloy expressed his views about suffering (Jewish and otherwise) without "overwhelming emotion."[134] She was struck by the feelings that the pages incited rather than the content of the theology communicated. Maritain insisted that what drove Bloy's writing was a desire for his readers to experience and feel this reality themselves, and that his texts were purposely aimed at being experiential. She wrote that Bloy's novels and other writings were excessive and exaggerated as a way to "force the imagination to 'feel' in some way or another those incomprehensible contradictions of Christianity."[135] Maritain agreed with another key idea of Bloy's, that others "hid" dark, grave matters under a "whitewash of sociability."[136] By consistently emphasizing the emotive impact of Bloy's texts on the imagination of the reader, she formulated some of her earliest thinking on aesthetics, thoughts she would come to articulate much more fully in her later writings.

At this point, Maritain was a twenty-two-year-old burgeoning aesthete who did not yet have a theory to describe how this disturbing material about Jewish abjection incited her imagination. As with Péguy, other assimilated Jewish intellectuals on the left would find something oddly appealing about Bloy, not so much for his theology of Judaism as for his vivid, evocative rage against modernity. In 1924, after reading the "splendid exegesis" of Bloy's satirical *Exégèses des lieux communs,* Walter Benjamin claimed that "a more embittered critique, or rather satire, of the bourgeois could hardly have been written."[137] Later, Emmanuel Levinas cited Bloy's "admirably bold" vision of femininity in *Lettres à sa fiancée.*[138] Franz Kafka also admired Bloy, reporting that he "possesses a fire that brings to mind the ardor of the prophets—an even greater ardor, I should say."[139] Like Maritain, Lazare, and Julien Benda, many nonobservant Jewish men and women were attracted to revivalists like Bloy and Péguy and were thereby drawn into a particular kind of antibourgeois Catholic philo-Semitism in early twentieth-century France. To enter this world was to immerse oneself in images saturated with suffering and with Judaism, and though some found it abhorrent, others, like Maritain, would go as far as conversion.

ATTENDING TO MARITAIN'S OWN VOICE AND THE CONTEXT from which it emerged releases her 1906 conversion from compartmentalizing dismissals of it as "incongruous" and opens it to explanation. If Maritain's transformation from an antireligious seeker, to an apostle of the great secular Jewish philosopher Henri Bergson, to a devotee of Catholicism focused on radical suffering is surprising, it is not beyond understanding. The explanation, in part, lies in her immersion in the widespread critiques of secular positivism and her curious and powerful ability to connect freedom and the affections, particularly suffering, a connection that gradually intensified and deepened over time. Maritain's encounter with Bergson enabled her to move away from secular positivism and reframe the suffering she had experienced while a student as positive evidence of intellectual resistance. Moreover, through her work with Bergson, Maritain gradually came to understand premodern Christian and Greek mystical writings as the most commanding alternative to the stuffiness of the Sorbonne, and as best exhibiting Bergson's rich descriptions of the inner life. Péguy's Judaized *suppliant,* wounded and heroic, opened up conversations about the powerful *mystique* of Jewish affliction as a counterweight to all that was mediocre about the modern world: its fear of suffering, its bourgeois complacency, its *politique*. But it was her intense friendship with Léon Bloy that brought her to the doorstep of the church. Bloy's messianic imagination introduced Maritain to the notion of the destiny of the suffering Jews' acceptance of the "King of Abjection."

People like Péguy and Bloy do not merely provide the background necessary to illuminate Maritain's ideas and understand her conversion; they also exhibit a mode of embodied and affective thinking that is absolutely central to her vision. Her relationships and the ideas her friends and mentors embodied were strong galvanizing forces throughout Maritain's whole life. My interest in how these intense personal relationships animated Maritain's life, and the *renouveau catholique* as a whole, draws from Frédéric Gugelot and also, more recently, the historian of religion Constance Furey. Furey claims that while scholars of religion regularly analyze the disciplining role of societal norms and practices in the formation of religious selves, bonds of "intense, sustained relationships" are less frequently taken seriously as an analytic framework. *Relationship,* she hastens to add, "seems like a friendly word only insofar as the scholar's ear inclines toward friendly relationships, avoiding the unequal distribution of resources, the injustices, conflicts, aversions, repugnance, and rejection that relationships also entail."[140] In the world of Raïssa Maritain, not only fascination and love but the pressures and breakdowns in communication typical of any intimate relationship influenced her route to conversion.

Finally, before continuing with the story, we must acknowledge the extremely fraught legacy of this intellectual impulse. The theme of suffering sanctity, as Maritain and other French Catholics invoked it, was not politically neutral; nor was it merely a safe haven from the coldness of secularism. As this story shows, early on the Maritains' foundational community included an eclectic array of critics of the Sorbonne's scientific positivism from all sides of the ideological spectrum: anti-Semites (Massis and Surin) and philo-Semitic Dreyfusards (Péguy), clergy, decadent literary figures, and the precursors to surrealism. The legacy of these early years is deeply ambiguous. Many people, from the Right and the Left, drew on the wide-ranging critiques of modernity to advocate for an extreme anti-democratic politics that continued to exercise its pernicious influence as late as the Vichy regime. The community's valorization of Jewish suffering also proved problematic, as chapter 5 will explore. Péguy and Bloy's brutal and sordid descriptions of Jewish wounds, abjection, and commitment to *mystique* raise questions about the total effect of such a discourse: Does it produce fatalistic, submissive acceptance of suffering and injustice? Provoke sympathy and outrage? What did Maritain do with this religious *imaginaire,* particularly in the decades that followed, the late 1930s and beyond, as the European horizon darkened? But before we answer this question, another demands our attention. It is clear from any reading of the literature of the French Catholic revival, by Bloy, Jacques and Raïssa, Péguy, and many others, that it prominently associated suffering not only with Jews but also with women. Feminized suffering predominates in the French Catholic revival writings. What did Maritain make of this?

CHAPTER 2

"She Who Weeps"

Feminized Suffering in the Thought of Léon Bloy and the Maritains (1906–35)

In December 1906, six months after their conversion, Léon Bloy introduced Jacques and Raïssa to his beloved devotion to the Virgin Mary of La Salette. La Salette is the name of the French village where, on September 19, 1846, the Virgin allegedly appeared to two impoverished children, Mélanie Calvat and Maximin Giraud, weeping, with her face in her hands, and wearing a crown of thorns.[1] This occurred on the eve of the Feast of the Seven Sorrows, a holy day celebrating the most sorrowful events in the life of the Virgin (symbolized in the popular iconographic image of seven swords piercing Mary's broken heart), and the timing of the event gave the apparition more legitimacy and intensified its import. As the children described her, Mary appeared just as afflicted as the familiar iconographic images depicted her. At La Salette, Our Lady mourned the impiety of the nineteenth-century French republican society, the erosion of religious observance, and the moral laxity of the French people. Not only sorrowful for the state of the modern world, Mary of La Salette was also angry at the church. In the midst of the apparition, the Virgin allegedly whispered a secret to young Mélanie: "The priests," the girl claimed Mary had told her, "by their bad life, by their irreverence, their impiety in celebrating the holy mysteries, by love of money, love of honor and of pleasures, the priests have become cesspools of impurity."[2] Our Lady of La Salette predicted apocalyptic doom if the clerical orders were not purged. A local cult grew around the site of the apparition, and the church sanctioned the public and more orthodox message about moral laxity but never approved of the anticlerical secret Mélanie claimed to have heard. The secret was eventually transcribed and printed into a booklet, but in 1905 Mélanie's booklet was placed in the Index of Forbidden Books, and in 1915 further research on La Salette was banned. The church eventually rejected Mélanie as insane and a fraud.

La Salette was only one among many of the villages in Europe's "siècle de Marie" in which the Virgin Mary is said to have appeared, drawing multitudes of devout men and women on pilgrimages.[3] But above all others, La Salette held special appeal for the French Catholic revival. La Salette's marginal status within official Catholicism endeared the site to J.-K. Huysmans, Léon Bloy, and eventually, the newly baptized Maritains. Bloy wrote in his journal that the La Salette phenomenon had been the "central concern of my life!" and confessed to a friend that it had been "the starting point of my intellectual life, and as much as I can see, of my religious life."[4] Bloy discovered La Salette when he was thirty years old and made his first pilgrimage to the shrine after the death of his young son. He eventually published two books on Mélanie and her vision, *Celle qui pleure (She Who Weeps)* (1908) and *La vie de Mélanie (The Life of Mélanie)* (1912).

In 1907, a year after her baptism and in the midst of her first life-threatening illness, Raïssa Maritain, at Bloy's urging, made a novena to Notre Dame de La Salette. She attributed her sudden recovery to the Virgin, and the speed at which Raïssa and Jacques developed a devotion to La Salette and the child seer Mélanie was astonishing. The following spring they made a pilgrimage of thanksgiving to the shrine and there dedicated themselves to the Virgin as her "slaves," just as their godfather had done. They had a statue of Our Lady, a large wooden carving of Mary's sadness and grief, placed in their home in 1911. The mournful Virgin and the girl Mélanie became a major focus of Jacques and Raïssa's attention. By 1912,

Jacques finished a document on the events surrounding the apparition that ran to seven hundred pages. In 1917, at the height of the First World War, Raïssa convinced Jacques to present his research to Pope Benedict XV in an effort to get the ban on La Salette research lifted.[5] The effort did not succeed.

At the center of the phenomenon of La Salette are the images of two afflicted females shrouded in holiness: Mary, tears streaming down her face, burdened with sorrow and rage, and her child seer, Mélanie, scorned, shunned, rejected as insane by the official church. It was precisely the affliction and marginalization of La Salette's women that drew Bloy, the Maritains, and other revivalists to them. Mary and Mélanie are but two images of suffering femininity that lie close to the heart of late modern French Catholicism. Much as Péguy and Bloy were fascinated by Jewish affliction, throughout the nineteenth and twentieth centuries many French theologians, lay intellectuals, poets, novelists, and even modernist philosophers relied on feminized symbols of agony to communicate truths about human nature and the divine.[6]

In the introduction, I argued that scholars have tended to see the women and girls entangled in these discourses in terms of the doctrine of vicarious suffering and to take the modern perspective that their illness and anguish render them passive victims. Within a framework of the doctrine of vicarious suffering, sufferers are seen as submissive and as bizarrely accepting of the blows that come their way. If suffering women are active, it is mainly through their suffering, which redeems sinful others in the eyes of God. In this mode of piety known as *douleur rédemptrice,* vicarious sufferers do the necessary work of suffering in a Christian cosmology that depends on it.[7]

Yet I argue that the image of the suffering woman can be more polysemic than this equation would allow.[8] Using La Salette as the starting point in this chapter, I extend my investigations outward to explore how the symbol of suffering femininity, broadly conceived, variously functions in the writings of Léon Bloy, Jacques Maritain, and Raïssa. The doctrine of vicarious suffering played a role in energizing and elaborating French Catholic symbols of suffering, but those symbols also drew from a range of literary, theological, and historical sources, none of which can be understood as simply rendering women active or passive, resistant or hopelessly entangled. There were more options than these two avenues allow. First, Léon Bloy's decadent literary deployment of prostitutes, impoverished widows, and scorned young girls, all of whom appear in his texts as aesthetic and highly vivid prompts to the faculty of memory, relate femininity to holy suffering in complex ways that I examine in detail below. I then turn to the reflections of Jacques, whose writings on feminized holy suffering converged mainly around Raïssa and the many illnesses she endured in the early years of their marriage. Drawing deeply from medieval models of women's piety and from the countless *vitae* the couple devoured in their early apprenticeship as Christians, Jacques was not interested in having his sins atoned for by Raïssa's suffering. For him, when Raïssa re-emerged into the world from her cycles of sickness and healing, she had knowledge of supernatural matters that would have been beyond his grasp if he had not learned of them through her.

Finally I turn to Raïssa Maritain's investment in these models of suffering femininity and the ways she adopted and transformed them.[9] I focus on Maritain's first three decades as a Christian, in the years before 1935. Maritain drew deeply from the French Catholic fascination with female suffering, but she also departed from it in crucial ways. She was a conscious contributor to a narrative that saw suffering as holy for women (as well as men), but she also exhibited a capacity for critique when she challenged the conventions of this gendered theology by using Catholicism's own resources. Her discovery of Thomas Aquinas in 1909 ultimately enabled her to centralize the role of the intellect—something that does not typically figure into feminized notions of anguish. Furthermore, representations of *souffrance* and *peine* in Maritain's writing are indebted to the seventeenth-century French school of spirituality (with its roots in the mysticism of the Spanish Carmelites) in that she locates suffering interiorly, within the will, rather than in feminized flesh in pain. This pairing of suffering-centered devotionalism and Thomas's theory of connaturality creatively bridges the rift between suffering-centered, feminized Catholicism and its intellectual counterpart, which has been typically gendered masculine. As we will see, the divisions between suffering femininity and masculine rationality were deep and were extremely embedded in French discourse. By seeking to heal the gendered and disciplinary divides of Christian history, Raïssa Maritain made a creative contribution to the revival of mysticism in twentieth-century France.

SPECTACLES OF DISTRESS: DECODING SUFFERING
FEMININITY IN LÉON BLOY'S NOVELS AND LIFE

Like the abject, wandering Jew, prostitutes locked up in insane asylums, widows mistaken for vagrants, and young girls dressed in rags are among Léon Bloy's most consistent literary vehicles to communicate theological truths. Echoing his theology of Judaism, Bloy describes these abject women and girls, in page after page, as sites of power and holiness. Consider a passage in his work *Le sang du pauvre (The Blood of the Poor)* (1909), which Bloy began just shortly after meeting the Maritains. Here Bloy describes what he calls "the Indignation of God."

> [The Indignation of God] is a haggard girl famished with hunger [C'est une fille hagarde et pleine de faim], and all doors are shut to her, a true daughter of the desert whom no one knows. . . . She has wrung her hands before every threshold, begging to be taken in, but she has found nobody to have pity on the Indignation of God. She is beautiful, nonetheless, but cannot be seduced. The Indignation of God is clothed in rags and has almost nothing to hide her nakedness. Her eyes are dark gulfs and her mouth no longer utters a word. Whenever she meets a priest, she grows paler and more silent, for priests condemn her, finding that she is ill-kempt, intemperate . . . : she knows so well that henceforth everything is in vain.[10]

In the theological imagination of Maritain's godfather, such young girls dressed in rags are like the child seer, La Salette's Mélanie, shunned by the clergy but holding an awesome, divine power.

Bloy's most famous novel and the text that drew the Maritains to him, *La femme pauvre (The Woman Who Was Poor)* (1897), is about the sanctification of the protagonist, Clotilde, a violent process that inspires something equally harrowing in her husband. Bloy not only renders Clotilde's suffering but exults in it and describes it again and again. He wants to elicit every last drop of shock, distress, empathy, and compassion, as well as pleasure and relief, from his readers. While her husband nearly goes blind and her first-born son dies, Clotilde descends into poverty and loses her home. Later, her husband dies in a heroic display of martyrdom, rescuing people from a fire. After this spectacle of distress, Clotilde's sanctification radically intensifies. "Make me a Saint!" she cries out to God; then "flames roared and surged about her, devouring all around."[11] These flames are spiritual and metaphorical rather than actual (as in her husband's death), and she suddenly gives all she has to the poor and becomes a mendicant. After this transformation, Clotilde is mistaken in her town for a madwoman—"dérangée d'esprit"—and a vagrant. Police are afraid of her, but some are "bewildered at her power" and consider Clotilde a saint. Even a priest goes away "dazed with Divine Love" when she shocks him with the pronouncement that has become one of the most famous lines in the book: "I am completely happy. One does not enter into Paradise tomorrow or the next day, or in ten years, but on *this day*, if one is poor and crucified."[12] Clotilde's suffering exhibits a self-annihilating model of sanctity, and in the excruciating detail central to the literary movements of realism and decadence Bloy urges his readers to imaginatively identify with her despair.

To take another example, Léon Bloy's first major novel, *Le désespéré (The Desperate Man)* (1886), introduces Véronique, an impoverished prostitute who becomes a site of mysterious religious power for those around her. As Véronique becomes a "glorious vessel" of God, she gradually succumbs to madness. Yet this seems to only deepen the holy alliance between Véronique and the divine. Once she is committed to an asylum, a visionary in the novel whispers, "The Church is locked up in a hospital of madwomen" (L'Église est écrouée dans un hôpital de folles).[13] Invoking the sacrament of the Eucharist, Bloy pairs the vulgarity of prostitution with the sacred when he refers to "la présence réelle de Véronique."[14] Even ugliness is divine in *Le désespéré,* for the once-beautiful Véronique freely transforms her body and has all her teeth extracted and her head shaved, willfully rendering herself completely repulsive, while deepening, Bloy writes, her experience of love and intimacy with God.[15]

The novel was based on Bloy's experiences with the prostitute Anne-Marie Roulé, the first woman with whom he had a deep relationship. They lived for two years in what he describes as a state of religious ecstasy until she went insane in 1882 and died in an asylum. Two years later, Bloy met another prostitute whom he rescued, revered, and planned to marry before she too died. His experience of the prostitute as a Christ figure was never far from his imagination. "I want to show, to the wonder of mediocre souls," Bloy wrote after *Le désespéré*, "the miraculous connection that exists between the Holy Ghost and the most lamentable, most despised, most polluted of human creatures," and according to Bloy, the most rejected by bourgeois modernity, "the Prostitute."[16] Bloy's association here of the Holy Ghost with abject women, prostitutes in particular, echoes his association of the Holy Ghost with forsaken Jews. They are brought in from the margins and placed in a new, sanctified center.

Untangling the theory of aesthetics that Bloy aimed for in his texts can at least partially illuminate his symbols of suffering women and girls so that we see the world Maritain came to know. It would be tempting to see them in terms of vicarious suffering alone—these women suffer so that men do not have to—but Bloy had something more complex in mind. As he described it, he hoped that the eroticized and grief-stricken female characters in his novels would have a transformative effect on those who read about them—and not just *via* vicarious redemption. The most effective tool of his literary craft, Bloy claimed, was imagination, which he called the artist's "master faculty." Women, suffering, and sanctity never converge in a general way in his texts but do so around a specific woman, such as the prostitute locked up in an asylum or the destitute widow mistaken to be a vagrant. Further, Bloy claimed that "the artist who considers only the object itself *does not see it*. To say something worthwhile it is essential to exaggerate it, that is, to carry one's scrutiny beyond the object."[17] Extremes of hyperbole and exaggeration, Bloy believed, would spur the imagination toward the Absolute. Ultimately, Bloy saw the ideal encounter with art, particularly art that depicted graphic suffering, and the response of the imagination as redemptive.

The faculty of memory, as Bloy understood it, aided in the transformative work of his imaginative texts. More biographically, he explained, "Philosophy wearies me, theology bores me to death. . . . God gave me imagination and memory and nothing else."[18] He maintained that the hyperbolic, abject figures in his art (mainly women and Jews), after working on the imagination, awakened the reader's memory, particularly memories of suffering: "From the depths of the seas of memory, suddenly there surge forth the almost forgotten sweet charms of yesteryear . . . the burning desires for martyrdom, the indescribable tenderness and then rain of holy tears which poured forth on a far-off day, gone beyond recall."[19] Bloy describes how this process works in *La femme pauvre*. In one of the novel's earliest passages on the power of La Salette, he highlights the links between memory, suffering, and healing prompted by an image of a suffering woman. In the novel, the character Marchenoir (based self-consciously on himself) makes a pilgrimage to La Salette.[20] Marchenoir is apparently devastated by the recent death of his one-year-old son (echoing Bloy's own devastating experience) but is hardened against emotion. When he sees the anguish and grief of the Virgin of La Salette, his despair, as he describes it, suddenly "[unwinds], strand by strand," presumably as he remembers his son: When "I saw the Mother seated on a stone, weeping, her face in her hands, with that little fountain that looks as it if flowed from her eyes, I went up to the railings and threw myself down, and spent myself in tears and sobs." His grief intensifies, but, as he reports, "I no longer suffered" (Je ne souffrais plus).[21] A kind of cathartic healing takes place through the weeping, grief-stricken Virgin, whether through consolation or the relief of purging his grief. Bloy seems to be suggesting that an encounter with the suffering other draws up memories of one's own suffering and opens a path to healing and transcendence.

For Bloy, identification with the suffering of the Virgin excavates memories of suffering, and he insists that everyone has such memories, even if they are buried below consciousness: "We are all creatures of misery and desolation [tous des misérables et des dévastés], but few of us are capable of looking into the abyss of ourselves. . . . You don't even know your own hell. One must be, or have once been, devout, to be well acquainted with one's own abandonment, and take full count of the silent troops of devils we all carry about within us."[22] Suffering comes to consciousness in the confrontation with the hyperbolically afflicted other, which stirs memories of one's own affliction, the first step toward intimacy with God.

Moreover, there is a distinctly erotic tone to Bloy's work. The grief-stricken prostitutes, widows, and girls are all sexually charged. Drawing on the long-standing association between suffering and love in Christian mystical literature, Bloy in his work on La Salette narrates Mary's anguish at the foot of the cross in explicitly erotic language.[23] Consider, moreover, Bloy's claim that women's sexual parts are "the tabernacle of the living God."[24]

The suffering women in Bloy's texts neither repay an Anselmian debt nor suffer on behalf of sinners. Women—or anyone else—could never suffer in another's place, for anguish, grief, and affliction are far too central in Bloy's vision of sanctity. Instead, these women ideally evoke empathy and heightened emotions, such as sadness and grief, and thus accomplish union with God (or at least the possibility of such union).[25] Moreover, the women in Bloy's texts are not simply carriers but also *models* of sanctity to emulate for men and women alike. Of course, feminist theorists have long insisted that symbols of gender can be "about" things other than relationships between men and women, and here Bloy's symbols of suffering femininity seem to have modeled the recognition of one's own grief.[26] Further, poor, insane, and vagrant women were symbols used to mount scathing critiques of bourgeois republicanism. Bloy's fascination with La Salette, prostitution, weeping, and forsaken women—all seen as powerful, holy, and transgressive—traveled within the literary currents of realism and Catholic decadence, which came together in a shared antipathy for the bourgeois ideals of the secular republic. It pays to consider these movements in more detail.

SUFFERING FEMININITY
AS ANTIBOURGEOIS SYMBOL

In chapter 1, I described how critics of French republicanism could relish the details of Jewish particularity over and against the *laïcist* ideal of assimilation as a prelude to secular citizenship. Historians such as Caroline Ford have recently added to this conversation by analyzing how, in addition to religious particularity, gender became crucial to the religious and aesthetic traditions opposed to the *laïcité* ideals.[27] Ford explores the discourses of masculinity, femininity, and religion that sustained the debates around *laïcisme* in nineteenth- and twentieth-century France, arguing that beginning with the French Revolution, representations of feminized Catholicism played a crucial role in the articulation of French secular republicanism. In the speeches, novels, newspapers, and films of many anticlerical republican men, Catholic women (real or imagined) became associated with both counterrevolution and religion, and both were depicted as unreasonable and incompatible with the secular aims of the republic. The feminization of Catholicism in the nineteenth century underpinned the rejection of the church by secular, republican men who worked to keep politics and the public sphere animated by reason alone.[28] In these discourses, Catholic women were seen as hysterical and irrational ("fanatiques et dévotes imbéciles") but also as ultimately powerless and ineffective, an "other" easy to dismiss.[29]

The republican promotion of the feminization of Catholicism was part of the imaginative apparatus of the *laïcité*, but that does not mean it was merely a fantasy. Claude Langlois has demonstrated how women really *were* more actively religious than men in nineteenth-century France. It was women in France that led the resistance against de-Christianization campaigns following the Revolution, and in the nineteenth century the growth of women's *congrégations* was astounding. The number of nuns in France increased from fewer than 13,000 to over 130,000 between 1808 and 1880.[30] Partly because of Napoleonic support for the socially useful—as opposed to contemplative—orders that staffed orphanages, hospitals, and schools, women flocked to religious orders. As Langlois argues, these orders fulfilled religious needs that had been nearly wiped out in de-Christianization campaigns, and they offered status, responsibility, and pay to women who were afforded few such opportunities elsewhere.[31] From the republican perspective, Catholicism and women were closely linked in both discourse and material reality, and *both* should be kept out of the rational, masculine public sphere.

While the association of Catholicism with femininity was derogatory from the republican perspective, the church and other countercultural movements like the decadent movement harnessed their own feminized symbols to the purposes of subversion. Invested in differentiating themselves from French secular republicanism, the church's leaders and supporters saw *themselves* as "other" to the anticlerical extremes of the radical *laïcité*.[32] The church took up the disparaging stereotypes hurled at it by the secular republicans and exulted in them to demarcate itself from the church's enemies.[33] Take, for instance, the symbolic opposition between feminized Catholicism and rationality deliberately suggested in the 1854 Declaration of the Immaculate Conception. In an address on the Declaration, Pius IX invokes the Virgin Mary to "uproot and destroy this dangerous error of Rationalism."[34] On both sides of the ideological battle, therefore, Catholicism was the domain of women and was hostile to the calm, cool, and intellectual atmosphere of rationality. Feminized religious symbols became one of the most striking contrasts to what was regarded as the rationalism of the French state.[35]

The church's religious symbols not only tended to be gendered feminine but became linked with suffering in a way that deepened the church's opposition to secular rationalism, for what could be more dissimilar to male reason than the suffering body of a religious woman? In the nineteenth century, a range of French Catholic devotional works emphasized the suffering of Catholic women as counter to the aims of the sinful republic.[36] Suffering mothers, nuns, and the Virgin Mary herself were seen to agonize over the sins of the impious, male, French republic grounded in rationality. Sylvain-Marie Giraud (1830–85), a superior of the Missionaries of La Salette, published a popular devotional periodical that described "les douleurs de Marie" at the foot of the cross as redemptive for a nation in sin.[37] In 1849, the widely read *De la douleur,* by Antoine Blanc de Saint-Bonnet, a friend and correspondent of Léon Bloy, depicted suffering as a pathway to "le sublime" and suggested that excessive suffering in the world, often that of women, was a useful offering to a God who was offended by the French nation's impiety.[38] La Salette's tears over the immorality of modern French society similarly fit here.

In the late nineteenth century, a group of artists and writers tapped into these ideological battles and mined Catholicism's symbolic resources for their countercultural capacity to critique the secular republic. For these literary figures, Catholicism provided a wealth of ready symbols to hurl at the bourgeois *laïcité.* Realist authors such as Émile Zola rebelled against the seeming optimism of bourgeois modernity by drawing upon images of everything that was most denigrated by secular liberalism and glorying in their grisly detail.[39] Gender was crucial to these symbols: prostitutes, sick girls and women, and the female *hystérique* all occupied a prominent place in naturalistic novels to subvert the values of the French republic.[40] Similarly, some authors, such as Huysmans, went so far as converting to Catholicism in their flirtation with taboo and began to give a supernatural dimension to everything that bourgeois modernity opposed (crime, sickness, madness, female mystical visionaries, poverty).[41] Jules Amédée

Barbey d'Aurevilly's popular novel *Les diaboliques* (1874) is a dark imaginative exploration of women committing violence; like Sade's idealization of crime and sin, it expresses a yearning for a space beyond morality.[42] Barbey d'Aurevilly's book was responsible for the Catholic conversions of both Ernest Hello and Bloy. For his part, Hello went on to translate and promote the writings of one of the most graphic of the suffering-centered female mystics of the medieval period, Angela of Foligno (1248–1309).[43] (In her *Memorial,* Foligno meditates not only on the Crucifixion but on the tiny pieces of Christ's flesh that were pierced by the nails into the cross.)[44] Through Léon Bloy, Maritain became acquainted with this literary world, immersing herself in the writings of Ernest Hello and, primarily, of her godfather.

The relationship between real women and this theological and literary imagination in Bloy's thought cannot be assumed from a reading of his novels alone. Women are at once the source of astonishing suffering, pleasure, and transformation. They are radically other, a sex set apart and the source of real power, models of sanctity that point to salvation and incite religious experience. Prostitutes, impoverished widows, and the weeping Virgin Mary provoke an imaginative identification with them, bringing heightened emotion and the perceived possibility of redemption for those who encounter them. In the works of the decadent literary movement, agonized women take center stage but do not carry the burden of others' sins. Instead, *souffrance* among these authors is bound up with critiques of bourgeois liberalism and rationality and a new valorization of those on the margins of society.

Despite the literary power of some women in Bloy's texts, it is not hard to appreciate Hannah Arendt's critique of Bloy as "absurd and crude." Arendt rejected what she saw as Bloy's claim that women "should either be saints or whores and while saints may be forced by circumstances to descend to the level of the whores, and whores may always become saints, the honest woman of bourgeois society is lost beyond salvation."[45] There is no disputing that Bloy held this view; furthermore, one could see how Bloy's vision would set up women to see *souffrance* as their special destiny and vocation.

But it is worth noting that the irony of women's position within the Catholic Church was never lost on Bloy. His was a rare voice pointing out the hypocrisy in the fact that the institution located divine power in (suffering) women but denied women ecclesiastical authority. Bloy pointed to these divergent standings of women throughout his life. For instance, he had in mind both the Virgin Mary and the child seer at La Salette when he wrote satirically: "After she spoke, men then rose up who had miters on their heads and held in their hands the crooks of the shepherds of Christ's flock. And these men said: 'Now that's about enough! *Taceat mulier in Ecclesia!* Let a woman remain silent in Church! We are the Bishops, the Doctors, and we have need of no one, not even of Persons who are of God. . . . Your little shepherd will receive from us, even in her old age, only contempt, calumny, mockery, persecution, poverty, exile, and finally oblivion!'"[46] Bloy was outraged by the church's contempt for and silencing of La Salette's child visionary. He saw only hypocrisy and fear on the part of the clerics who stifled Mélanie's message, dismissed her as insane, and placed her writings on the Index of Forbidden Books in 1905. "On one side a whole world, allegedly religious [prétendu religieux]," Bloy wrote in a letter to the Maritains, "and on the other, a humble and holy girl stripped of human power."[47] From about 1906 to 1915 Léon Bloy dedicated himself to her cause ("I have been chosen among all to be the advocate of our Lady of La Salette"). Predictably, the publication of his books on La Salette made little impact on the clerical world, who continued to dismiss Mélanie. In his own way, Bloy saw himself as an advocate for these women shunned in the margins. But beyond giving a positive valence to their suffering, it is not clear what he wanted for them: health, power, safety? Such ideals were too bourgeois in this imaginative world and thus were completely scorned.

Furthermore, the real women who read Bloy or were otherwise drawn into his *imaginaire* were not only passive surfaces on which Bloy, or anyone, could press the destiny of suffering. Literary and devotional texts can come to life in unexpected ways in the experiences of the women and men who read about them—sometimes merely deepening the prescriptions of the texts, sometimes subversively resisting them, often somewhere in the middle, and sometimes hardly touching them at all. To approximate this realm of women's experience, one must engage the journals, correspondence, and writings of a woman like Raïssa Maritain herself to see how she shapes these discourses and images and how they shape her.[48] Before doing this, I turn to the image of "suffering femininity" in the early writings of her husband Jacques to get a sense of the complexity of the symbol of suffering femininity that Maritain encountered. The symbol of the afflicted woman was central to Jacques, just as it would be to most French Catholic revivalists, but it functioned differently than it did for Bloy, centered as it was on his fascination with, and devotion to, Raïssa. Like the figure of the suffering Jew, the symbol of the abject woman was marked by its instability.

"L'INTERMÉDIAIRE TERRESTRE":
RAÏSSA AS JACQUES MARITAIN'S LOCUS OF GOD

Two months after their baptism, in August 1906, Jacques and Raïssa departed for Heidelberg on a fellowship for Jacques's studies. The two-year period in Germany would always be interpreted by Jacques and Raïssa as a retreat into solitude and exploration, away from Paris and especially the judgments of their shocked, left-wing parents and friends, who were still reeling over their conversion and their affiliation with Bloy. It also freed them from immediately embracing a settled Catholic community or parish. For Jacques, Christians themselves were an obstacle to Christianity. For Raïssa, most Catholics seemed simply to be obsessed with order, a far cry from the radical lives of the saints and mystics that inspired her. Much as the lecture halls at the Collège de France, Léon Bloy's bohemian, destitute apartment, and Charles Péguy's bookshop had done previously, the relative isolation of a household in Germany provided a refuge outside the settled orthodoxies of both the church and the republican Left. But the couple took Bloy's writings with them, corresponded regularly with him, and remained involved with Péguy's life.

However, just as Jacques and Raïssa began to experiment with their new identities as Christians, in November 1906, Raïssa succumbed to a terrifying bout of enteritis, an inflammation of the small intestine, and almost died. Jacques's new wife's health was so poor that he needed help, so he enlisted that of Raïssa's sister, Véra, who moved to Heidelberg to live with them. Véra had also been baptized with them in Paris, and immediately Jacques, Raïssa, and Véra formed what they called "notre petite comunauté laïque" (our little lay community), or their "petit troupeau de trios" (little flock of three), a trio that would remain intact for the next fifty-two years. Véra lived with Jacques and Raïssa until her death in 1958.[49] It is difficult to overstate the importance that Raïssa's early experience of illness, near death, and eventually healing had on the *petit troupeau.*

It was the first and most dramatic among many episodes of Raïssa's sickness and healing that would follow, and it confirmed Jacques's suspicions that immediate experiences of God were the particular province of his wife. Jacques understood Raïssa's suffering body as the site of divine power, a power that he felt to be beyond his own grasp. Symbols of suffering femininity were crucial to his religious imagination, as they were for Bloy and other revivalists. But these symbols functioned differently than did Bloy's decadent spectacles of distress.

During Raïssa's first and most dangerous bout of enteritis, the couple wrote letters to their new godfather imploring his prayers for her health. Bloy responded, urging his goddaughter not to merely endure the suffering for its salvific rewards but to pray to Our Lady of La Salette for a cure. In a letter to Bloy's daughter, Raïssa claimed she had begun praying to La Salette "just twenty minutes after" she read her godfather's advice.[50] A few weeks later her health was in even further decline, and she received the sacrament of extreme unction. During the sacrament, in January 1907, she said a novena to the Virgin of La Salette, and this experience brought about a total transformation—a "new baptism" as she called it, which she claimed completely and miraculously restored her health.

Through this experience of sudden recovery, she and Jacques both noted in their journals that her bodily healing could not be disentangled from the even more profound inner experience of intimacy with God that had lasted for two days. Raïssa wrote a letter to Jacques's sister immediately after she felt healed, claiming that in the midst of the novena to the Virgin, at the height of her illness, "My soul felt truly liberated from sin, wholly united with the will of God!"[51] Jacques expressed in his journal both fascination and gratitude, since he too, along with Véra, experienced a sudden supernatural intervention into their household—certainly a new experience for the three of them: "[Raïssa] is suffused with grace and with peace. Ineffable grace of total abandonment to God and of the joy of suffering. Véra and I feel its victorious gushing forth; we are, as it was, enraptured in paradise. As for the body, the improvement is sudden and undeniable."[52] Jacques also wrote a letter thanking Bloy, since they attributed Raïssa's experience to her new devotion to the Virgin of La Salette: "For two days," Jacques told his godfather, "she lived in continual intoxication of the love of God [l'ivresse continuelle de l'amour de Dieu]. And all three of us were in the heart of Jesus, abandoning *everything* to Him and glad for everything that would please Him."[53] From Jacques's perspective, his wife had moved from near death, to total ecstasy in God, to full bodily recovery. Raïssa was not, nor would ever be for Jacques, a prophet or a direct voice of the divine, but her interior contact with the supernatural would represent another world in a way that he could never access on his own. "How she looked at us from afar," Jacques wrote just after her cure, "from the other side of the world! What beatitude in her eyes, what love and what detachment!"[54]

After the miracle of healing, Jacques began describing Raïssa in a new way, as someone set apart from himself and Véra. "Yesterday morning," Jacques wrote, "Raïssa was like a sparrow on the roof, between Heaven and earth, suspended in a kind of starry sadness [une sorte de tristesse étoilée]. . . . It is as if she were dead for an inappreciable instant," he continued, "and now the purified and strengthened soul has retaken possession of its temple and has re-erected it without effort."[55] As this passage indicates, Raïssa's suffering body, once afflicted and ill, had become the site where the divine entered and acted, a power that could be felt and experienced by those around her. Jacques noted that her contact with God was interior but inseparable from its physical manifestations. Jacques did not relish the aesthetic details of her distress, as Bloy might have, but he imagined that somehow her closeness with God, brought on by illness and proximity to death, enabled her to radiate something mysteriously salvific to others. Jacques became increasingly explicit about the redemptive role his wife played in his life, calling her an "earthly intermediary" (intermédiaire terrestre) between himself and God: "My beloved Raïssa!" he wrote. "I will know only in Paradise what I owe her. Every good comes from God, but *everything* has come to me through her as an earthly intermediary, from her heart, from her reason, from her prayers, from her counsels, from her example, from her sufferings [de ses souffrances]."[56] Raïssa's anguish did not compensate for his sins; instead, her anguish, illness that took her nearly to the "abyss" of death (to borrow Bloy's phrase), authorized her as religious teacher.

Even before the "intoxication of the miracle," as he called it, Jacques saw Raïssa as religiously and morally superior to himself. In the fall of 1906 he wrote his own *vita* of Raïssa, undoubtedly modeled on the medieval *vitae* of holy women the couple were "devouring" while in Heidelberg. In his *Introduction à la vie de Raïssa,* published decades later in Jacques's *Carnet de notes,* he saw her as a radical embodiment of everything they had learned from both Bergson and Bloy. Clearly channeling Bergson, Jacques wrote that Raïssa's "genius tends always to intuition. As she is wholly interior, she is wholly free. Her reason can be content only with *le réel,* her soul only with the absolute." Drawing on Bloy and other decadent writers, he described her as both a "feminine genius" and a "true Jew," who "loves Poverty and loves Tears" (aime la Pauvreté et aime les Larmes).[57] Jacques borrowed Bloy's insistence that the annihilated woman is, mysteriously, a powerful locus of God, but he avoided Bloy's erotic, ecstatic raptures. Jacques's theology of the suffering woman is vivid but ultimately sober-minded and cautious. These medieval *vitae* would have reinforced Jacques's sense that after the illness the more technical matters of the spirit were Raïssa's special domain. In Heidelberg, Raïssa was seen to be the one with the vocation of prayer and contemplation, a role that solidified as the years went on. "I have the clear impression," Jacques wrote in 1910, "that Raïssa will never have happiness except in establishing herself in a state of the contemplative souls, and in making prayer the permanent foundation of her life."[58] While in Heidelberg, she gradually took on more and more the role of the authority in matters of the spirit. As Raïssa, Jacques, and Véra increasingly saw themselves as a community of prayer "in the world," it was Raïssa who devised ways to form their daily lives according to the liturgies of the hours and daily prayers.

Jacques's idea about Raïssa's special access to God through her bodily suffering remained largely intact for the remaining years of their marriage. Raïssa struggled on and off with illnesses for the rest of her life—various gastric problems, a serious pharyngeal blockage, chronic headaches, and other problems only vaguely diagnosed. In his introduction to Raïssa's posthumously published *Journal,* Jacques wrote in 1963 that Raïssa's lifelong struggle with illness "was like a seal on her whole life." Even at her deathbed in 1960, her continual sickness radiated for Jacques "God's mode of action." "To everyone that came near her," Jacques remembered after her death, "she invariably gave some sort of impalpable gift which emanated from the mystery in which she was enclosed. Throughout that time she was being implacably destroyed, as if by the blows of an ax, by that God who loved her in his terrible fashion, and whose love is only 'sweet' in the eyes of the saints, or of those who do not know what they are talking about."[59]

Jacques's lifelong insistence that Raïssa's illnesses corresponded with spiritual gifts draws deeply from the medieval *vitae* of holy women that the couple had immersed themselves in reading. These gendered constructions of sanctity came alive in the household of the Maritains, and for Jacques they lingered for decades. Medieval historians such as Caroline Walker Bynum, Amy Hollywood, and John Coakley have shown how discourses of bodily suffering, illness, and even eating were central to medieval constructions of female piety because they were statements asserting women's inherent physicality.[60] In the history of Christianity, some theological traditions held that women represented materiality and the body, while men represented the soul or mind. Articulations of female sickness and bodily affliction expressed a conception of women that emphasized this association with embodiment.[61] In the medieval period, male clergy, confessors, and husbands also often understood women's fragile physicality, especially their illness and weakness, to correspond to a special supernatural power.[62] Women's suffering was a state of special separateness, a liminal space between life and death, far removed from the status and power that were understood to be largely the domain of men.[63] Through their suffering and illness, some medieval women were seen to critique and provide a counterweight to the male attachment to pride and power. Christianity has a long history of afflicted and ill women providing friars, confessors, husbands, and priests with visions, advice, and comfort. For the men, connecting with these women was seen as connecting with the divine, and they could return to the mundane world with teachings and illuminations gathered from women's bodies and souls.[64]

In a very similar way, Jacques always insisted that his wife's experience of illness took her to the threshold of death, confirming for Jacques that she had always gone "farther into the thickness of the cross" than he ever had in his life. When she "returned to the surface," as he put it, her experiences with God gave her knowledge and endowed her with an authority from which he could learn. Raïssa's suffering and its positive influence on Jacques would extend even to his intellectual life, for he explained that all of his philosophical work had "its source and light" both in Raïssa's contemplative prayer and "in the oblation of herself she made to God" (dans l'oblation qu'elle a faite d'elle-même à Dieu).[65] There was certainly something vicarious about the redemption Jacques experienced from Raïssa's suffering, but he did not understand it in the cosmological sense of atonement and reparation.

Although for Jacques the idealization of suffering women centered primarily on Raïssa's illnesses, it also endeared the marginalized child seer Mélanie to him, just as it had for his godfather. This illuminates at least some of Jacques's ambivalence and complexity regarding women in the church. As noted earlier, Jacques wrote a seven-hundred-page document on the apparition and cult of La Salette, defending Mélanie, who, as an adult, had been disgraced by the church. Having been appointed professor at the Catholic Institute in Paris in 1914, Jacques took a risk in defending Mélanie against her powerful ecclesiastical critics.[66] One of Jacques's early mentors, the conservative Dom Paul Delatte from the Abbey of the Solesmes, wrote to Maritain to warn him against continuing his research on La Salette, claiming it could damage his reputation as a professor. In this letter, Delatte expressed his suspicion of "tout ce qui est le surnaturel de voie féminine" (anything supernatural from the feminine perspective). "Let them say what they will," Delatte wrote of women visionaries, "the church has no need of this type of supernatural and it often does wrong to the other."[67] These cautions went unheeded, and Jacques insisted on pursuing Mélanie's cause. In his own writings on Mélanie and the Virgin, Jacques's approach was more measured and cautious than Bloy's. He downplayed Mélanie's alleged insanity, her abjection, her terrible life (all emphasized and relished by Bloy) and simply insisted that she spoke truth—like Raïssa, Mélanie was a teacher whose illuminations came from the margins. As late as 1946, the Dominican journal *La Vie Spirituelle* published a centenary issue on La Salette. Several of the essays were deeply critical of Mélanie and referred to her "désordres psychiques" and her fabrication of the Virgin's secret. Jacques protested vigorously against

those who declared Mélanie an *hystérique,* insisting that Mélanie, even in
her poverty, humility, and appearance of madness, "speaks like a Thomist!"[68] But *La Vie Spirituelle* refused to publish his essay. Like the idealization of Jews, the idealization of marginal women and girls who were
sick or poor would be a key reason that French Catholic revival intellectuals sometimes fit uneasily into the orthodox theological projects of the
mainstream seminary clergy.

MARITAIN'S MYSTICAL LANGUAGE OF AFFLICTION
AND HER INTELLECTUAL INTERVENTIONS

Clearly, when Maritain converted to Catholicism in France in 1906, she
entered a vast, complex world of discourses and practices that centrally
featured the holiness of suffering women. It came to her from all sides:
the novels of her godfather, the gaze of her husband, and long-standing
devotions of the Catholic Church, whether officially sanctioned or marginalized. However, Maritain is a rich case study for interrogating the issue
of feminized *souffrance* in French Catholicism. She cannot be understood
simply as an object of the fantasies of others, for she sought out and actively embraced this kind of Catholicism. And suffering femininity was
not just an aspect of French Catholicism that lurked in the background;
it occupied a vital, explicit place in the various theological and literary
worlds she inhabited and created. But she also transformed it.

The close connection between illness and the supernatural in her life
was not exclusively a fantasy of Jacques. Maritain herself also claimed that
her early proximity to death had led to supernatural provocations: visions,
dreams, direct experiences of the divine. In the midst of her first bout of
enteritis in Heidelberg, for instance, Maritain claimed to have dreamed
she was covered in blood and to have awoken to a vision that she was
grasping for a "host held by two celestial hands."[69] While some scholars
such as Richard Burton would see this as a sanctification of illness in modern terms of passivity and weakness, in the context of Christian piety illness was not just a means of destroying the body, of rendering the disciple
passive, but an opportunity for the disciple to merge with the pains of
Christ, of *imitatio Christi,* which Caroline Walker Bynum describes as "an

effort to plumb the depths of Christ's humanity at the moment of his most insistent and terrifying humanness—the moment of his dying."[70] We can detect in Maritain a similar sense that her health struggles deepened her experience with Christ. In the midst of her first major illness, she wrote, "I no longer recognized my faith, it was no longer mine," and added, "It was that of the Heart of Jesus."[71] Moreover, as Maritain came to understand it, her own devotion to the anguished La Salette led to an experience of healing and transformation, not passive acceptance of an afflicted body. Her experience remotely repeated Bloy's encounter with La Salette ("Je ne souffre plus!"). The suffering here turned into an ecstasy that also allegedly healed.

While Maritain could straightforwardly accept and express a relation between suffering and holiness, she often ignored or resisted a gendered sanctification of suffering. In an illustrative journal entry in 1919, Raïssa described the mundane details of an episode of one of her illnesses that continued to hound her well after 1906. Jacques, who oversaw the publication of the volume, added a footnote drawing out similarities between the holiness of Mary and that of his sick wife in the midst of medical treatment.[72] Jacques's footnote bursts through Raïssa's otherwise factual, sober-minded prose about the endless rounds of hospital visits and shuffling between doctors. He burdens her prose with theological meanings that it otherwise lacks. Jacques undoubtedly experienced grace through Raïssa's suffering and prayer, he saw her as bringing spiritual truths out of her suffering, and he was grateful that he could be close to her. This clearly was a genuine and profound reality for Jacques, one that lasted for the entire fifty-six years of their marriage. But it did not seem to always be part of Raïssa's self-understanding. Raïssa fits in with the many holy women in the history of Christianity who were seen to be sources of divine power and truth for those around them, but she also shared her predecessors' abilities to modify or ignore, at least at times, these objectifying discourses and practices in favor of a resolute dedication to her own soul and God.[73]

Along these lines, as more and more people came to know the Maritains, Raïssa's health struggles gradually emerged as a core part of others' perceptions of her. As a result, curiously, some friends in the Maritains' circle came to her as a kind of guide when they themselves struggled with mental or physical ailments. For example, Raïssa carried on an intense correspondence with the poet Catherine Pozzi, who at the age of twenty-eight was diagnosed with tuberculosis, from which she suffered intensely until her early death at age fifty-two. In their intimate exchanges in the years before Pozzi died, they discussed poetry, metaphysics, and the life of the soul, but Pozzi also continually confided in Maritain the depth of the pain and depression that ravaged her for decades, nearly without respite. In 1931, Pozzi confessed to Maritain that she wished finally to die and prayed to Christ for an easy death, that she could not handle the suffering.[74] Maritain responded tenderly, expressing a wish that she could provide her with something that could protect her from all that wounded her but urging fortitude: "You must not wish to die yet, you have so many beautiful things to learn about life down here." She encouraged Pozzi on her recent book and promised to visit her.[75] Maritain later confided in Pozzi about her own depression after her mother's death and her struggles with a range of undiagnosed illnesses. In a period when illness and proximity to death were sheer facts for many of these religious seekers, it was often the language of comfort and commiseration that guided their discussions. The "suffering body" did play a role in Maritain's private and public writings, but it fits uneasily into the inherited doctrine of vicarious suffering.

Nonetheless, the figure of the "suffering holy woman" as an isolated object of theological analysis occupies a much less prominent place in Maritain's own corpus than it does in that of her male contemporaries in the *renouveau catholique*. Scholars such as Burton and Griffiths are right in pointing out the prominence of words like *souffrance, tristesse, agonie,* and *anéantissement* in Maritain's texts, but these terms take on a different resonance than in the writings of Bloy and Jacques. For Raïssa, *suffering* and *sanctity* often referred to the inner annihilation of her will as a means of deepening her intimacy with God—something she had longed for as early as 1906. Drawing on the mystical traditions of the French school and the Spanish Carmelites, she understood suffering to reflect the darkness that she began to see as the condition of being transformed by God.

In 1908, after the couple returned to Paris from Heidelberg, Maritain met the man who would become her first spiritual director, the French Dominican Humbert Clérissac (1864–1914). Maritain remembered that there could have hardly been anyone more different from her first religious mentor, Léon Bloy. "The Christian life is based on intelligence," Clérissac explained to her. "Before everything else, God is truth."[76] Clérissac urged Maritain to turn her attention away from the affective, agonized holy women and mystics she had read with Bloy and directed her instead toward more intellectualized mystical authors, especially Thomas Aquinas and his Dominican interpreter John of St. Thomas. Clérissac contended that these Dominican writers adhered to a vision of the spiritual life more intellectualized but also more "simple," whereby God's activity could "simply operate in the soul."[77]

Maritain plunged into Thomas Aquinas and his Dominican interpreters with enthusiasm. She recalled her first encounter with Aquinas in 1909: "It was not without trembling with curiosity and foreboding that I opened the *Summa Theologica*'s 'Treatise on God' for the first time. Was not scholasticism a tomb of subtleties fallen to dust? From the very first pages I understood the emptiness, the childishness of my fears. Everything here was freedom of spirit, purity of faith, integrity of the intellect enlightened by knowledge and genius. . . . Everything was luminous for me in what I read, and it was with incessant thanksgiving that I pursued my reading."[78] Maritain derived immense pleasures from these new resources Clérissac suggested to her, especially Aquinas's *Summa,* which gave intellectual and systematic coherence to her otherwise relatively inchoate Christian faith. If feminized suffering was the "other" to the cold rationalism of the French state, intellectualized Thomism gave Maritain a very different resource.[79] Yet Maritain was reluctant to dispense with the affective female mystics and Bloy, as Clérissac advised, claiming that Clérissac misunderstood their descriptions of the "secret sufferings of the soul."[80] Instead, she insisted the two perspectives could work in partnership. She remembers "wedding together," for example, the work of Aquinas to the praises of St. Gertrude, a German Benedictine mystical author whose work she also immersed herself in throughout 1909.

This new cluster of influences brought together a set of writers not usually paired in the history of Christian thought. On the one hand were Bloy's riotous texts about prostitutes and widows, the harrowing dark nights described by the Carmelite mystics, Angela of Foligno's graphically portrayed desires to merge with crucified Christ, and Gertrude the Great's dramatic visionary experiences. Now the sober, sparse intellectualism of

Clérissac's scholasticism and that of his master, Thomas Aquinas, joined the choir of influences. Maritain claimed these two modes of thinking initially came together in their shared "severity," given that each demonstrated a "heroic faith" and "intransigence" concerning obligations to truth. Above all, she saw that each of these spiritual writers—whether male or female, and whether seen as "intellectual" or "affective"— exhibited, like so many who impressed her, a sort of Nietzschean impatience with the mediocre. These spiritual writers were bound up with her own youthful intellectual revolt.

In the history of Christianity, these two different kinds of mysticism, intellectual and affective, are often aligned along the axes of gender, the former seen to be the domain of men and the mind, the latter the domain of women and the body.[81] The tensions between these two kinds of piety and their gendered articulations became apparent to Maritain in 1922 during conversations with the Dominican theologian Réginald Garrigou-Lagrange (1877–1964). Maritain's journals describe how Garrigou-Lagrange confessed to her that he was reluctant to include women in the Thomist retreats she and Jacques had been planning. Afterwards, she reflected on this episode: "A great theologian preaches Love to women but teaches Intelligence to his disciples. The two ought to be preached and taught simultaneously." "These poor intellectual women!" she added, "How people mistrust them!" (Ces pauvres intellectuelles! Comme on se méfie d'elles!)[82] Love, the affections, and suffering were seen as shaking the stability of the mind and rational soul. Later that year, Raïssa wrote a letter to Jacques claiming that the tension between *la vie intellectuelle* and *la vie mystique,* where affection, love, and suffering predominate, was *the* intellectual problem of the twentieth century.[83] Maritain needed conceptual resources to bridge the rift in French Catholicism between feminized affections—love and suffering—and the masculinized intellect— rationality and the mind.

We know from Maritain's *Journal* and her earliest writings on Thomas Aquinas and John of St. Thomas that she claimed she found in these materials the resources to bring together what had previously been disparate parts of her own religious and intellectual formation. Since their conversion, the Christianity of Jacques and Raïssa had almost exclusively consisted of the ferocity of Bloy and the treatises of female early modern and medieval saints that he showed them. Bloy's deeply suffering-centered and feminized Catholic imagination blew their minds, inspired them, but did not offer up the kind of metaphysical, ontological level of reflection they sought. Yet when Clérissac introduced Thomism to Maritain she did not see it as a more mature, more modern, or even more compelling kind of faith. She saw it as bringing in a piece that had been missing, and she was determined to integrate it with what she and Jacques had been introduced to earlier.

The texts of John of St. Thomas were Raïssa's primary interlocutor for interpreting Aquinas, and John of St. Thomas is known for his emphasis on the affective dimensions of Aquinas's epistemology. Aquinas's theory of the *intellectus* was not the sterile rationality of the Sorbonne but something much more expansive. His faculty of the *intellectus* has a cognitive dimension but is also grounded in the will or desire.[84] As Maritain came to understand it, the process of learning truth is grounded in the affections, in the desire to know more and more, or to draw ever closer to infinite Truth, Goodness, Love, and Beauty—a process that can never be fully complete. This resonated with Maritain, who had had a deeply affective, highly emotional relationship with learning ever since childhood.

While this emphasis on the affective dimension of learning initially attracted her to Thomism, she focused her own intellectual efforts on seeing how the intelligence could cohere with feminized, suffering-centered Catholicism. The first book she coauthored with Jacques, *De la vie d'oraison,* is the fruit of these efforts. Originally intended as a resource for the Thomist retreats at the Maritains' home that began in 1914 (but expanded significantly in 1919; see chapter 3 for elaboration), the text eventually reached a wider audience with the 1922 version. From what we have seen about Raïssa's authority in the household in matters of the spirit, and from her unpublished notes and writings from the late 1910s and early 1920s, it is clear that she was the primary researcher and author for this work.

As Maritain explains it in *De la vie d'oraison,* according to Thomas, spiritual and intellectual progress requires that the natural, human faculty of the intellect be passive because the object of mystical life, God, entirely exceeds the capacities of human knowing. Since the faculties of knowing are utterly disproportionate to the object of contemplation, only when the intellect is passive can it receive or know God. Maritain emphasizes that rendering the intellect passive does not mean abandoning it. Instead, this faculty is "supernaturalized" when God infuses it with grace to strengthen the intellect *qua* intellect, "implanting" a deeper knowledge of Truth. The soul knows God connaturally, through the infusion of divine Wisdom.[85] Crucially, Maritain wants to insist that the process of passivity, transformation, and expansion is experienced as deeply painful. But because Aquinas describes this process "purely in a formal way," according to Maritain, he does not communicate the psychological and experiential suffering that one must endure. Maritain had by now, for more than a decade, been immersed in the Christian spiritual tradition that would give her resources to understand and think through the process of expansion. In *De la vie d'oraison,* she brings these disparate resources together. She moves from Thomas Aquinas to the mystical writers, many of whom echo the ravishing intensity of Bloy, to mine for language that is more intensified and explicit than that of Aquinas. For example, Maritain shifts the Thomist notion that the intellect must be *passif* to the claim that it must be more than passive; it must be *annihilé* or *anéanti* (shattered, annihilated). Mystical texts that she had learned about through Bloy—deeply emotive and graphically centered on suffering—are texts that describe this harrowing ordeal whereby the natural faculties are annihilated to ready the self to receive the grace of divine Wisdom. That is why the "sanctifying Spirit" (l'Esprit sanctificateur), as she puts it, "is also the sacrificing Spirit" (aussi l'Esprit sacrificateur).[86] On an experiential level, she writes, in order to render our will passive, God "purifies us, sacrifices us, and," she claims, echoing John of the Cross, this is the "night" of our soul.[87] The intellect, "the most spiritual of our faculties," as she calls it, seems to the person to dwindle, darken, and even become extinguished. The experience of "annihilation" at this level can feel "aride et douloureuse," and for this reason the individual must be merged with and strengthened by "Jesus Crucified."[88] The intellect therefore intensifies, reaching new levels of truth through prayer and the suffering felt so acutely on the psychological level. Maritain claims that the spiritual books of Teresa and Gertrude describe at the level of lived psychological experience what Aquinas explains metaphysically in epistemological terms. Mary's grief becomes a symbol to illustrate this process of purgation. Throughout *De la vie d'oraison,* Aquinas is paired with the great female and male mystics, just as the soul's capacity for the pure, ineffable connaturality of God is paired with the crucified humanity of Christ. The most graphically suffering-centered language in Maritain's text must be understood in interiorized terms, not as separate from intellectual life.

This pairing of suffering-centered devotionalism and Aquinas's theology of connaturality loosens the binary that aligns women with affective, embodied mysticism and men with intellectual mysticism. Even the dedication page of *De la vie d'oraison* illustrates Maritain's method. The epigraph is a passage from Petro Calo's *Vita sancti Thomae Aquinatis*. Calo's *vita* emphasized that Aquinas's theological science arose from prayer and suffering. According to Calo, Thomas "poured out tears [répandant des larmes] in order to discover divine secrets."[89] This image—the towering, stoic Aquinas, bowed down in tears and prayer as he prepared his *Summa*—was a vivid way to begin her project. Not only the Virgin of La Salette but also Aquinas weeps, and he does so in preparation for his astonishing intellectual achievements. This suffering is undergone, not to atone vicariously for impious men's sins, but to ready the intellect to know God.

By seeking to heal the gendered and disciplinary rifts of Christian history, Raïssa Maritain contributed to the revival of mysticism in twentieth-century France in creative, interventionist ways. Early on, it was her attraction to Aquinas that focused her writing. In 1921 she translated from the Latin and published *Des moeurs divines: Opuscule LXII de saint Thomas d'Aquin,* attributed to Aquinas, and, in 1925 she embarked on a translation of the seventeenth-century disciple of Aquinas, St. John of St. Thomas, that she entitled *Les dons du Saint-Esprit.* She published the latter as a series of articles in 1926 and as a book in 1929.[90] In 1925 Maritain selected and presented portions of Teresa of Ávila's texts for *La Vie Spirituelle,* the new Dominican journal dedicated to mysticism and asceticism.[91] In her treatments of Thomas and his interpreters, Maritain consistently emphasized the role of the affections. In a much later publication, *L'ange de l'école ou Saint Thomas d'Aquin,* Maritain detailed the "taxonomy of tears" one can learn by studying the texts of Thomas Aquinas and his life.[92]

Maritain published all of these texts on Thomism and the intellect anonymously, under the initials R.M., or as Jacques's coauthor. Were Christian women expected to write on the affections and affliction, but not on Aquinas? Maritain's first publication under her own full name (discussed in detail in chapter 4) was a poem, "La couronne d'épines" (The Crown of Thorns), published in 1931, a graphic, moving rendering of Jesus's fear on the Mount of Olives that described "all the misery laid bare before him." Fitting within the idioms of the revival, Maritain surfaced as a sole author when she offered a poetic reflection on the suffering Jesus, but her efforts within the Thomist revival would always remain more hidden.

MARITAIN'S *SOUFFRANCE* OF THE WILL

In *De la vie d'oraison,* Maritain shows how she grappled with the gendered associations in mysticism in her intellectual writings. But what of her own experience? In 1914, once Jacques became professor at the Institut catholique in Paris, Jacques and Raïssa began to enter the inner circles of the Catholic elite. For Raïssa, the first of these important connections was with the famous Dominican Pierre Dehau, who became her spiritual director in 1916, as Clérissac had died in 1914. Dehau, after telling her he had "never seen someone so supple in the hands of God," recommended that she significantly increase her daily time allotted to total silence and contemplative prayer. Dehau's advice, Maritain recalled, "changed my life in a remarkable way."[93]

With Dehau, Maritain became further immersed in the French school of spirituality, which drew on the long tradition of Christian mystical theology and stressed interiorized *souffrance* as a way to participate in the inner life of Christ. Familiar phrases such as *souffrance, tristesse, agonie,* and *anéantissement* circulated in this theological world, but the annihilation that Maritain sought was not physical, nor was she passive in the face of it; it was interiorized and related to desire and the will. In one of her earliest journal entries, Maritain draws on this tradition's meanings of *souffrance* when she argues that "in annihilating oneself [s'anéantissant soi-même], one finds Him whom one loves. The ego [le moi] is an obstacle to vision and possession."[94] She copied down a phrase from Pierre Dehau, "Our suffering [notre souffrance] has no other reason for its existence except to lead us to this death of the will."[95] In fact, Father Dehau seems to have made an explicit effort to encourage Raïssa to think of *souffrance* only in terms of the interior, psychic pains of transformation of the self before God. This therefore directly speaks to those who insist that the discourse of feminized suffering propelled Raïssa irresistibly to embrace illness and bodily pain as a means of salvation for those around her. In 1919 Dehau warned Jacques to tell his wife:

> God *does not want* bodily mortifications [mortifications corporelles] for her. Above all, let her not attempt them, let her not even think of them. Contemplative prayer, full stop, that is all. She is not to think of anything else. Remain with Jesus. Offer as mortification all Our Lord will determine himself through the sufferings of prayer [les souffrance de l'oraison] (no time for many things which seem necessary, periods of aridity, anxieties, temptations). Accept all that in a spirit of mortification. And only that. . . . It is not necessary to make the body suffer [il ne faut pas viser à faire souffrir le corps].[96]

Raïssa seems to have heeded his advice. In the journal entries that follow, she describes *abnégation, souffrance, mortification, annihilation,* and *transfiguration* as experiences felt on an inner register. Writing in 1921, she insists, "All possible mortification, *interior* [Toute la mortification possible, *intérieure*]. In fact, it depends entirely on my own self to create the 'desert.'"[97]

Although the *souffrance* in her journal is spiritualized, located in the will and not necessarily physical, she does revitalize Bloy's intense, ravishing language to describe this inner process. In Bloy's aesthetic renderings, although the women are figures of his imagination, they experience harrowing events in history: poverty, prostitution, the death of a spouse, being driven to the edge of sanity. Maritain, on the other hand, uses Bloy's graphic images to metaphorically describe the process of inner transformation she so deeply desires. She describes sanctity as something ecstatic and simultaneously agonizing. In her private writings, she takes up her own flights of imagination toward the ecstatic and, like the writers of the decadent literary movement, often emphasizes eros, death, and violence with an intensity that differs from Dehau's more measured approach (and certainly that of Clérissac).

For example, in a prayer she transcribed in 1917, Maritain describes her own yearning for a self-annihilation that will be a "faithful holocaust" and burn away her former self in the process of union with Jesus:

O Jesus, how necessary your Passion was. How necessary it was that your adorable heart should be pierced for me. O Jesus! O Jesus! your sorrowful and bleeding heart tells me not to be afraid and to have confidence. . . . You know what a living heart is, a heart of flesh and blood where earth and heaven battle. You know that the human heart which seeks you has to suffer, to die a thousand deaths in order to find you [pour vous trouver, souffrir, mourir de mille morts]. And if you are all torn and bleeding it is not only because you suffer for our sins. . . . But you have also wished, in your infinite mercy, to show us that you have a heart similar to ours so that we can go to you with confidence. That is why I open my heart to you without any fear. I cry out to you with all the strength of my being and I would rather die than offend you. I abandon my heart to you, ready to suffer, to be wholly consumed in a faithful holocaust [prête à souffrir qu'il se consume entièrement en un fidèle holocauste] until the flame of divine charity soars above the cinders of all my earthly powers.[98]

Bodily suffering—here her own living heart and Jesus's torn and bleeding body—provides the images to illustrate the inner journey Maritain desires.[99] She echoes Bloy's yearning for the ravishing, ecstatic transformation represented by the Passion: to love God, she claims, should be an "*extase*. Going out of ourselves, we ought to transport ourselves into Him."[100] Images of Christ's passion reappear as the only metaphors that can describe properly this experience of love, suffering, and the ravishing longing for union.

In the years that followed, Maritain's spiritual journal details this long, arduous, and even harrowing process of being "wholly consumed," which for Maritain centered on deeper and deeper intimacy with the suffering Christ. Beginning in 1917, she draws on the mystical language of erotic devotion: she recalls a moment in prayer when, inspired by a passage from a devotional book about placing one's lips "on the wounded side [au côté blessé] of Christ," she "imagine[d] being quite close to the Savior, kissing his wounds."[101] This imaginative practice echoes a medieval devotion centered on the veneration of Jesus's side wound as a way to inculcate feelings of intense love of Jesus's suffering humanity.[102] As Maritain details her experiences of feeling the wounded Jesus "so close" to her in 1917, she mines the Christian mystical vocabularies of simultaneous pain and delight that segue easily into Léon Bloy's decadent imagination (recall his claim that we enter paradise in a "swoon of pain and delight"). In her encounters with Christ she "wept and was exalted," declaring, "O my only Jesus, how pleasurable and painful at once is this state!"[103] And later that year, "Nothing is so good as to weep before God."[104]

Yet the suffering engendered from these transformations becomes increasingly painful. "My company is the darkness of the grave," Maritain writes at the end of a 1928 entry, reflecting on the agonized lamentation psalm, Psalm 88, notable for its absence of hope.[105] Another entry only offers the brief cry "Agony! Agony!" The dissolution of her will, as she seeks to annihilate it before God, is experienced as a "tearing out, breaking off, an indescribable rupture."[106] Maritain sees this as the war of her interior life: "I wanted to be gone, to die."[107] By the early 1930s, Maritain not only feels the "impression of being quite close" to Jesus but comes to see herself as entering the very scene of Christ's crucifixion: it is as if she were on the cross ("comme sur la Croix"), as if she herself were "fixed by the heart with a lance" (fixée par le Coeur comme avec une lance).[108] Later she describes an experience in which the suffering Christ enters and inhabits her very own body and soul: "One would think Jesus wants to enter into me, with all his destitution [toute sa misère], with all the blood that covers him [avec tout le sang qui le couvre]—it is unendurable."[109] "It is terrible," she adds in 1934, " to be assimilated by him."[110] She concludes later that year that God desires "perfect assimilation" to his passion, and she recounts that she has heard Jesus tell her in prayer, "I will espouse you in blood."[111]

These vivid experiences of Jesus again draw on medieval devotional practices whereby the Christian explicitly aims to internalize Christ's passion as an explicit effort at *imitatio Christi* and participation in the redemptive work on the cross.[112] In some medieval traditions, practices of sharing in Christ's sufferings centered on the belief in the power of *bodily* pain such as mortifications of the flesh and other ascetic practices of ritual penance that were understood to have a cleansing, purgative power. Through mortifications of the sinful body, one could align the body and soul more and more closely to Christ's suffering on the cross.[113] But Maritain departs from this tradition of somatic suffering; instead, her engagement with interior *souffrance* draws especially deeply on texts of the French school of spirituality, founded by Pierre de Bérulle (1575–1629). While those texts (like the writings of the decadent literary movement) concentrate intently on *souffrance* and *peine,* and often gender them feminine, they do not offer a theology of co-redemption and substitutionary expiation and do not emphasize the physicality of suffering. This school emphasized interior spiritual suffering, particularly *anéantissement* (annihilation, sometimes also translated into English as "shattering"), but had little to say about physical and emotional anguish.[114] Influenced by the Spanish Carmelites, it emphasized interior annihilation as a way to incorporate oneself into the interior life of the suffering Christ. And partly because of the extraordinarily high Mariology promoted by one of the French school's founding figures, Louis-Marie Grignion de Montfort (1673–1716), inner annihilation and mortification of the will were presented as the proper ground for Marian devotion. Christian suffering in this school of thought was primarily a matter of self-disciplined and rigorous efforts to mortify and empty the will as a means of deepening one's relationship to Mary and subsequently her Son. The sins of others, central to the doctrine of vicarious suffering, were also not critical to this version of spiritualized anguish.

Maritain's inner experiences of the suffering Christ can also be usefully illuminated not only by the vivid language of the decadents and by the French school of spirituality but by the category of fantasy. In her recent work *The Fantasy of Feminist History,* Joan Wallach Scott understands fantasy as the setting of the fulfillment of desire, where one's identity undergoes a desired transformation in an imagined scenario.[115] As Maritain draws closer and closer to Christ, she imagines herself not only as *with* Christ, or in pursuit of him, but actually as *becoming* Christ himself. In this fantasy setting, Maritain steps "across the threshold" to participate in a wider scene of her desires, here a desire for intimacy with the divine. This devotional context or fantasy scenario enables a new experience of selfhood that is "systematically askew" with ordinary reality.[116] One feels "as if" one were in the desired scenario, which is not quite an alternative to or subversion of reality but is not exactly "reality" either.[117] This is Maritain's language precisely: her earliest vision, in 1907, of being covered in blood began in a dream, and the passage cited above similarly has a dream-like quality: it is "as if" she were speared with a lance, and it is not that Christ enters her, but that "one would think" or "one could say that" (on dirait que) Christ wanted to. In this setting, it is not simply that God consumes her; rather, "it has seemed to me" (il m'a semblé) to be so. Yet these metaphors and fantasy scenes cannot quite be understood *only* "as if" or *only* as something "one would think." They seemed to have genuinely inculcated new experiences and dispositions for Maritain: "Agony! Agony!" in her journal corresponded to something real. There were times when Maritain's spiritual life felt so painful that she would stay in bed for days, turning away those who came to visit. As early as 1917, she struggled to describe the relation between these painful supernatural experiences and reality: on one spiritual retreat, her friends assumed she was experiencing the "sweet joy" and rest common to most retreatants, but Maritain later claimed in her journal that in secret, during prayer, she had experienced an "incredible violence" and a "real martyrdom of the heart" that amounted to the *plus grandes souffrances* and generated real tears.[118] Readers encountering the abundance of Maritain's language of affliction enter these private scenes of fantasy and imagination.

Crucially, and in contradiction to what some scholars see in Maritain, others were a *threat* to her prayer and suffering, not the motive. This suffering was meant, not for the salvation of men around her, but for increased intimacy between her own soul and God. Maritain did not describe suffering and sanctity in the other-oriented language of vicarious suffering. Rather than offering redemption to the impious men in her life to make cosmological reparation, her life of interiorized affliction was marked by solitude and even secrecy. "I am truly never at rest, in peace, spiritually active except alone, in silent prayer," she wrote in 1916. "[God] induces me so strongly to be alone with him that I prefer those moments of silence to everything in the world and cannot break them without regret."[119] These desires were so far distant from the widely understood motive of suffering for the sins of others that they sometimes ground against a duty Maritain felt to support others in her life. She wondered, in 1919, whether she could possibly "live like a recluse among my family" or whether she was bound by "duty to be at Jacques's side."[120] What is surprising then, is how private she was about her experiences in her prayer life, hiding her interior suffering even from Jacques. Reading

Raïssa's private notebooks after she died in 1960, Jacques wrote three years later, left him "dazzled and a little baffled [un peu égaré]." Jacques had always insisted that Raïssa "entered deeper into the Cross" than he did, but he experienced the journals as a "revelation" of something he knew, but "only in a way."[121]

SUFFERING FEMININITY RECONSIDERED: CONCLUDING REFLECTIONS

The vocabularies of *souffrance, douloureuse, annihilé,* and *anéantie* circulate freely in Maritain's texts, as they do in the works of Bloy and Jacques. Many revivalist writers made gender crucial to these discourses of suffering, and each of them endowed affliction with a certain kind of ecstatic, supernatural power. But a careful reading of their formal and informal writings reveals that the symbol of suffering femininity was multivalent, deployed in divergent ways, even within a tight, close-knit spiritual family like this one. We need to be attuned to the instability of this gendered symbol and to the creative ways Maritain engaged the highly mobile theology of *souffrance,* just as we cannot assume that the theologies and practices of suffering played out in her life in a predictable, uniform way.[122] In this chapter, I have argued against a too-easy equation between the agonized images in women's texts like Maritain's and the cosmological doctrine of female vicarious suffering. An exclusive emphasis on vicarious suffering does not entirely capture the different engagements of the women's texts with *souffrance* and *douleur;* these images and ideas are too complex in the lives of those who encounter them to be neatly explained by one cosmological doctrine of expiation and reparation. Moreover, this chapter clearly refutes the view of Raïssa Maritain as an unwitting recipient, entirely passive under the pressures of this theological association. Like her husband and godfather, Raïssa Maritain drew from and deepened a long-standing set of associations in Christianity between suffering and holiness, a tradition that was revitalized in a particularly feminized form in nineteenth-century France. Should her work, by virtue of her being female, be considered only as a tightening of the screw, a strengthening of the persistent association between women and suffering? Or can her interventions at the theological level, and at the level of practice—she herself was an intellectual—be counted as transformative of the tradition?

Certainly they must be considered as both. In her early years as a Christian, Maritain undeniably recognized salutary effects of her sickness through the dreams, visions, and immediate experience of the divine that she saw her proximity to death engender. Moreover, according to Maritain, her illness had practical fruits that deepened their religious lives: because of being bedridden during another bout of sickness she had time to pour through the *Summa* and urged Jacques to read it; because of her frail health they were later allowed to have a private chapel built in their home for Mass; and because of her physical fragility she had to withdraw regularly from the enormous social demands placed increasingly on the Maritains. These periods of silence and seclusion required by her illness were also the bedrock of her spiritual life.

On the one hand, all of this sanctification of her sicknesses could be seen as rendering Maritain helpless, passive, or overly submissive to a debilitating way to live. But in a world in which medical interventions often helped her only a little, what more could we ask of her?[123] When she could, she went to doctors, who often did not help, and the Christian connection between the agony of Christ and her own experiences of fragility shrouded an otherwise grim reality with an aura of power.[124] Men in her life endowed her with this power, a power that gave her a foothold in the revival as a writer, teacher, and intellectual. These men were captivated with Raïssa's spiritual gifts that were understood to have emerged from her suffering. From Bloy's fawning praise of Raïssa's Judaism and her frailty, to Jacques's fascination with her sickness, to her confessors' claims that they had never seen someone so "supple in the hands of God," this fascination with the frail and powerful Raïssa, a woman and a Jew, carried forward throughout her life: her godson, friends, even all of her obituaries refer to her struggles with health but typically acknowledge that her soul, in the words of her godson, "was a vertical line from earth to heaven."[125] In 1931, Jacques confessed to a priest his worries that his demanding schedule caused Raïssa undue suffering, both mental and physical, because it disturbed her prayer life. "No," the priest assured Jacques, "it is not a distraction for her, she is wholly supernatural."[126] The relationships between Raïssa and so many men were marked by a fundamental tension between power and fascination. This both constrained and enabled her: she partially subverted it by merging Aquinas's affections with the agonized suffering of the mystics. In addition, Maritain's legacy is more than suffering: she was a woman organizer in the Thomist retreats (they were her idea), an intellectual, a writer.

Maritain's own writings concern themselves less than those of other Catholic revivalists with sickness, vicarious suffering, or the administration of aesthetic shocks to the bourgeois republic, though they often place an ecstatic, vivid, if metaphorical emphasis on eros, death, suffering, blood, and the Crucifixion. This did much more than refer to her own suffering body as her special supernatural destiny. For Maritain, in her first decades as a Christian, suffering referred to the mortification of her own will in prayer. She wrote little about the prostitutes and insane women of Bloy in her first decades as a Christian, but as we will see in chapter 5, during the Shoah she presented Bloy at his most graphic and radical on this topic. Moreover, the fact that intellect was understood to be outside the domain of suffering-centered mysticism, and outside the domain of women, troubled her (people mistrusted "ces pauvres intellectuelles!"), and she intervened to transform this long-standing binary in the history of Christian thought through her discovery of Thomas Aquinas in 1909. In her public writings, she linked the affections (especially love and suffering) with the faculty of the intellect—an integration she learned from Aquinas—and underscored that even Aquinas had prayed, suffered, and wept before he wrote. She forged an improbable and innovative combination of Thomistic metaphysics and Bloy's deeply feminized, agonized sanctity, creatively dissolving the rift between feminized affect and masculinized intellect. Maritain is an example of a situated use of critical detachment and analysis in relation to a powerful cluster of associations between suffering and women in the Catholic theological imagination.

Yet it must be added that, despite Maritain's creative interventions, it is doubtful if her writings would have ever been read at all had they been entirely outside the grammar of suffering. The association between femininity and *souffrance* was, arguably, too powerful in modern French religious discourse and practice for Maritain to have made a way for herself in the French Catholic revival without engaging it.[127] From literary figures like Claudel, Bloy, Huysmans, and Zola, to the new translations of the *vitae* of medieval holy women that flooded Paris's intellectual scene in the late nineteenth and early twentieth centuries, to the church's own promotion of the weeping Virgin Mary, suffering femininity stood at the center of late modern French Catholicism. It is difficult to find voices of Catholic women in Europe whose theological writings did not engage in discourses of *souffrance*. Suffering enabled Maritain to be heard in the limited way women were recognized and authorized—by her godfather, her husband, and by her own contemporary readers. In this way, just as she transformed the discourse of female suffering by incorporating an emphasis on the intellect, Maritain also deepened and extended the long-standing association between women, suffering, and holiness, since her own writings never fully steered away from these themes. Finally, conceptual tools such as fantasy, imagination, and devotion remind us that the suffering-centered discourses at the center of Maritain's spiritual life can be "askew" in their relationship to reality. Through these discourses and images, the Christian can cross into a new scenario and imaginatively enter into the experience of the suffering Christ in a way that sits unpredictably and uneasily with the everyday reality of history.

CHAPTER 3

Building a New Tribe in the Gathering Storm

Raïssa Maritain and the Complexity of Interwar
Philo-Semitism (1923–39)

Nearly every Sunday, from 1923 to 1939, men and women from all walks of life took the forty-five-minute train ride from Paris to attend the famous salon Jacques and Raïssa hosted at their home in Meudon, France. It had been seventeen years since their conversion, and Jacques was a full professor at the Institut catholique of Paris. At the start of their salon, Raïssa had spent much of her earliest intellectual energy aiding Jacques with the first writing projects that would establish his career. In 1921, she had completed her first large independent scholarly work: a translation of one of Thomas Aquinas's lesser-known works, *Des moeurs divines (The Ways of God)*. The following year their coauthored *De la vie d'oraison* appeared in pamphlet form. By 1923 the Maritains' reputations were growing; people flocked to Meudon to participate in the Maritains' Sunday afternoon discussions and, if they were lucky, to be invited by Raïssa as one of the five or six asked to stay late for a private dinner and more intimate conversation.[1] The salon was frequented by an unpredictable cast of artists and philosophers; exiled Russians, homosexuals, wavering

Catholics, clergy, Protestants, and Jews all took the train to Meudon in interwar France. "The Maritains," one such pilgrim remembered, "had a
tremendous power of attraction, and magnets draw everything."[2]

Some of the Maritains' guests included more or less active members
of the Jewish faith, such as Benjamin Fondane and Marc and Bella Chagall, but many more of the émigrés in their circle were, like Raïssa, Jewish
near converts or converts to Catholicism.[3] This was no coincidence: the
Maritains' salon was for many Jews a key site of attraction to Christianity
in the interwar period, and Frédéric Gugelot has argued that Jacques and
Raïssa's 1906 conversion laid a foundation for many of the interwar baptisms in Paris.[4] As Jacques remembered, "The baptisms rained down" (Les
baptêmes pleuvaient) in Meudon from 1923 to 1939.[5] Some people in
France even speculated that the Maritains were conspiring with the dio-
cese to bring the faithless into the fold.[6]

A Jewish convert herself and eventually a writer on Jewish-Christian
relations, Raïssa, by her presence and her intellectual work, made crucial
contributions to this phenomenon. As one pilgrim remembered her, she
was a "pioneer of Judeo-Christian relations" and an outspoken critic of
anti-Semitism as early as 1931, but she also directly or indirectly ushered
in countless Jewish conversions to the church.[7] As with the whole of the
French Catholic revival, deep ambivalences mark Raïssa Maritain's thinking on Jews and Judaism. Here I analyze how Maritain and her interwar
community of Jewish-Catholics and philo-Semites both inherited and
transformed the classic multivalent features of modern French Catholic
philo-Semitism established by Bloy and Péguy: the valorization of Jewish
suffering and Bloy's insistence on a unity dependent upon conversion. In
particular, I analyze how Maritain's interwar essay *Histoire d'Abraham*
(1935) seeks to establish what she called the *lien vivant,* the living bond,
between *juifs* and *chrétiens.* For Maritain, the bond emerged from the familiar terrain of *souffrance, douleur, peine,* and *misère,* but the ecstatic, joyful
encounter with interiorized affliction of the early years (see chapter 2)
began to fade from her work, and in the 1930s her conceptions of affliction became inextricably entangled with Europe's darkening future.

Finally, in considering the conversions more broadly, I diverge from
those who see the widespread Jewish conversions around Meudon primarily in terms of self-loathing and the attempt to expel Judaism from

one's identity. I argue that the sources reveal a more complicated story.[8] By the interwar period, many of these intellectuals, Raïssa Maritain included, understood themselves as a community of "juifs chrétiens dans l'Église catholique," Christians who still held on to their Jewish identities even after their baptism into the church. I argue that we may best understand the interwar Jewish attraction to Catholicism by situating it in multiple contexts: the role of Catholicism in furnishing critiques of secularism and *laïcité,* the draw of Catholicism as exotic, and, in a spirit of profound optimism, the hope that the church could become universal. Catholicism had appealed to Maritain as an exotic source for critiques of secular republicanism since 1906, but the notion of the universalizing capacities of the church was new. This community hoped to integrate Judaism within a *nouveau christianisme* that could embrace all religions, but especially the religion that lay "au fond du christianisme." These ideas about Catholicism's universalizing capacities were fairly unique to the experimental atmosphere of the Jazz Age, but they also drew on a classic supersessionism as old as Christianity itself: the idea that *l'accomplissement* of Judaism resided in the Christian Church.

Taken together, the ideas about Jews and Judaism held by Maritain and her community are worth thinking through because they illustrate not simply the "good" philo-Semitism of Catholicism against its "bad" anti-Semitism but also, as the recent work of historian Richard Crane has shown, the conflicts, tensions, and constraints at the heart of French Christian thinking on this issue.[9] This community resists a simple appraisal; it fits uneasily into contemporary notions of religious tolerance. Certainly we cannot discover among these revivalists a purely progressive Catholic position on Judaism. Not only were Jewish conversions often central to the aims of these philo-Semites, but the movement was not unified or static. The revivalists battled and split from one another; anti-Semitism of the most vicious sort, for example, circulated freely alongside defenses of Judaism and philo-Semitism.[10] The movement produced not only a range of philo-Semitic texts but also Georges Bernanos's rabidly anti-Semitic *La grande peur des bien-pensants (The Great Panic of the Moderates)* (1931).[11] My analysis aims to untangle the multivalence of these endeavors and to track how the revivalists' thinking underwent significant revisions in the years before the Shoah.

Despite the problematic aspects of these ideas and practices, this community of Jewish converts and philo-Semitic Catholics tried to wrest the conventional, long-standing anti-Jewish discourse from the Christian imagination and create a more tolerant alternative. Theirs were early experiments to validate Judaism and Jews for their religion, not despite it.[12] Their writings were episodic and imperfect, but they exerted a force that cracked the massive edifice of Catholic anti-Semitism in France (indeed an edifice so massive that Julie Kalman's recent work suggests that Catholicism and contempt for Judaism have been largely synonymous for most of modern French history).[13] Revivalist thinkers were consistently daring aesthetically on this difficult theological and political issue and attacked it head on. Yet their prescience in this respect is balanced, if not tragically overwhelmed, by the extent to which their labors were vulnerable. Indeed, the eventual failure of Catholicism in 1940–45 to pursue these early prewar attempts at universalism and cosmopolitanism would evoke outrage in the twilight years of late modern Catholicism's golden age. This topic therefore presents us with an ideal moment to consider the opportunities and limits, risks and rewards, for "thinking with" the Jewish converts and philo-Semitic Catholics of the revival like Raïssa Maritain, and the enduring, if troubling, link between *souffrance* and Judaism that they maintained.

THE APPEAL OF THE EXOTIC

The Jews who converted to Catholicism and circulated through Meudon were mainly intellectuals (writers, artists, composers, scholars) with remarkable careers who exerted a massive impact on the revival and even on the interwar avant-garde more broadly. Well-known names include, for example, the Polish sculptor Marek Szwarc (1892–1958), who converted in 1919 after he met Jacques and Raïssa and went on to become a member of the famous community of artists, L'école de Paris.[14] Three members of the Menasce family from Egypt were converts and friends of the Maritains: Jean de Menasce (1902–73), a historian of religion who was baptized in 1926 and ordained a Dominican priest the following year; his uncle Abbé Jean-Marie de Menasce (dates unknown); and his cousin the orientalist Georges Cattaui (1896–1974).[15] The German writer Roland Hill (1909–78) and the Polish theater critic Jan Kott (1914–2001) must also be included. The Jewish converts in the Maritains' circle included French-born citizens, some of whom were from elite Jewish families. Max Jacob (1876–1944) had converted with his daughter in 1909, close to the time of the Maritains' own conversion. A founding member of the Maritains' Thomist circles, the poet Jean-Pierre Altermann (1892–1958) converted in 1921 and eventually became a priest. The French essayist René Schwob (1895–1946) can also be included here; he would later serve as the god-father (with Raïssa as the godmother) at the 1935 baptism of Achsa Bel-kind (1905–90), a paleontologist and linguist who came from a family of famous Zionist pioneers. This community also included the French Jewish writer Maurice Sachs (1906–45), the journalist André Frossard (1915–95), and the actress Suzanne Bing (1885–1967).

These Jewish converts whom Raïssa knew exemplified no single way of identifying with Catholicism or Judaism. Relations to religious traditions were naturally multivalent, involving men and women, immigrants and French citizens, the working class and the elite. Certainly, there was a great deal of variation in each experience of these "catholiques de volonté," as they were often called.[16] Moreover, this community of seekers, converts, and near converts was far from being representative of Jewish life in Paris in the interwar period, for many Jews were highly critical of the Jewish attraction to Catholicism.[17] As a young man in 1936, Emmanuel Levinas wrote an essay "Fraterniser sans convertir," in which he mounted a serious attack on Christians who contaminated the spirit of interwar Jewish-Christian friendships with proselytization aimed at conversion.[18] Many Jewish converts hid their baptisms from their communities and shocked parents. The Jewish intellectuals who came to the Maritains' salon and converted represented only a part of the religious and cultural scene in Paris.

In terms of Raïssa's role in this community, many friends remembered her as more reticent and quiet than Jacques, frail and sometimes ill, but for Meudon guests interested in Judaism, "le centre lumineux de ce cercle était Raïssa," as one friend recalled.[19] Her layered identity proved irresistible. For Georges Cattaui, Maritain was a "Jew in the heart of Jesus."[20] One émigré convert described Maritain as a woman "of Jewish

descent and born in Russia" who had "retained her native tongue and culture. She was therefore most helpful to me." But Maritain provided more
than comfort. The same convert recalled that she was both "firmly rooted
in her race" and a "pioneer of Judeo-Christian relations. No one had a
deeper insight than her into the mystery of Israel."[21] Another convert from
Poland wrote with a similar emphasis: "If ever in my lifetime I have met
a saint, it was Raïssa. Born into a Hasidic family, she had converted to Catholicism as a young girl, but she had retained the ardor of both faiths."[22]
Maurice Sachs, whom Maritain would usher into the church, saw her
through the prism of Léon Bloy: "Raïssa Maritain was a Jewess and it is
to her that the admirable work of Léon Bloy is dedicated: *Le salut par les
juifs*. To me she seemed what the holy Jewish women of the early Christian
age must have been: beautiful, the burning brightness of her race, but re-
served, loving, all spirit. . . . She was truly one of those Jewesses consumed
by the mystic flame, whose soul was a vertical line from earth to heaven."[23]
Sachs's quixotic, even orientalist rendering of the *femme juive* carries forward from Bloy's initial impressions, resurrected years later.[24] She was seen
to embody much of what the French Catholic revival intellectuals yearned
for—as a woman, a Russian, and a converted Jew, she was the proximate
other, and for a community that rebelled against bourgeois standards and
celebrated those on the margins, her otherness only contributed to her
allure.

Maritain's success also must be partly attributed to the fact that as
"l'hôtesse du cercle de visiteurs" she, like many of her guests, fit uneasily
into existing categories of the Catholic (or secular, for that matter) milieu.
A Russian-born Jew who still spoke her native language, Maritain hosted
a "Catholic" salon that was certainly unconventional. By the time the Maritains moved there, the town of Meudon was home to a growing and vibrant community of Russian artists and writers, many of them Jews who
had moved to Paris as exiles from the Russian Revolution in 1918. Marc
Raiff has argued that the Maritains' home drew countless numbers of
Russian émigré Jews largely because the "Russian-Jewish" atmosphere
that they encountered there was a welcome familiarity.[25] Raïssa and her
sister still spoke fluent Russian and often did so at home, and Raïssa
referred to herself as a Jewish-Christian long after her baptism. The
Russian-Jewish friendships in Meudon were Raïssa's initial forays into

the broader community in interwar Paris of Jewish émigré artists and intellectuals who came from Egypt, Germany, Lithuania, and Poland. By 1920, Paris had become one of the largest Jewish centers in the world, and the Jewish population in the city doubled between the turn of the century and 1930.[26]

Neither a mother nor a nun, Maritain's identity was also unconventional because as a married but childless intellectual and contemplative she eschewed traditional Catholic gender roles. Maritain also assumed a leadership role at Meudon that would have been difficult for a woman to attain in the university and ecclesial settings of the 1920s. Although she was the *hôtesse,* Maritain was almost entirely freed from domestic duties. These fell to other women, especially Véra and her mother, Hissia, who had moved to live near the Maritains after her husband died in 1912. Véra and Hissia prepared the large Sunday meals and weekend teas for guests, cleaned, and cared for the children who sometimes appeared at the doorsteps of Meudon with their parents. Maritain was free to dedicate herself exclusively to intellectual and spiritual work and to her relationships with the cast of artists, intellectuals, and religious seekers who passed through their doors.

In the memoirs and correspondence of many of the émigré Jewish converts who circulated through Meudon, one can detect echoes of Maritain's description of her own upbringing in 1909: "Je ne reçus pour ainsi dire pas d'instruction religieuse."[27] As with Raïssa, for many of the Jewish émigré intellectuals in Paris the Jewish faith had not survived the exile, and the émigré community had gradually come to align their behavior with that of their fellow French citizens of the secular *laïcité.*[28] Moreover, many of the émigré intellectuals circulating through Meudon were affiliated, some more than others, with philosophies on the left, and for Jews, as far as religion was concerned, these offered assimilation as the goal.[29] As a result, the sense of Judaism among some intellectuals in Maritain's circle was often nominal, and the detachment from religious tradition under the pressures of French assimilation was often experienced as true disillusion: "Je n'étais de nulle part" (I was from nowhere), mused Maurice Sachs.[30] Assimilation, religious indifference, and in some cases, a yearning for an alternative more accurately describe the background for their conversions than a robust Jewish identity.[31]

In the perceived atmosphere of religious rootlessness, many inter-war converts were deeply attracted to the aesthetic dimensions of Catholic devotionalism, which was understood to be capable of reorienting them and plunging them into the exotic and the medieval. The Jewish convert Paul Loewengard's widely read *La splendeur catholique: Du judaïsme à l'église,* published in 1910, just five years after Maritain's own conversion, de-scribes feelings of awe in his confrontation with the perceived beauty of Catholic rituals, chandeliers, stained glass, and even the intricacy of the elaborate dogmas. Yet this yearning for the exotic was often not ethically or politically neutral: Loewengard's echoed an old, anti-Semitic sentiment in France that Catholicism's elaborate panoply of rites generated interi-ority, whereas those of Judaism were empty and legalistic. "On the one side," Loewengard explained, "there was the sweetness of the Catholic re-ligion" and on the other, Judaism: "dry, cold, frozen."[32] The fascination with the splendor of Catholicism and its perceived capacity to galvanize the inner life taps into a similar fascination with the architecture of great medieval churches seen among the Jewish intellectuals who came to Péguy's bookshop, like Bernard Lazare, Raïssa Maritain herself, and Julien Benda. Much more than Jacques, Raïssa marshaled the aesthetically, eroti-cally, and exotically charged representations of Catholic piety, particularly for artist converts who came to Meudon like Maurice Sachs. Sachs was a Jewish disciple of Jean Cocteau, who introduced him to the Maritains at Meudon in 1925, and he converted to Catholicism that summer (his con-version was short-lived). Jacques and Raïssa's home was an attractive salon for young writers and artists like Sachs because of the Maritains' willing-ness to take seriously the desires and questions of young intellectuals, re-gardless of their background. (Sachs, after all, was a homosexual, a drug user, and only nineteen when Raïssa took him on as a project.) Raïssa, more than Jacques, seems to have taken up Sachs's spiritual quest imme-diately and in earnest. They began a lengthy correspondence in August 1925.[33] In the course of the short month to his conversion, Maritain gave Sachs a rosary, sent him a copy of the *Imitation of Christ,* and showed him pictures of Chartres Cathedral. She stressed the emotive, aesthetic aspects of Catholicism, just as her own godfather had done for her. Maritain wrote lengthy letters to Sachs in which she transcribed the entire cele-bration of two masses for approaching feast days, part in Latin and part in French, including the introits, the prayers, psalms, epistles, and Gospels.

On August 13, 1925, Maritain explained the Feast of the Assumption of the Virgin to Sachs, but after a long transcription describing the rejoicing of angels as Mary is transported into heaven, it was not doctrine she emphasized but the feelings that the passage elicited: "My dear friend, do you feel the sweetness of these words? For me, they are ineffable."[34] Her role in conversions from Judaism to Catholicism must be understood at least in part by her capacity to evoke this aesthetic, exotic tradition to the *déjudaisés* who yearned for it.

Sachs's own letters to Maritain en route to conversion reveal that he was concerned less with a shift from Judaism to Christianity than with Raïssa and Jacques's austere, antibourgeois lifestyle, which he held in awe. He was attracted to its exotic and aesthetic dimensions but also to a radical vision of Catholicism rooted in the decadent literary movement, the piety and theology that Maritain had carried forward from Léon Bloy. "The Church," Sachs recalled in his memoirs, "has sanctified extreme passions, blessed the frenzied, acclaimed the neuroses it has previously canalized. Nothing, it seemed, could stop me at its door. Nothing."[35] Catholicism, for young people like Sachs, was the experimental and radical aesthetic alternative to liberal modernity. Sachs assured Maritain that her gestures to explain Catholic rites, art, and devotions were for him "rays of sunshine. I cannot speak, and I don't know anything, but my silences are from such profound emotions that they do not leave the heart."[36] He expressed to Maritain how much the devotional objects generated emotional intimacy, although his emotions were primarily directed toward his godmother rather than toward God. His new devotional objects, he asserted, made him feel that "you perpetually surround me, Madame Maritain, my soon-to-be godmother!"[37] Maritain and Sachs rarely discussed Jewish or Catholic doctrine; Sachs was simply intent on expressing the "overwhelming, enormous emotion I have had getting to know you."[38] As he counted down to his baptism, he looked forward to the moment when he would finally be able to be connected to Jacques and Raïssa "in body, mind, and soul." As for Maritain, she assured Sachs that the feelings were mutual, although her private writings reveal she was more apprehensive.[39]

Sachs's fascination with the church echoed a widespread attraction to interwar primitivism and exoticism circulating through Meudon.[40] Scholars of French interwar exoticism tend to focus on the common yearning for truths located in a geographic or temporal elsewhere, but Catholicism itself, although internal to the history of France and evoked in nationalistic terms, also harbored something of the curious, the romantic, and the risky.[41] The devotional and aesthetic dimensions of pre–Vatican II piety practiced at the Maritains' home fed interwar yearnings to locate meaning in a region of proximate otherness. Sachs's exasperation with mediocrity and his fascination with a tradition in which holiness was overlaid with the erotic, the degenerate, and the exotic were well-known territory for his soon-to-be godmother.

Along with the exotic and aesthetic dimensions of Catholicism, Maritain's letters to Sachs stressed affectivity and interiority, and her attention to the inner life and emotions seemed to be focused on urging Sachs to tend to his own soul, to care for it, to cultivate new dispositions to interiorize God. "Make a monk's cell in your heart where you can go, at any time, and be alone with God," she advised him. Sachs was baptized into the Catholic Church on August 25, 1925.[42] Maritain's correspondence with other religious seekers (many, though not all, Jewish) similarly show her urging them to simply develop an inner life, advice seen by many as long-awaited nourishment. Catherine Pozzi wrote to Maritain in 1931, telling her that her letters were like "a flower that falls on the soul," and later added in her journal, "An indescribable grace guides Raïssa. When she leaves, I feel lifted up, stronger, and almost well."[43]

These impressions of Raïssa as someone otherworldly, inspiring, and exotic are crucial for understanding the conversions to Catholicism at Meudon. Like Maritain herself, pilgrims such as Maurice Sachs count among the "Jewish" converts to "Catholicism," but in both cases it seems less of a journey from one stable religious tradition to another than an embrace of the radical spiritual ideals embodied in their awe-inspiring mentors and an attraction to the panoply of art and objects from Catholic devotionalism—all of which threw into sharp relief the perceived sterility of secularism.

THE ATTRACTION OF CATHOLICISM'S POTENTIAL UNIVERSALITY

During the interwar period, Jews' attraction to Christianity that Maritain helped instigate was also fueled by a curious, widespread optimism about

Catholicism in its Parisian idiom. Salons like the Maritains' thrived in the mid- and late 1920s in what has been called Jazz Age Paris, "le temps de ferveur et de frénésie," "l'époque de toutes les sensations nouvelles," and crucially, a time of *rapprochement* between the Catholic Church and the French state.[44] This atmosphere created a lasting impression that modern cosmopolitanism was bound to French Catholicism. Consider, for example, the German Jewish novelist and essayist Joseph Roth, who moved to Paris in 1925. In May of that year, Roth wrote a rapturous letter from Paris to his editor and friend Benno Reifenberg in Germany. "Here," he wrote, "Catholicism is at its worldliest. In Paris," he explained, "Catholicism is a cosmopolitan religion that embraces all religion."[45] Roth did not convert but spent much of his life pursuing the realization of Jewish-Catholic cosmopolitan religiosity. As his biographer put it, he both believed in the equation "Catholicism ≈ Judaism" and deeply desired that it be true. For Roth this strange and vague formula did not erase the traditions' differences entirely: he arranged to have not one but two funerals, one Catholic, one Jewish.[46] He added, "European Catholicism brought about the wonderful mixing of races, the colorful confusion of all the differences of life. . . . Everyone [in Paris] carries in himself the blood of five different races, young and old, and every individual is a world comprising five continents. Each can understand each, and their society is open; no one is forced to take up any particular position. This is assimilation at its best: A person may remain as different as he is and feel at home."[47] In 1928 Roth wrote exuberantly, "I am a Frenchman from the East, a humanist, a rationalist with religion, a Catholic with a Jewish brain, a real revolutionary."[48] This perception was neither personal nor unique to Roth. Dennis Dunn argued that among the 150 Russian émigrés who converted to Catholicism in Paris in the 1920s and 1930s (from Judaism but also from the Orthodox Church or atheism), it was a common hope that a new era of internationalism and openness would be bound to Catholicism and that Catholicism had the capacity to include difference rather than erase it.[49]

Likewise, many converts in Maritain's community saw themselves not as true converts but as creative combiners of Judaism and Christianity. Take, for example, the case of the Jewish Polish sculptor Marek Szwarc, who had immigrated to Paris from Poland along with his wife. The two were (secretly) baptized Catholic in 1919 after meeting Jacques and Raïssa.

They raised their daughter, the writer Tereska Torres, as what they called a "juive-chrétienne." As an adult, Torres wrote at length about this unusual upbringing, nourished in the salons of the Maritains and of Stanislas Fumet, who was also married to a Jewish convert.[50] Torres recalled, "I was Jewish. This was something I knew very deeply. I could be as French and Catholic as any other girl in my school, but it didn't change the fact that I was also Jewish. I was a Sephardic, Jewish, Polish, Catholic, French girl! I felt much richer than those other children who were only one thing, 'Jewish,' or at most, two things, 'French and Catholic.'"[51] Torres recalls that she and her family saw themselves as "a new tribe of Jews in the Catholic religion."[52] Similarly, the Jewish convert Jean-Marie Lustiger, the future cardinal, theorized in the interwar period about the dignity of the "juifs-chrétiens" in the Catholic Church, seeing them as guardians of both the Old and New Testaments who would never completely sever ties with their tradition. Maritain continued throughout her life to refer to herself as a *juive-chrétienne* and, according to some perceptions of her, she carried in her person the possibility of that generation's hope for a new kind of internationalism and openness.[53] On the one hand, the refrain "Le catholicisme constitue l'accomplissement du judaïsme" is part of an old, familiar Christian story, one that was revitalized in France in the nineteenth century. In 1876, the Jewish convert Joseph Lémann wrote, "The Jew who becomes a Catholic does not change his religion, he supplements it. . . . In becoming a Catholic I want to become a perfect Israelite."[54] On the other hand, in the interwar period assimilation was more widespread than it had been in the previous century, and one heard more frequently of Jews claiming to have *discovered* Judaism in and through Catholicism, as opposed to merely aiming for its fulfillment in Catholicism. Writing in 1946, the French Jewish playwright Jean-Jacques Bernard described the Jewish conversions to Catholicism in the earlier part of the twentieth century: "Of the many unbelieving Jews who came to Christ . . . they had just shrugged their father's mantle from their shoulders. Judaism had become for them an empty word, in a sense. But when they opened the doors of the Church, what did they find within Christianity? Their Judaism."[55] Maritain wrote something similar in 1941: "Suppose that a Jew should, as is so often the case today, have become a stranger to the Mosaic Faith and hence indifferent to the destiny of Israel. If such a Jew becomes a Christian he begins only then to understand the depths of his debt to

Judaism—the idea of a God at once transcendent and personal; the revelation of the supernatural universe, the roots of his new theology, the beauty of his new liturgy; and only then does he do justice to his people's greatness, and become proud to belong to it."[56]

As with Péguy and Bloy, a range of opinions surfaced about what exactly this new Jewish-Christian optimism entailed: Christianity's replacement or assimilation of Judaism? The creation of a new religion combining both? These questions would take on an urgent ethical and political cast in light of the ascendency of anti-Semitism in the late 1930s and later the Shoah. But in the early interwar period, Maritain continued to believe in her godfather's claims about the completion of Judaism in Christianity. In 1925, for example, just weeks before Maurice Sachs's baptism, her mother, Hissia Oumançoff, who had moved with the Maritains to Meudon after her husband died, finally relented under pressure from her daughters and son-in-law to convert to Christianity. Nine years later, in 1934, Maritain wrote a poem entitled "Élisabeth-Marie," in which she described her mother's "serious mind" (grave esprit) that traveled "slowly the way from the Old / to the New Testament" (fit lentement le chemin de l'Ancien / au Nouveau Testament). The poem continues, "O that day when you at last said to us, the Gospel / open on your lap— 'I am ready.'"[57]

PHILO-SEMITISM IN THE GATHERING STORM: MARITAIN'S *HISTOIRE D'ABRAHAM*

If the 1920s was a time of unbounded optimism about the capacities of Parisian Catholicism to accommodate Judaism, the 1930s were ominous for both Jews and philo-Semitic Christians.[58] Jacques's international travels and the religious and ethnic diversity of the Meudon community gave the Maritains a unique perspective on European political developments. They understood earlier than most the increasing intensity of European anti-Semitism as it gained ascendancy. Their friendship with several members of the German clergy alerted them in 1933 to the existence of the Dachau concentration camp, which housed some of these priests in addition to German Jews.[59] By 1934, the news of anti-Semitism's escalation was beginning to be felt inside the borders of France. That year *Mein Kampf* was translated into French, and the notion that Jews were "unassimilable" began to resurface in Paris.[60] In 1935, the Nazi Party passed the Nuremberg Laws, which deprived German Jews of citizenship, creating thousands of refugees at France's borders. From this year onward, many voices in France urged that the Jewish refugees be denied entrance to their country.[61] Some of the anti-Semitism had an explicitly theological cast. In 1930, the German writer Alfred Rosenberg published *Der Mythus des zwanzigsten Jahrhunderts (The Myth of the Twentieth Century),* endorsing the Nazi Party's Program of 1920. According to that program, the party stood for a "new, positive Christianity" that would abolish the "Jewish Old Testament" and purge the New Testament of "Jewish" as well as pacifist themes.[62] During the Shoah, the theologian Henri de Lubac leveled a scathing critique of Nazism's gross misreading of both Christianity and Judaism, exposing pseudoscientific theologians who aimed to purify Christianity from its putatively corrupt Jewish roots.[63] "Bloody filth," he would later call it.[64]

In general, from the earliest stages, French Catholic intellectuals in the Maritains' community demonstrated a mixed response to the developments on the political horizon.[65] Some of the hateful fascist literature emerged from Catholic presses whose writers Jacques and Raïssa knew well. Their former colleague and ally from their Sorbonne days Henri Massis, for example, was a leading spokesman for French anti-Semitic movements.[66] For their part, the Maritains resisted these events early on and unequivocally, and although their voices were rare among the Catholics they were not alone. In the 1930s some Catholic youth publications, including *La Vie Catholique, Le Monde Ouvrier* (part of the Jeunesse ouvrière catholique), *Le Bulletin Catholique International,* and the Dominican weekly *Sept,* joined ranks with Jews to fight anti-Semitism.[67]

In this increasingly ominous climate, in the 1930s many philo-Semitic Catholics and *juif-catholique* converts in Maritain's community began to study the sacred texts and traditions of Judaism more seriously and moved away from language of replacement or untheorized assertions of unity. The Maritains' friend and Jewish convert Jean de Menasce began publishing on Judaism in the early 1930s with his celebrated study of Hasidism, *Quand Israël aime Dieu,* seeing within the tradition of Hasidism—little known at the time— the warmth of ritual art and the emphasis on inner life that had become familiar to him through Christian mysticism. Marc Chagall, although never a convert (or even close), began for the first time to take up explicitly Jewish themes in his work in the early 1930s, most famously in his extensive illustrations of scenes from the Hebrew Bible. Joseph Roth wrote his most famous novel about Jewish life, *Job*, in 1930. Maritain's acquaintance Henri de Lubac, S.J., would argue in his 1938 classic *Catholicisme* that Christianity could be revitalized through contact with its roots in the Hebrew Bible; for Lubac this meant the return to the predominantly *social* notion of salvation history, which was for him a thoroughly Jewish concept.[68]

In 1935 Raïssa Maritain joined these efforts, and her thinking evinces a similar continual revision of her understanding of the relationship between the two traditions. The foundations for articulating Jewish-Christian unity in the face of anti-Semitism had been established by Léon Bloy and Charles Péguy, and Maritain had her own personal confrontations with it beginning in 1931, when her friend Georges Bernanos published *La grande peur des bien-pensants,* a deeply anti-Semitic text celebrating Édouard Drumont. Maritain responded to Bernanos with a letter arguing that, despite Bernanos's claims to the contrary, Mary and Jesus were not "outside their race." Aware of the anti-Semitic tendency to highlight the *differences* between Judaism and Christianity and to avoid acknowledging Christianity's debts to Judaism, she insisted on the Jewishness of both the Old and New Testaments, which had "furnished the church with its prophets, and its evangelists."[69] This fairly mild rejoinder was one of Maritain's first responses to the anti-Semitism within her Catholic milieu (in the coming years her reactions would intensify). It was left to Joseph Roth to condemn Bernanos's book with more outspoken rage: "He wanted to exterminate the Jews," Roth commented. "So much Catholic faith for the devil, and so much principle for nothing! So much heroism for cowardice! So much insight for blindness: what a sorry waste of a life!"[70]

At the urging of her friend Abbé Charles Journet (1891–1975), a Swiss theologian and future cardinal, Maritain began working on her first book on Judaism, *Histoire d'Abraham ou La sainteté dans l'état de nature.* The authorization Maritain obtained from her more established male (in this case, also clerical) colleague was critical, and something she deeply desired. In June of 1935 she sent Journet a sample of one chapter and asked, "Tell me, do you think I should continue this work?" To which he replied,

"These pages are splendid. . . . Of course you must continue! I'm *asking you* to do it, for me and for the countless minds that they will illuminate."[71] A few months later, Maritain published it with the academic press Journet was involved in.

In *Histoire d'Abraham,* Maritain moves from the book of Genesis to the Pauline letters to highlight what she calls the "living bond" (lien vivant) between the Old and New Testaments. In Maritain's hands, this notion of the *lien vivant* is multivalent, bringing to the surface both the opportunities and the constraints Catholics face as they try to forge new understandings of Judaism.[72] In this work Maritain places the figure of Abraham at the center, claiming that the Patriarch unites the Old and New Testaments ("Il unit l'un à l'autre les deux Testaments"). In the emphasis on unity rather than replacement, Maritain's treatment of Abraham works to break down the theological underpinnings of a typical Christian super-sessionist notion of the New Law replacing the Old. Illuminating the faith of Abraham, Maritain moves to dismantle two other Christian charges against Judaism: its putative legalism and its moral degeneracy or infancy in comparison with Christianity. She begins by addressing the puzzling presence of immorality in the book of Genesis—the lies and infidelity, the incest and violence. Maritain wants to avoid using these unsavory scenes as proof of the superiority of Christian morality, but she refuses to sweep them under the rug. "Of the lie Jacob told at his mother's behest," she writes, "St. Augustine said: 'It is not a lie; it is a mystery.' Let us have the courage to say: It is without doubt a mystery, but it is also a lie."[73]

Genesis, she argues, makes clear that faith exists in a "different regime" than ethics; the protagonists in the Hebrew scriptures are models, not of morality, but of theological faith. To this end, Maritain limns the story of Abraham and Isaac with particular care and passion, presenting Abraham as the archetypal model of faithfulness. She had read Kierkegaard's *Fear and Trembling* when it came out in French translation earlier that year (1935). She and Jacques were close friends of the surrealist writer Benjamin Fondane, who was, like Raïssa, an émigré, a poet, and a Jew (he never converted and was later killed at Auschwitz). Fondane was a student of the Jewish thinker Lev Shestov, a preeminent interpreter of *Fear and Trembling.* This Jewish reading of Kierkegaard seems to have been an influence for Maritain. According to Maritain, Abraham's faith during the "nuit obscure" of God's terrible demand was a faith most radical and pure. It was "naked, arid," stripped of consolations, and purged of everyday understandings of morality. Of Genesis 22, she writes:

> All this happened at night, for next it is said that "early in the morning" Abraham arose. It was the night of his agony. The night in which the mere man in him died. The night of a transfiguration! . . . The Abraham who went to bed in the evening was not the same Abraham who arose "early in the morning." . . . He believed, and in his faith he began to die. He died to his happy life, to his abundant life according to the flesh. He died to the light of his simple thoughts, to his too natural thoughts, to his still too simple knowledge of good and evil. In that great darkness, his faith grew greater yet, and its roots struck ever deeper into his soul. And with his son Isaac, Abraham gave to God the very soul of his life and of his joy; he consented to the destruction of all his hope.[74]

In *Histoire d'Abraham,* Abraham's apophatic faith is a dark faith shorn of comforts, of human concepts of good and evil, even of happiness, and is reminiscent of the aesthetics and spirituality of Bloy. Certainly immorality is present in these stories, but the figures are operating in a different, almost mystical realm.

In *Histoire d'Abraham,* Maritain links Abraham with other figures, both Jewish and Christian. As with Abraham, Maritain wrote, "so too with Mary in the Annunciation; with Joseph in his dream; with the apostles, called one by one to believe in the mission of Christ; with Joan of Arc, charged with the temporal salvation of a people. In each instance, the act of faith is stripped of all visible assistance and is carried out in anguish of conscience."[75] The unity here is a community of faithful Jews and Christians who have gone through the dark night—the interior anguish where even hope is destroyed, reminiscent of her own inner journey described in her posthumously published *Journal.* The *souffrance* here again resurfaces as an interior experience of being plunged into the deeper, darker realms of mystical faith, something she sees as shared by the best Jewish and Christian figures alike. In this panoply of heroes, the Jews Abraham and Joseph do not merely prefigure more traditional Christian heroes such as Mary and Joan of Arc. Maritain lists her saints side by side, out of temporal order. This cluster of Christian and Jewish figures together subverts the expected linear progression from Judaism to Christianity. Here Jewish figures do not submissively bow down to the demands of Christianity; they actualize Christianity's most radical goals.

With careful attention to Abraham's inner life, Maritain also subverts traditional Christian readings of Judaism as legalistic. She explicitly takes on this ancient charge in *Histoire d'Abraham,* arguing that legalism is "not a temptation of Jews *qua* Jews." "Any community," she insists, "that holds in honor the law of God risks falling victim to it."[76] The struggle to render the Law interior and spontaneous is the struggle of every individual. "To integrate within oneself the whole of this morality, to assimilate it into the intimate life of the soul, and to bring it to the living springs of grace much love is needed." Love is not, according to Maritain's reading of the tradition, Christianity's gift to Judaism; rather, it is at the heart of the Jewish scriptures themselves. "Hence the very soul of the Law," Maritain writes, "is the commandment of love," and she cites not the Gospels or the Pauline letters but Deuteronomy: "'You shall love the Lord your God' (Deut. 6:5)." Paul's notion of love and the Law is in Maritain's view nourished by Christ *and* the Jewish scriptural imagination. "Paul," she writes, "having known both the Mosaic Law and the Law of Christ," emphasizes the inextricable bond between love and the Law. "The Law is spiritual" (Rom. 7:14), she reminds readers. "Freedom and love" are the foundation of the Law.[77] Here her approach differs from that of her friend René Schwob, who wrote in 1929 that the "New Testament replaced the former because it replaced its legalism with a broad and deep universalism, because it offers food to the heart previously unknown, because its symbols are a true religion."[78] Maritain's analysis must be understood as a robust political *and* theological defense of Judaism as a faith that generates, rather than constrains, ethical and spiritual interiority. In *Histoire d'Abraham* her prose is that of a controlled theologian or exegete, a sparse style that could hardly clash more with the epithets that blaze through her godfather's books or with Péguy's yearning for the radical, passionate *mystique* of the Dreyfusards. Yet on another level, Péguy and Bloy's influences are unmistakable. Bloy's commitment to the sheer Jewishness of Christianity and the fundamental unity of Judaism and Christianity, something "most do not want to know," flowered in Maritain as an ethically and politically valuable concept in the face of anti-Semitism. Without Péguy and Bloy's rejection of anti-Semitism as a blasphemy, Maritain could scarcely have articulated this cry against the emerging horrors in Europe in the 1930s. But it differs from Péguy's evocation of the bruised Jewish body or the wounded *suppliant,* and from Bloy's evocation of the wandering, abject Jew embodying the Holy Spirit. The heroes of the Hebrew scriptures here are anguished, but in a way that refers to the darkness of a purged, inner faith. Péguy and Bloy did not have to worry about the potential of their rhetoric to fan the flames of anti-Semitic violence; since neither was of Jewish origin, neither was a physical target of increasing anti-Semitic hatred in the late 1930s. Moreover, Maritain has left behind earlier notions inherited from Bloy about carnal Jews and spiritual Jews who are already Christians at heart (as Maritain, in Bloy's view, was *déjà une chrétienne* well before her conversion). This old binary does not appear in *Histoire d'Abraham.* Bloy's fundamental messianism, however, remains central to her theological imagination: the "regime of the spirit," as she calls it, is "dependent on and fastened to" Christ's redeeming love.[79]

One wonders what political difference Maritain's theology about the unity of Christianity and Judaism—and not just Christianity's historical indebtedness to Judaism—could have made if it had been more well known in the 1930s. Spiritual unification with Jewish souls in the inner forms of faith could have been a persuasive claim to universalism and a powerful rejoinder to Nazi anti-Semitism. For example, one of the most reiterated Nazi tactics was the insistence on Jewish irreducible difference, including difference at the level of soul and spirit. The notorious 1939 Nazi propaganda film *Der ewige Jude,* for example, overlaid footage of Jews in the Lódź Ghetto with images of rodents to show that Jews "*differ* from us in body, but especially in soul."[80] Spiritual unity between Jews and Catholics pushes against that. We know that the pronouncement "Spiritually, we are all Semites" was one of the few papal utterances by the Vatican that took the side of Jews in the 1930s and even during the Shoah, a small sign of support that the resistance community hung onto dearly.[81] What if there had been more? Bloy and Péguy, in their own puzzling and ambivalent ways, had aimed to articulate this through all their complex proclamations of the unity of Christians and Jews. Maritain carried it forward, building a philo-Semitic version of Christianity that genuinely embraced Jewish political dignity and Judaism's spiritual value. Anguish was a part of this spiritual value, an anguish of a faith shorn of comforts that she had yearned for since her own baptism. But the language of anguish and Judaism was at this point far removed from the theory of vicarious suffering.

DEEPENING THE DISCOURSES
OF JEWISH *SOUFFRANCE*

As Raïssa published *Histoire d'Abraham* in 1935, Jacques's work also turned to public pronouncements against anti-Semitism, and not all French Catholics were on board with their philo-Semitic project.[82] On September 24, 1937, Jacques confided in his notebook that Father Réginald Garrigou-Lagrange, the couple's old friend, was "very worked-up against me. . . . It seems that Raïssa and Véra are being implicated as dragging me along by their influence. (Russian Jewesses, are they not?) This puts me in a black rage, which I do not hide."[83] Garrigou-Lagrange's venomous critiques of the Maritains' philo-Semitism show that not all Catholics who turned to scholarship about Judaism in the 1930s segued neatly into critiques of anti-Semitism. The turn to the Jewish past could be marshaled for a wide range of political and ethical projects: in 1931, Garrigou-Lagrange wrote a widely read book *Le judaïsme avant Jésus-Christ,* a long apologetic showing the need for Jesus's interventions in a moribund and morally bankrupt pre-Christian Judaism in Palestine.[84] In one of her last publications before she died Maritain would take issue with Lagrange's claims directly.

In the late 1930s, more pernicious and racist accusations from Garrigou-Lagrange and others were hurled at Jacques; Raïssa was devastated. Not only were some of her co-religionists attacking her as a spiritual poison and a racial pollutant, but perhaps even worse, very few Catholics publicly rallied to her defense. Raïssa painfully described this betrayal in racial and theological terms. On April 9, 1938, she wrote to her friends Pieter and Christine van der Meer de Walcheren:

We have been insulted before. . . . But now racism is at the bottom of the hatred, it is impossible for me not to see that this insult is addressed at *my* blood! It is intolerable. This insult is made to the blood of God himself, the author of life. What is intolerable is that they usurp the name "*chrétien*" to deliver these offenses. And on top of it all to see how *Jacques* is treated on account of my blood . . . If we left France today, those who would miss us would not add up to more than ten.[85]

Here it is clear that although Judaism for Maritain was about faith *(Histoire d'Abraham)* it was also about blood and biological inheritance. Two weeks after this pained letter to the Meer de Walcherens, she admitted to the Swiss Charles Journet, "For me the face of this world has suddenly shriveled up."[86] But her pain extended past personal hurt to include broader existential reflections. Thinking of those who tried to evade the reality of gathering darkness in the late interwar period, Maritain offered a critique in 1938: "The time of childish things is over, the time of playing games, of make-believe, of eloquence, of 'let's pretend.'" Did the Jewish-Christian experiments of the 1920s seem naive? A few months later, she repudiated the duplicity around her, arguing that reality had trumped illusions. "Every word of consolation," she wrote, "seems a lie."[87]

By the late 1930s, Maritain's language of *souffrance,* death, and affliction—always at the center of her spiritual life—had become entangled in the political crises of this period, the ascendancy of anti-Semitism, and the personal betrayals. "I find myself so alone, so wretched, so abandoned," she wrote in 1937, "that I wonder by what miracle I keep alive and on my feet; for my soul and my mind are then, as it were, drawn out of me and only my will remains with me and enables me to live and act [ma volonté seule reste avec moi et me fait vivre et agir]."[88] By September 1939, after the Nazi invasion of Poland, and as Germany was poised to invade France, the complicity of those around the Maritains, the silence around the cruelty and injustice, took Raïssa's *souffrance* to a new level, one that "drives one to desperation." As the voices denying Jewish citizens rights in France were raised to new heights, as the news from Poland and Germany worsened, she wrote in her journal, "Faced with death, will I be afraid? Should I be afraid?"[89] Later she described an experience at Mass in which she had offered God to take her own life in exchange for peace.

By the late 1930s, Maritain was poised to leave France for America on what would be a long wartime exile. In this period Maritain's thinking on Judaism made one final shift that would become more fully developed and subtly transformed during the years of the Shoah (to be explored in chapter 5). Her language of *souffrance* shifted as well: instead of describing the painful interior transformations of an anguished mystical faith that united Jews and Christians, she, like Bloy and Péguy, focused on historical suffering, persecution, violence, and death, though she was still at this point fundamentally connected to images of redemption and light. Here she merely planted seeds for what would become more developed in the war years: suffering and grief as essential to Jewish identity, something the French Catholic revival had long trained her to see and articulate. She began to echo the emerging sentiment of the community of Jewish converts to Christianity. "Persecution," Cardinal Lustiger wrote, "is a fact of our identity."[90]

FOR AT LEAST THREE DECADES PRIOR TO PIUS XI'S 1938 pronouncement that "spiritually, we are all Semites" and his 1939 "lost" encyclical on racism and anti-Semitism, *Humani Generis Unitas,* nonordained Catholics had theorized what a closer relationship between Catholics and Jews would entail epistemologically and theologically.[91] *Humani Generis Unitas* was never published, since Pius XI died before he could sign it and it subsequently went into the Vatican Secret Archives. Before these archives were opened in 2006 there was occasional speculation that it contained the lost material for what might have been a robust Catholic rejoinder to Nazism. But the revealed text only brings to light the lamentable state of church teaching on Judaism in the 1930s: among other things, the church remained alert to the "spiritual dangers to which contact with Jews can expose souls."[92] The French Catholic revivalists I have explored rejected this theology out of hand, and at the time the encyclical was written some had been constructing an alternative for nearly thirty years.

The Shoah is often seen as the terrible, shameful catalyst for Christian revision of the theology of contempt for Judaism, which partially bore fruit with the promulgation of the Second Vatican Council's *Nostra Aetate* (1965). Because of the religiously eclectic makeup of their community, and the foundation established by Péguy and Bloy, the French intellectuals associated with the Catholic revival pursued a new understanding of Jews and Judaism not after the Holocaust but at a much earlier point in the twentieth century. Furthermore, *Nostra Aetate* did not, and perhaps could not, capture the experimental and far-reaching character of these explorations, which asserted not just tolerance but a kind of unity between the two traditions. Such assertions were both radical and deeply problematic.

In analyzing the Catholic revival's alternatives to the teachings of the church on Judaism, I have focused on the turn-of-the-century forerunners Léon Bloy and Charles Péguy (chapter 1) and on Raïssa Maritain and her interwar community of Christian Jews and philo-Semitic Catholics. Regarding Jews and Judaism, Maritain both drew on and diverged from her early mentors. Bloy's insistence on the Jewishness of Christianity as a counter to anti-Semitism prompted Maritain's theologically vibrant reading of Judaism in *Histoire d'Abraham*. An anguished, tortured vision of Jewish faith segued easily into the radicalism of Péguy, Bloy, and their beloved community of suffering-centered mystics. We see a continuation in Maritain's portrait of Abraham: more darkness, more sacrifice, more anguish, but here she marshals these themes to very different ends. Rather than asserting unity through the vehicle of suffering alone, she engages in the exegetical work of dismantling anti-Jewish slander about legalism and immorality. Yet for all of the prescience of the French Catholic revivalists, Judaism in their thinking moves irresistibly toward a cosmopolitan, apophatic Catholicism, and one must ask if this project can be fully disentangled from the two-thousand-year-old Christian refusal to see Jews as Jews, in terms other than as potential converts or obstinate sinners.[93]

As for the converts and near converts themselves, such as Maritain, Joseph Roth, Maurice Sachs, and many others, although some scholars see the pull that Parisian Catholicism exerted on Jews primarily in terms of self-loathing and the attempt to expel Judaism from their identities, the converts I have come to know illustrate a more complex process.[94] The complexities of the place of Jews and Judaism in the French Catholic revival are best illuminated in the interwar contexts of yearnings for exoticism, widespread optimism about the universalizing potential of Catholicism, and the ascendancy of anti-Semitism in the 1930s that drove many intellectuals to turn to explicitly Jewish themes and texts in their scholarship.

Finally, at the height of this movement, Catholicism for some represented a chance to integrate Judaism into a universalized Christianity, a vision of a *nouveau christianisme* that offered a chance for assimilation into a unified community based on ethical and, even more importantly, *religious* ideals that were distinct from the assimilationist goals of the laicized French state. Gauri Viswanathan's research has shown that conversion in modern, largely secular societies (particularly conversion from a minority religion to the majority) can be usefully interpreted as an act of resistance to the assimilationist project of the secular nation, a refusal to ground one's source of identity only in humanity in general or in the interests of the state in particular.[95] In this chapter I have sketched the details of how, in the midst of this watershed movement in the Catholic Church, Raïssa Maritain and her community of religious seekers sought to elaborate an understanding of Judaism that would be assimilable, not into the secular culture of the nation-state, but into the piety of an internationalist Catholicism called to its *lien vivant* with Judaism. The world of Meudon was a place where *déjudaïsés* intellectuals could ground a new epistemological, ethical, and religious community, forged as an alternative to laicized universal citizenship. Jewish scriptures and traditions were not expunged in this assimilationist project, and this oddly gave Jews like Maritain an alternative way not only to maintain their identities but to actually *discover* religion and, ultimately, a particular kind of Christian philo-Semitic Judaism.

This ardent hope, however, began to shatter by the late 1930s. For example, in his 1939 memoir Maurice Sachs expressed regret that he had so eagerly signed a baptism certificate that read: "Jean-Maurice-Marie-Jacques Sachs . . . renounced the errors of the Jews." Reflecting on this phrase fourteen years after he signed it, he wrote:

> Renounced the errors of the Jews! I wonder. If I were to some day worship Him again, I would not praise Him in the Catholic Churches, nor the Protestant ones. . . . I would return to the temple of my fathers to pray with the Jews, for in times like these, when the Jews are recovering their greatest honor in martyrdom, one is prouder to be a Jew than during the days of the prosperity of Israel; and I should never forgive myself if, having decided to pray, I did not go and kneel with the sons of Abraham, my fathers.[96]

The rage and regret Raïssa Maritain's godson expresses casts a glaring light on Maritain's own abiding commitment to conversions, a commitment that endured even after the Holocaust. But in some ways it also echoes some of Maritain's own sense of deep betrayal of the philo-Semitic ideals of the 1920s. Both sets of feelings reveal how ephemeral and fragile these interecumenical experiments actually were. These experiments in being at once *juif* and *catholique,* plunging oneself into the exotic world of devotional Catholicism and assuming it could accommodate Judaism, would feel, by 1939, naive and inadequate. Moreover, stories of the converts and the philo-Semitic Catholics who befriended them show us that the French Catholic revival cannot be understood as exclusively a moment of Roman Catholic self-renewal in the face of modernity. Instead, it was the result of vast numbers of men and women from various national backgrounds—émigrés from Poland, Russia, Germany, and beyond—and religious traditions—lapsed Catholics, Russian Orthodox, and especially Jews—who suddenly came into contact with both Christian and Jewish discourse and practice and engaged it from entirely new perspectives. They aimed to do something new, and did so, even if they would see many of their aims defeated and their communities shattered.

CHAPTER 4

Poetry "in the Storm of Life"

Art, Mysticism, and Politics at Meudon (1931–39)

In 1931, at the height of the Meudon years and four years before *Histoire d'Abraham* went to press, Raïssa Maritain published her first poem, entitled "La couronne d'épines" (The Crown of Thorns), a vivid rendering of Jesus's fear on the Mount of Olives before his crucifixion. In describing "all the misery laid bare before him," Maritain writes that Jesus "sees himself abandoned," and the "darkness is full / All is given." Maritain transformed the elegiac themes we have seen in her journals, correspondence, and essays into the sparse, dark poems that would distinguish her primary intellectual work until her death in 1960.[1]

"La couronne d'épines" appeared in the inaugural issue of *Vigile,* a journal, founded the previous year by Paul Claudel, Charles Du Bos, and François Mauriac, that served as a Catholic counterweight to André Gide's prominent secular literary journal, *La Nouvelle Revue Française.*[2] Although it only survived fourteen issues (because of internal fights about which should take precedence, Catholic orthodoxy or art), *Vigile* was a rallying point for leading intellectuals of the *renaissance catholique.* The cover of the inaugural issue displays the name Raïssa Maritain along with five other

Catholic luminary *hommes de lettres:* Henri Bremond, the great Jesuit historian of spirituality; Étienne Gilson, the Thomist and historian of medieval Christianity; François Mauriac, the Nobel Prize–winning novelist; the playwright Henri Ghéon; and Jacques.[3] The only woman on the cover, Maritain was presented here as one of the very few who now labored alongside the distinguished men in her intellectual community, forging a new kind of Catholicism engaged with the latest developments in European arts and culture.[4] In 1931, Raïssa had now publicly stepped out of the shadow of Jacques and established her own distinctive literary and theological voice.

Throughout the 1930s, Maritain created and operated a "counter-space" of creativity that existed alongside her anxieties about Judaism and the ascendancy of anti-Semitism. She became a poet and a theorist of art. Sometimes this new aspect of her vocation intersected with her thinking on Judaism, as when she expressed in poetry her anguish over the betrayal of early philo-Semitic ideals, and sometimes her poems and theory of aesthetics operated at a remove from all of that, in a different register.[5] In the 1930s Maritain published sixty-four poems in Catholic and literary journals, and her reputation in the literary community grew primarily when her first two books of poetry, *La vie donnée* and *Lettre de nuit,* appeared in 1935 and 1939. By the time of her death, Maritain had published ninety poems in four volumes. In addition to her poetry, Maritain presented lectures and published articles on the arts, a domain where her influence extended beyond the French Catholic revival into wider intellectual communities in Paris, the United States, and Latin America. She presented papers on religious experience and aesthetics at the Sorbonne, and, joining Jacques on some of his international lecture tours, she gave lectures in Brazil and Argentina in 1935 and 1937. Her works on aesthetic theory and mysticism appeared in a range of French and English-language journals, and in 1938 she coauthored with Jacques one of her most widely read works on aesthetics, *Situation de la poésie.* While in the United States during the war years (1940–45), Maritain joined a small group of European colleagues who served as founding board members of the American Society of Aesthetics, created to model European intellectual societies dedicated to discussing the meaning of art and beauty in contemporary society.[6]

The fact that Raïssa Maritain became a poet and theorist of aesthetics in the midst of the intense personal and political crises explored in the previous chapter has seemed incongruous to some readers. Like mysticism, how could art—perhaps poetry above all—be anything but an apolitical activity, an escape even, from actually choosing to confront those horrors that were affecting her so powerfully in the 1930s? Mysticism and artistic activity are often indicted for their evasion of reality and their tendency to withdraw from the political, and such perceptions have also given rise to the assumption that Raïssa was primarily Jacques's apolitical partner. Particularly in the 1930s and during the Shoah, Jacques's state-focused political advocacy gained momentum and his philosophical work became increasingly focused on the juridical sphere, culminating in his participation in drafting the United Nations Declaration of Human Rights in 1948. Most scholars see Raïssa during these politically tumultuous years as Jacques's cloistered other half, disengaged from the mid-twentieth-century's traumas and choosing to instead inhabit the ethereal realms of prayer and poetry. For some, this was an indictment.[7] For others, like Thomas Merton (who eventually translated some of Raïssa's poems into English), the fact that Raïssa was "immersed in the supernatural," as he put it, stood in "sharp relief to this century of torment, duplicity, confusion."[8] For Merton, it was precisely the gap between Maritain's absorption in the spiritual, communicated through her poems, and the century of profane darkness that inspired his abiding admiration for her.

But Maritain's own writings in this period suggest that she aimed to articulate, elaborate, and give voice to the traumas in her midst. She claimed that her continued immersion in the realm of contemplation and the creation of her poems were essential to this process. Many intellectuals who survived this period in European history have argued that poetry was not a retreat from, but a witness and participant in, the ordeals of the twentieth century. Czeslaw Milosz, a friend of the Maritains, described his own experience of the reiterations of violence on the European continent between 1914 and 1944 as "an encounter of a European poet with the hell of the twentieth century, not hell's first circle, but a much deeper one."[9] He recalls these years as ones of profound disintegration, when old systems of knowledge were seen as outworn and fundamentally powerless to explain a world that was descending into chaos. In this context, according to Milosz, poetry "became as essential as bread."[10] Poetry may have given authors a more open-ended way to access and articulate this collapsing world, perhaps because of the metaphors, short lines, missing links, and stark images enabled by the poetic genre.

Throughout the late interwar period, Raïssa Maritain struggled to articulate the relationship between poetry and the crises in history. As she did this, she again reached for the symbols of suffering and affliction. On the one hand, she *did* see the role of art—especially poetry—as a kind of escape, a refuge from suffering, something that enabled men and women to remember life and its joy in the midst of trauma and grief. On the other hand, she envisioned poetry as having an urgent, even interventionist role in countering Europe's descent into violence and the ascendancy of anti-Semitism. Crucial to Maritain's understanding of the relationship between politics and art was her commitment to a certain realism—a realism indebted to both Aquinas and Bergson. Maritain saw the interior suffering that came from the habitual practice of silence as crucial for an intuitive knowledge of *le réel,* and she understood this knowledge as the source of artistic activity. Artists, according to Maritain, therefore had the capacity to describe *le réel* in all of its messiness, pain, and danger in a way few people could typically manage. In the 1930s, she grappled with this theme in various essays: "La poésie est-elle un mensonge?" (Is Poetry a Lie?) (1939); "Le poème en prose" (Poetry in Prose) (1935); "Le poète, et son temps" (The Poet and His Time) (1936); "Sens et non-sens en poésie" (Sense and Nonsense in Poetry) (1937); "Magie, poésie, et mystique" (Magic, Poetry and Mysticism) (1938); and "Message aux poètes qui sont à la guerre" (Message to Poets Who Are at War) (1939).[11]

Moving from Maritain's essays on aesthetics to her poems written in the 1930s, I also argue that her long-standing training in suffering-centered Christianity, far from being private or apolitical, enabled her to pull into her being and offer poetic witness to the escalating violence in interwar Europe. Maritain's theological imagination and devotional practices, schooled in awareness and elaboration of—even the yearning for— *souffrance,* generated the words and images that named something unimaginable—an abandoned people, immeasurable darkness, and the injustice of complicity. A close reading of Maritain's poems, "Pietà" (1937) and "Aux morts désespérés" (1939) in particular, illuminates how Catholic symbols of suffering captured unbearable pain, giving words to cries that would have otherwise been unarticulated on the eve of the Shoah. These poems, along with her *Journal,* suggest that Maritain's long-standing practices of suffering-centered piety shaped her "religious sensorium" in a way that transformed and, I would argue, deepened her cognitive, affective, and bodily experiences of the crises of the late 1930s.[12] In 1939, when she learned of the unfolding violence in Poland, Maritain claimed that the bitter taste ("goût amer") of poverty, misery, and death "filled my whole mouth and whole being" (avait empli ma bouche et tout mon être).[13] Religious practices centered in *souffrance* that had long trained her as a subject to interiorize the suffering other—Christ—now shifted and expanded as she drew into herself the pain of others in Europe. To be sure, this would not be Maritain's last word on the topic. As we will see in chapter 5, during the war itself Maritain joined the chorus of poets who witnessed the annihilation of European Jewry, a subject she claimed went beyond authors' capabilities of narration. Writers like Maritain claimed to have encountered a reality that, to use Milosz's terms, "rose up before them like a wall" and that in Maritain's terms constituted "Ce que l'âme ne peut soutenir / Ce qui ne peut ni s'imaginer ni se dire" (That which the soul cannot support / cannot imagine or say).[14]

TOWARD A DOCTRINE "FULL AND LUMINOUS"

Maritain's friendship with Jean Cocteau (1889–1963) was critical to her formation as a poet. Cocteau was a leading figure of the avant-garde community in interwar France and beyond who made significant inroads in the worlds of literature, film, theater, and design. Honored with literary accolades throughout his later years, in 1955 he was made a member of the Académie française and the Royal Academy of Belgium. He had befriended the Maritains in 1924. Through his friendship with Jacques and Raïssa during the Meudon years, he was converted, or rather he returned to the Catholicism of his childhood, though only briefly.[15] Indeed, the years of the Meudon salon were, as Michel Bressolette put it, "a time of *coups de foudre* among intellectuals and artists."[16] Cocteau's startling return to the church made big waves in the literary community in 1925.[17] While

Cocteau and Jacques's friendship was quickly made famous with the publication in 1926 of an exchange of letters between them, Cocteau was also
friends with Raïssa, both in combination with Jacques (Cocteau wrote to
Jacques in January of 1926, "Naturally, when I speak to you, I'm speaking
to Raïssa") and separately (they began a separate correspondence in April
1925, and poetry was often the subject of their exchanges).[18]

In April 1925, Cocteau wrote Raïssa a gracious, even tender letter
thanking her for her suggestion to change a word in one of his poems
(from *"le vide"* to *"la Vierge"*).[19] "You are right," Cocteau wrote, "'*le vide*'
does not work. I need to put in '*la Vierge*,' who for me is the image of the
whole sky."[20] Maritain wrote him shortly after, on September 7, 1925,
thanking him "for not seeming to find me stupid" (ne paraissez pas me
trouver stupide).[21] As with Bloy and Charles Journet, now with Cocteau
the encouragement from a leading male authority gave Maritain the confidence to start working on a new intellectual project. She mailed Cocteau
some poems she had been working on in secret for the past year, and in
September 1927 he replied, "My *très chère* Raïssa. Your letter is so good.
You are a great poet."[22] Around this period, Raïssa also befriended at
Meudon the surrealist, poet, and cubist Pierre Reverdy, who became
another major source of encouragement for her new vocation.

These friendships gave Maritain the confidence to consider publishing her poems, but she had been thinking at least on a theoretical level
about the relationship between Christianity and poetry as early as 1907,
when Léon Bloy sent her a chapter of *Celle qui pleure* in which he elaborated on the place of non-Christian artists, especially poets, in eternity.
When Bloy considered the traditional doctrinal claim that no one (presumably including artists) would make it to paradise unless they were
Christians, he exclaimed, "The very thought seems monstrous!" Bloy continued, "Poets will soar with true Christians together like a cyclone without
lull, a beatific whirlwind within the boundless goal of every aim, an assumption of cascades of love."[23] Bloy commented on art more generally
throughout his life, often adding that the only art was an art that merged
with his theological glorification of the margins. He characterized it as
"an exiled art, it is true, despised, subordinated, famished, fugitive, in rags,
an art from the catacombs."[24] Though Maritain had been thinking about
this for some time, she noted that contemporary Catholicism had frus-

tratingly little to say about art. She wrote in her journal in 1919: "The Catholics of today, when they are sound on doctrine, are as a rule narrow-minded as regards the proper domain of art. . . . They are hard on artists. It seems to me that Catholics ought to possess a genuinely informed doctrine concerning everything that is human, a doctrine that conforms with truth, taste and intelligence. No timidity. No pharisaism. No ignorance. No prudishness. No Manichaeism. But the full and luminous Catholic doctrine."[25] Maritain's first attempts to take on the intellectual task of creating an informed doctrine of art can be traced to her collaboration with Jacques on his famous book *Art et scholastique* (1920). Critics quickly acclaimed the work, plunging both Raïssa and Jacques into circles of the (not necessarily Catholic) artistic and literary elite. Many years later, just after Raïssa died, in his own journal Jacques admitted she deserved far more credit for her help on some of his earliest works. Reflecting on why he had been reluctant to add Raïssa as a coauthor, he wrote, "Fear of the established rules? Old masculine rudeness? It appears only under my name. I should have *required* that Raïssa sign it with me."[26] We know Raïssa partnered with Jacques on the ideas in the 1920 edition of *Art et scholastique,* and subsequent editions of the book increasingly bore her imprint both in content and as a recognized contributor. The 1920 edition of *Art et scholastique* has a small dedication to Raïssa on the front (although difficult to decipher because Jacques refers to her by her baptismal name, Gertrude: "Delictae Gertrudi meae"). The edition of 1927—the year Raïssa started writing poetry—includes a longer dedication to "Delictae Gertrudi Raïssae meae dimidium animae dimidium operas effecit" and includes a new chapter, "The Frontiers of Poetry." The final 1939 edition is filled with footnotes that cite Raïssa's own poems and writings on aesthetics. Finally, *Situation de la poésie* (1938) is largely a work that draws on the ideas developed in the various editions of *Art et scholastique;* it was published under both Jacques's and Raïssa's full names.[27]

But when she and Jacques first began to think about art in the late 1910s and early 1920s, they aligned themselves with other early twentieth-century theorists of aesthetics who rebelled against the modern tendency to turn all aspects of life, including art, into an opportunity to improve the world, to render it more humane, just, or loving.[28] Artists, they argued, should be fundamentally detached from human pressures and demands, and art is a rare domain of human activity where one can escape from being entrapped in "a system of nothing but the earth."[29] They positioned what they called the artist's "purity of intention" at the center of their aesthetic theory.[30] They denied that poetry had any direct moral effects, and this was in part what made the Maritains' salon attractive to the transgressive surrealists, symbolists, and decadents of Paris's avant-garde scene.[31] For the Maritains, art could be for *God* rather than for the moral improvement of the world, and beauty could continue the work of divine creation and still be at a remove from politics and morality. Raïssa reiterated this in her own essay published years later in 1937. "No doubt," she wrote, "in the case of poetry a certain knowledge of the created world is involved, but all this knowledge does not lend itself to love; it tends toward the creation of beautiful works."[32]

But as the city of lights dimmed in the 1930s, Raïssa began to express concern that art that abrogated its responsibilities to the world was not always morally or politically neutral. In one of her first essays on aesthetics that she published as the sole author, "Magie, poésie, et mystique" (1937), she began to consolidate this shift in her thinking: "We have said that poetic knowledge does not in itself lend itself to love, any more, for that matter, than scientific knowledge; but it must be added that all knowledge that is not finally turned toward loving is by that very fact a source of death. Thus the poem that does not arouse enthusiasm and a passionate desire to rejoin the essential unity gives way to another movement similar to that which drags man into the abyss [à l'abîme]."[33] As her reference here to the dramatic binary between the "essential unity" and death suggests, Maritain considered the relationship between poetry and history in dramatic and metaphysical terms.

In "Magie, poésie, et mystique" and other essays published roughly concurrently, Maritain forged the link between the artistic and moral/political realms through a retrieval of two concepts, intuition and *le réel,* borrowed from her first mentor, Henri Bergson (with whom she had renewed contact in 1935). Although she consistently wanted to relate the poet to both *le réel* and what she alternatively called "son temps" (her time), Maritain claimed that true artistic creation could not begin with didactic, political, or moralizing goals. Instead, withdrawal into silence or *recueillement* was the poet's first step in the act of creation. Through silence one could penetrate "these depths of all spirit and life," and the capacity to do so was "a natural disposition," although it "must be cultivated."[34] Habitual removal from activity, a discipline of silence akin to that required for contemplation, created the necessary condition for artistic creation.

For Maritain, the subject had an intuitive structure—something she had learned from Bergson and Thomas—that enabled him or her to make contact with the most fundamental structures of reality. But intuition required penetration beyond the surface of the everyday and into the depths of silence; then art, poetry, music came to the artist as if from without. "He who would know the depths of the spirit, or if you will, the spirituality of being, begins by entering into himself. And it is also in the inwardness of life, of thought, of conscience, that he encounters Poetry if he be destined to encounter it."[35] One of the converts that came through Meudon, Jan Kott, referred to this when he said that Raïssa had taught him how "poetry emerges from a metaphysical flash: a flash full of the beauty of metaphysics."[36] Maritain's insistence on this point endeared her to other philosophically inclined poets in their milieu. Writing to Catherine Pozzi in 1930, Maritain confessed, "I remember the fullness of our joy when we heard Bergson only say, 'Metaphysics is possible.' And I sense that for you a similar joy is present just as it was for us."[37]

For Maritain, there was consequently an experiential, even mystical dimension to poetry, and poets were like mystics insofar as both ideally began by entering a state of withdrawal that stimulated the faculty of intuition.[38] At the same time, Maritain consistently tried to avoid Christianizing poetic withdrawal; she identified the silence of the poet with Aristotelian catharsis, the diffuse spirituality of the surrealists, the yearnings of Baudelaire, Cocteau, and Reverdy, and the cries of the Psalmists and Dante. Although they both began in silence, mysticism and poetry had their fundamental differences. For the mystic, the object of his or her silence was contact with God that could fructify in love; the silence of the artist, on the other hand, touched the "reality of the world in all its mystery and complexity," and the experience fructified as art. "Thus the poet, returning from his withdrawal into himself, will write a poem; but the mystic, moved, stirred by his God, will intensify his contemplative life and love God and men more deeply."[39]

The starting point for Maritain's theory of aesthetics is inseparable from the way she understood her own artistic process during the creation of her poetry volumes *La vie donnée* (1935) and *Lettre de nuit* (1939).

Throughout the 1930s she described her abiding commitments to the practices of silence with accompanying interior pain elaborated in great detail. She claimed that these experiences constituted the fertile grounds of her poetry and needed to be expressed eventually as poems. "For some months now," she writes in July 1934, "I have had the feeling that deep below the surface, almost without my being conscious of it, I am undergoing profound, important transformations, destined one day to come into full light and be expressed."[40] She continues, claiming that the words she will express have passed through "the sufferings of a soul [l'ardeur et les souffrances d'une âme] in order to become one day, elsewhere perhaps, luminous truths capable of serving men."[41] Two months later she published *La vie donnée* and then almost immediately began the poems that appeared in *Lettre de nuit*. Maritain clarified this in a 1937 letter to her friend Albert Béguin, Emmanuel Mounier's successor at the personalist journal *Esprit*. "I know that it was not in the continual clamor of the imagination, but in the heart of silence, when that silence attained a certain degree of depth and purity, that nearly all the poems in *Lettre de nuit* and *La vie donnée* were born."[42] And Maritain added in her journal, "Poems are made in the most naked silence when it has attained a sufficient degree of depth and purity. . . . I have spent so many years mortifying the imagination to create in myself the silence propitious to being alone with God."[43]

What did this have to do with the realities of the world and its dramas? According to Maritain, the moral and political worlds remain relevant to the artist's practice of withdrawal because what he or she experiences in silence is not subjective. Something felt to be "given" from the world to the artist constitutes an intuitive knowledge of *le réel*. Artistic creations make a claim about reality, and creation has to do with knowledge of reality or is itself gleaned from the intuition. Art therefore shows what is in some sense real—poetry for Maritain has essential, ontological ties with *le réel*.

These reflections did not stray far from Maritain's 1909 commitments to Thomism. They merged neatly with the Thomistic insistence that the external world was real and not just subjective impressions of the human mind. It was Jacques who would make famous this merging of Thomistic aesthetics with avant-garde trends in art. This theory of aesthetics was not always welcomed by the Thomists who came to Meudon. In 1934,

Étienne Gilson confessed to Henri de Lubac that he saw Raïssa as "an angry angel [l'ange courroucé] driving out everyone of the Garden of Eden" with her "flaming sword of poetry."[44] He claimed Raïssa had really "goaded her husband toward a theory of aesthetics that had little to do with St. Thomas."[45] (Gilson later admitted, after Raïssa died, that he had simply "never liked her.")[46] Whether "Judaizing" (chapter 3) or "corrupting" Jacques with her aesthetics and her poems, in some circles of Catholic orthodoxy Raïssa's influence was seen as deleterious.

But Raïssa herself seems to have been less preoccupied with her status among the Catholic neo-Thomists than with discerning a role for poetry amid the increasing violence. What would be the role of poetry, she asked, "among the sorrow of men" (parmi la peine des hommes)?[47] In an essay written at the eve of the war, "Message aux poètes qui sont à la guerre" (1939), Maritain claims that poetry emerges from the "nocturnal navigations" of the artist to the realm of *le réel* and intuition. When this experience is exteriorized as a poem, it must bear the trace of its origin. The poem then is ideally a "life-bearing sign" that can conduct the one who receives it back to the artist's intuitive experience of the hidden dimension of *le réel*. Maritain insists that the penetration into *le réel* that is typically concealed in ordinary time makes a difference in a time of war. This means the artist has the capacity to describe reality in all of its menacing qualities and danger, something most will not or cannot do. For Maritain, artists who attend to the *réel* can hear a "distant murmur that imposes itself little by little and secretly."[48] For the poet on the verge of creation, "everything seems to be given to it at once, as it were, from the outside. In reality, everything was there, in the shadow, hidden in the spirit and in the blood; everything that is going to be manifested in operation." In hearing this, she claims, the artist has a mandate: "It must be described." Maritain claims that Europe poised for war needs to find a voice to pierce the "void" surrounded by "bitterness" and to describe it in all of its reality, complexity, and darkness. The voice, she claims, "will be found among you." "You," she appeals to her fellow poets, "will be the voice that carries us to safety, like the poor saint who carried Christ and the whole world on his shoulders."[49] The poet, having emerged from silence, cannot look aside from suffering and darkness but must name it. For this reason, those who withdraw from the world out of "contempt for their time" have a loneliness that is "sterile," but the "true solitary, the contemplative, the poet, are mysteriously connected to the life, work and the hope of men today."[50]

Maritain insisted that the practice of silence could enable the artist to see what was hidden in everyday life, even when that life was shot through with suffering, death, and destruction. Thinking of those who tried to evade the escalating darkness of the late interwar period, Maritain wrote in 1938, "The time of childish things is over, the time of playing games, of make-believe, of eloquence, of 'let's pretend.'" A few months later, she repudiated the duplicity around her, arguing that illusions had trumped reality. "Every word of consolation," she wrote, "seems a lie."[51] This critique of falsity and denial captured Maritain's yearning for realism among Catholics in the late 1930s, when most were still responding to the Nazi threat and the prospect of impending war with indifference and denial. Although the worst would not happen until the early 1940s, after Maritain was in the United States, concentration camps had been open since 1933, the Nuremberg Race Laws had been enacted (1935), Jewish shops and businesses had been boycotted or prohibited (1936–39), and forced labor had been decreed (1939). "These are appalling times," she wrote in 1939.[52]

In addition, for Maritain *le réel* that artists can intuit is dark but contains a hidden grace, a glimmer of light, what some have described as a vision of sacramental realism. In the late 1930s, Maritain positioned her dark realism within a narrative of Christian salvation history and clung to the belief that reality, no matter how grim it might appear, always hid a promise of redemption. According to Stephen Schloesser, this "mystical realism" or "dialectical realism" marks much of French Catholic revival writing. Schloesser describes this vision as pairing that which is present in the *réel,* in all of its darkness, with that which transcends it, what can be imagined or hoped for beyond what is explicitly there.[53] Those who are in touch with this hushed *réel* can detect not only the darkness on the horizon but also light and can imagine another vision that might be possible.

Maritain's own poems and journal entries in the late 1930s gesture toward this vision of melancholy in a world infused with a memory or a hope of goodness and transcendence, beginning with this dialectical realist vision in an untitled 1937 poem:

In the darkness of human life
A faint light glimmers
Like a star sending down its rays
From unimaginable distance.[54]

Similarly, in the poem "Méditation" (1936), Maritain again suggests the hidden presence of God amid the mysterious persistence of evil:

Darkness from below, darkness from the heights;
Beneath the Archangel's black wing
The divine plan unfolds.
Infinite paradox of the creation:
Eternity is being built with time,
And good—imperishable—with evil's assistance.
Mankind trudges along toward justice
Through the lazy curves of iniquity,
Today's error is at the service
Of truth to come;
The bit of good,
Seemingly powerless to vanquish
The misfortune of days,
Keeps on being the seed
Of Love's everlasting tree.[55]

The darkness in her poetry "beneath the Archangel's black wing" is shot through with narrow flickers of eternity. The good is present but only a "bit," and it is "seemingly powerless," merely a seed of love amid the present's misfortune.

Other poems in the later interwar period speak directly to her own experiences in contemplation, which she identifies as the ground of recognition for a mystical realism. Consider "De profundis" (From the Depths) (1936), where she describes the soul's lament for God:

God my God the distance between us is not endurable
Show me my path, straight and bare and boundlessly true
From my soul to Your spirit—without the screen

Of anything men have raised between earth and heaven.
I am poor and divested and everything wounds me
All that is spoken is too hard
And too human for my distress.
Pain has torn away my childhood from me
I am only a soul mourning her joy,
In the terrible and strict way
Where hope is just alive.
Barely enough to raise my eyes to You!
. . . .
And while You veil Yourself in all these shadows
The world You have made shines with its countless stars.
And the dizzy abyss grips my soul
And I cry unto You, my God
From the depths of the abyss.[56]

Desire and the hope for its fulfillment pierce through the soul's lament, but the hope is modest, "barely enough," just as in "Méditation" the good was ephemeral and vulnerable. Maritain echoes the poem's image of mourning over a more childlike, less realistic faith in this 1939 journal entry: "If ever I felt the 'comfort' of the spiritual life, that feeling has long ago left me. A spiritual destiny is a light bridge thrown across the abyss, or the peak of a rock rising above the ocean. . . . She has a view of the world that makes her dizzy, whether it displays itself to her in its beauty or its madness." The sense of the world's simultaneous beauty and madness also appears in a poem she wrote that same year, "All Is Light":

All has been given.
The anguish stilled.
Death fulfilled.
How my soul weighs light.
Everything is bright.
Darkness and light merge.[57]

In 1939, for the first time, Maritain deployed this dialectical realism as a way to reflect on the condition of European Jewry. Reflecting on the themes of Judaism in the paintings of her friend and fellow Russian émigré Marc Chagall, her poem "Chagall" gestures toward the vision of dark *souffrance* understood in the historical sense of persecution. But again, it is always permeated with joy, in a dialecticism she came to articulate as the essence of Jewish life. The poem is explicit in its attention to the violence and dangers posed to European Jews by this time.

> Chagall came with long strides
> Out of melancholy Russia
> With a pack on his back
> Full of violins and roses
> With lovers lighter than angels
> And frock-coated beggars
> Musicians and archangels
> And synagogues.[58]

The poem continues for several stanzas to describe Chagall's dances, horses, and circuses: "And nothing is left out, all the colors of the sun are dancing there." Then she moves to describe his famous crucifixion scene, introducing a sense of foreboding and cruelty that envelops the poem:

> Then he has a Christ
> Spread across a lost world
> In a vast ivory space
> At his feet a candlestick is lit
> With six candles by mistake
> While in the sky desolate men
> Watch what goes on.
> At the four corners of the horizon
> Fire and flame
> Poor Jews [De pauvres Juifs] everywhere go their way
> No one asks them to stay
> They have no place left on earth
> Not a stone to rest on
> Hence they must lodge at last in heaven
> The wandering Jews [Les Juifs errants]
> Whether alive or dead.[59]

Here "les Juifs errants" (the wandering Jews), the old anti-Semitic symbol that Maritain first encountered in 1905 when reading her godfather's *Le salut par les juifs,* resurfaces thirty-five years later. Like Bloy, who aimed to recast this ancient trope to express a kinship between the Jews and the "wandering" and "restless" Holy Spirit, Maritain deploys it positively. Her style is always more cautious than Bloy's shocking aestheticized invective, and in her poem the suffering Jews wander beneath Chagall's Jewish Christ, taken from his famous and controversial 1938 painting *White Crucifixion.*[60] In the painting, Chagall depicts Jesus as a crucified Jew, holding a Jewish prayer book, and watching over a village being ravaged: a burning synagogue, Jewish refugees scattering in every direction, a dead, unburied body, and a mother shielding her baby from the soldiers. The Maritains were close friends with Marc and Bella Chagall (he and Raïssa carried on a vast correspondence in Russian), and through the Maritains Chagall may have been introduced to the Christian attempts to rediscover Jesus's Jewish heritage in the 1930s.[61] But the immediate setting for his painting is the 1938 synagogue burnings in Munich and Nuremberg, and Maritain's 1939 poem taps into this controversial Christological reading of Jewish suffering to ignite sympathy from her largely Christian readership for those *pauvres Juifs* who "have no place left on earth." Three years later, Maritain expanded her reflections on Chagall in a lengthy prose piece in which she echoed her underlying theological vision of Chagall's painting and her Christological framing of sympathy: "Misery without remedy. The synagogues burn, the Jews flee to the four corners of the horizon. No one calls them. Alone the compassion of the Crucified One shines and takes to himself their sorrow."[62]

In the late 1930s, her poetry makes clear her faith in the presence of light, even if little, barely, in the midst of darkness. But privately, Maritain seems to have struggled to keep both sides of the dialectic alive—the madness threatened to eclipse the beauty. She confessed to Maurice Sachs in 1939, "I admit that I am living in anguish. There is too much cruelty on earth, too many people tortured and in the throes of death—how could the heart rest for a moment in any joy whatever? I feel as if my soul were living outside myself wherever people are suffering anguish, agony, and death. Do not think that faith and hope are the seat of spiritual comfort. Certainly, they remove despair, but anxiety for such comfort would be more than likely to make them disappear."[63] For Sachs, Maritain quickly channeled this grief into the familiar frame of redemption, marshaling the dialectic of light. Thinking about the impending war and the possibility of exile, she assured him, "Mercy will have the last word . . . and the fact remains that the great and royal road accessible to all is in the Gospel, in the life of Christ and in the life of the Saints."[64]

This optimism is less visible in her private writings and would be stretched to the point of rupture in the next two years. We also know from her journal in the late 1930s that her spiritual life was unremittingly painful, a domain where very little light shone in. In this period, Maritain began to describe her spiritual experience of silence in the most graphic, almost unendurable terms. In 1934, she described feeling "all the bitterness of death." She continued: "God asks me more than my life: to accept living death, existence in a barren desert. That is more than giving one's soul. *Amartiudo amarissima.* Tortured, sobbing, I felt at the end, as it were, a faint whisper coming from the Lord. . . . The relief, the appeasement in which this prayer ended. But this *oraison* is all my life now. And death is proposed more every instant on God's side. I can accept it—and enter into the world of Jesus—or refuse it and begin to live the life of this world."[65]

Outside the privacy of her journals, through her public writings on poetry and aesthetics, Maritain still responded to this increasingly foreboding decade—politically and spiritually—by insisting on the dim presence of goodness, no matter how faint. But from her correspondence and journals during that time, it seems as if silence offered nothing but pain and only art could revive pleasure in an ominous world. In some places, Maritain insisted that poetry, theater, music, and paintings could be interventionist and could thrust us into the realms of light, however dim and distant.

We see this, for example, in Maritain's letters of 1938, a year we know was terrible for her. In the deepest spiritual agony, just two months after Maritain learned that Jacques had been accused of being "Judaized" by his wife, and just weeks before she confessed to Charles Journet that she wanted to flee France (see chapter 3), Maritain wrote a letter to her good friend Arthur Lourié (1892–1966), the composer and fellow Russian Jewish convert to Catholicism. On March 25, 1938, after attending his symphony, Maritain wrote, "I am happy as can be, my very dear Arthur," sounding not at all like a devastated intellectual ready for exile or a spiritually ravaged disciple. The concert, as she described it, was potent enough to overpower her grief: "I received all the music on me, in me, as one receives the rays of the sun and the sounds of the sea." The music, she continued,

> was like a sunrise over the sea, with the caresses of the light and the soft, mysterious noise of the waves that come and go. Everything gradually heightened, the earth began to live, life flowed from everywhere, near and far. A host of beings peopled the resonant space in which one was trapped with no loophole for escape. Life rose up in the heart of men, coming from the depths of the ages, with their own spontaneous song, hinted at, dropped, taken up again; astonishing in its fragility and delicacy, then in its gravity and religious amplitude. A whole world had come from your heart to ours and was advancing toward us as the day proceeds from one dawn to the next.[66]

Lourié's symphony called forth a feeling that "rose up" from her "heart," something that came from the past, or down deep ("from the depths of the ages") that enabled "life" to return (from the "archives," as she put it elsewhere). She described this as revitalizing memories of pleasure and evoking a time when "the earth began to live" (again). Such redemptive moments of absorption in art stand out in her writings in the late 1930s as some of the only signs of genuine joy in this decade of increasing pain.

For Maritain, the best art, rather than seeming untouched by suffering, communicated radiance and beauty in the midst of it. As she wrote in her journal just afterwards, "Music slightly loosens the bonds of spirit and body, and the soul catches a glimpse of rapturous, eternal love."[67] Even if the art engendered feelings of mourning and suffering, it still brought great relief. Of avant-garde composer and friend Erik Satie, Maritain stated that he "sparkled," although he "seemed to carry on his shoulders a long mysterious past of suffering and disillusionment."[68] Art and silence enabled a realistic vision that included danger and loss but also hope in other possibilities. Even Maritain's own poems communicated something of this transcendence amid suffering, thereby giving pleasure and relief to some of her readers: Catherine Pozzi wrote to Maritain expressing her joy at reading Maritain's first published poem in *Vigile,* "La couronne d'épines," and stating that Maritain's line describing Christ's assimilation of sin through his death was life-giving to her, summarizing her entire philosophical outlook.[69]

SUBJECTIVITY AND THE SUFFERING OTHER

So far, we have seen that Maritain's metaphysical understanding of art keeps the artist tethered to reality, a reality that although dark and foreboding still contains a glimmer of hope. The artist communicates something of that reality with his or her art, and this voice "pierces" the void of bitterness and denial. In this final section, I turn to another way to access the relationship between Maritain's suffering-centered piety, her poetry, and the crises of the impending war. On one level, I argue that in her poetry Maritain drew on the symbols of *souffrance* that had been central to her religious *imaginaire* since her conversion in 1906. Over thirty years later, the language of suffering enabled her to see and express what was happening in the late interwar period. Yet even more than that, her years-long immersion in the practices of suffering-centered Christianity enabled her not only to understand and speak for the suffering but to experience it herself bodily and affectively and to exteriorize such experiences in her poetry. Maritain's devotions to the suffering Christ were intersubjective, moving in both directions.[70] We know from her journals that she had long been immersed in practices that trained her soul to move "outside herself" and occupy the other before her—the suffering Christ. She claimed that this process of placing her soul in the hands of Jesus, or emptying herself so that Jesus might enter, entailed a kind of "death" that she could "accept" so that she might "enter into the world of Jesus." Such transformations of the self, I suggest, enabled Maritain in the late 1930s to "accept" and incorporate into her being the sufferings of others, in the way that she describes in the 1939 letter to Maurice Sachs: it is as if "my soul were living outside myself wherever people are suffering anguish, agony, and death."

Consider another example, more explicit: On October 5, 1939, days after the Nazi invasion of Poland, Maritain reflected on an experience at Mass:

> At Mass I was gripped by a feeling I had never experienced before. It was as if the bitter taste of poverty and misery had filled my mouth and my whole being. A total and all-enveloping misery [une misère totale et enveloppante], a dense wall with no opening to let in fresh air or the faintest glimmer of consolation. Then I saw Marie (our Polish maid) pass by, going to take up her place in church; a humble, touching little figure, her clothes of some dark, indeterminate color that became even dimmer as they brushed against the benches. She too appeared to me as defenseless poverty—the image of her country, devastated Poland. Marie, a little creature alone in the world, with no relatives, with no country. No one but us—and we are probably going away! I followed the Mass with my heart shattered [le coeur brisé] with pity and bitterness, thinking of our friends over there, those in Warsaw—in Laski, no doubt tortured to death, or still alive and enduring all kinds of fearful ordeals. So these things happen! Ah, those whose names one knows always seem nearer to us! I think of my dear Sophie Landy, in religion Sister Teresa of the Carrying of the Cross. What a name! What a destiny! And Abbé Kornilovicz, and Marylski, and Mère Czapska, the blind nun, light of her community. I dwell on the bitterness of their mortal anguish [leurs angoisses mortelles].[71]

As Maritain explains it, the "taste" of misery filled her "mouth" and what happened in Warsaw left her shattered (brisé). These are themes we have seen before, of being enveloped by misery in the midst of silence before God. But here these familiar marks of her spiritual life cross the threshold into the experience of collective suffering. The moments that seemed so private in Maritain's spiritual life—an interior merging with the suffering Christ—now become inseparable from the public events of history. Her practices of self-dissolution before the abject God—an act of imaginative identification with the suffering other—shift here to an imagined self-dissolution before afflicted individuals in wartime Poland. Far from being private or apolitical, her long-standing training in suffering-centered Christianity enabled her to take others' suffering into her own being bodily, affectively, and spiritually. It must be in part true that the political and historical context shaped her spiritual life, but it is also true that her years of laborious self-transformation into the suffering Christ changed her relationship to politics and history.

Maritain's newfound poetic voice meant that this experience did not have to remain private. Her experiences at Mass bore fruit in the creation of her 1939 poem "Aux morts désespérés," a cry of anguish for the victims of Nazi raids in Poland. Her poetic voice became a final means of self-extension, or to draw from her own theory of aesthetics, an instance of exteriorization. As she wrote poetry, what she understood as an entirely transfigured self, assimilated to suffering, began to occupy a space much larger than her body and soul:

> Our sorrow is so great, the sun astounds us.
> O God, its comfort is no more remembered!
> What fabulous, ingenious yesterday
> Sent forth these rays? They are too slight
> To cover up the coffins of our dead.

In juxtaposing the shining sun to the coffins of the dead, Maritain's poem asks implicitly how the unthinkable atrocities of 1939 in eastern Europe can be thought of in everyday frameworks, alongside something as simple as the rays of the sun. She lays bare for her readers the grim fact that the rays of the sun, the most powerful force in our physical lives, are rendered suddenly inadequate by the horror that confronts us. Maritain's poem continues,

> The desperate dead, who did not want to surrender,
> Their agony still unforgotten.
> Our hearts give shelter to so many restless shades,
> With the unceasing clamor of their blood
> Poured out by slaves.
> Immeasurable darkness covers life,
> It is not grief that drives to desperation,

It is injustice
And not calamity, but cruelty
It is not dying, but the desolation
Of the dread silence of complicity.[72]

In these final lines, Maritain seems to suggest that grief, agony, and death are not the forces that drive one to despair. There is something new in the suffering she describes in 1939, which now includes cruelty, injustice, and the silence of complicity. She and Jacques had been speaking out against anti-Semitism and had warned of the seriousness of the threat throughout the 1930s. By September 1939, after the Nazi invasion of Poland and as Germany was poised to invade France, the complicity of those around her, the silence surrounding cruelty and injustice, took her *souffrance* to a new level, one that "drives one to desperation."

To turn to a final example, one of Maritain's most moving poems centered on suffering shifts from the autobiographical and metaphysical to enter into the pain of another. In 1935, her friends Pieter and Christine van der Meer de Walcheren suffered the death of their thirty-year-old son, their second son to die suddenly. (Twenty years earlier, during the First World War, their two-year-old son had died.) Pieter and Christine were Maritain's "spiritual siblings," both bohemian artists from Holland who had been baptized under the influence of Léon Bloy, and the two-year-old had been Maritain's godson, "whom I loved so much." Now, with the death of another son, Pieter and Christine's grief was so great that, as a challenge to God in face of their unbearable loss, the couple decided to "give him our cloaks too." This meant that they shaved their heads and entered the religious communities of two different monasteries, enduring a two-year separation and sacrifice of their marriage. This greatly distressed Raïssa, who thought that more suffering was a terrible idea and that the love of one another was the only good they had in the world. She helped convince both Pieter and Christine's religious superiors to order them to reunite after two years.

In 1938, Maritain wrote the poem "Pietà," for Christine, in which she connected her son's death to that of Christ, and the tears of his mother to those of Mary. In "Pietà," Maritain describes "La reine de compassion" with her dead son heavy on her "genous fragiles" (frail lap).[73] The poem was an invitation to grieve, to tap into and generate feelings of affliction in a moment of unthinkable loss.

> Come wails lamentations and tears
> Come sobs and cries rise up like the sea
> Sweep away with your waves our bitter refusal
> Flow abundantly from the source of the soul.
> Death has touched the docile Victim
> God gathers all around the night of the Cross
> And he deposited his Son into your arms . . .
> And your tears will wash his bloody face.

Maritain ends the poem on a note of chilling quiet:

> Stunned silence keeps you company
> In your exile, Queen of Compassion.[74]

Maritain identifies the suffering of her friend with the figure of Mary at the foot of the cross, capturing something of the unbearable pain and loss of a woman in mourning. By writing poetry in the midst of unspeakable horror, whether that of her friend or of her Polish maid and her country, Maritain gave words to the brutal singularity of another's pain that would have otherwise gone unarticulated, accompanied only by "stunned silence."

Placed together, "Pietá" and "Aux morts désespérés" urge readers to reconsider the boundaries we draw between personal and political writing. In *Against Forgetting: Twentieth-Century Poetry of Witness,* Carolyn Forché claims that modern readers tend to distinguish between "personal" and "political" poems, the former the domain of emotional love and familial relations of the private sphere, and the latter calling to mind public relationships and juridical politics centered on state political action and intervention. The "poetry of witness," Forché claims, often occupies a space in between these two realms. "We need a third term," Forché argues, "one that can describe the space between the state and the supposedly safe havens of the personal. Let us call this space 'the social.' . . . The social is a place of resistance and struggle, where books are published, poems read, and protest disseminated."[75] In this space grief is articulated and the losses endured from violence are recognized for how fiercely singular they are for those who experience them, however directly they map onto larger social and political forces. The suffering is intensely personal, but through poetry like Maritain's it does not have to remain private.

TO LIVE IN THE "STORM OF LIFE"

Raïssa Maritain's art is rarely "religious" or "political" in the overt sense of content. More often, she presents realistic snapshots of singular events and people: a mother holding her son's lifeless body, coffins beneath the sunshine, the sound of a bird's wing. The images often reroute readers back into the ordinary realms of life and experience. Both Jacques's and Raïssa's immersion in the world's pathos and pleasures (which were there as well)—what Raïssa once described as living in the "storms of life"— was central to the allure and persistence of their vision.[76] Even in Maritain's theoretical reflections on aesthetics, the realm of life and experience turns out to be crucial. Only through experience, the experience of silence, can one encounter the real and make contact with—receive—an art that can then make a claim about the world. Artistic creation and mystical withdrawal enable a view of reality that is otherwise hidden—a reality that many concealed in the 1930s.

We know that Maritain was a subject produced through a range of discourses and practices. Many of her religious practices were traditional disciplines of piety aimed at incorporating Christ's suffering (silent prayer guided and interpreted through medieval hagiographies and mystical writings: for example, Eucharistic devotion). These kinds of pious disciplines were central to her private writings for at least three decades. What I have tried to show in this chapter is how her experiences of self-transformation and self-dissolution, which had previously seemed interior and personal, crossed the threshold into the public events in history. Maritain's vocation as a poet enabled her to exteriorize these experiences into poems that rendered her interior life public and communicative—poetic communications that were theological, and highly Christological, reflections on the crises in history. I have described the relationship between Maritain's religious experience and the social political context as mutually conditioning and intersubjective.

I emphasize these terms to avoid the pitfall of seeing Maritain's religious experiences of self-transformation and of the suffering Christ (explored in this chapter and in chapter 2) as *merely* a representation or a reflection of larger social events and forces: the history of Christian mysticism, the decadent literary movement, her relationship with her confessors, the impending violence, the ascendancy of anti-Semitism. This kind of social analysis of religious experiences and thought, according to Michel de Certeau, "eliminates them as real factors of history. They become additions and secondary effects, precious only insofar as, through their transparency, they shed light on what instigated them."[77] It makes the specificities of religious ideology and experience "unthinkable" as Certeau puts it, because it transforms them into something else (the result of cultural history, gender relations, war). These have all been crucial analytic tools to tell Maritain's story, but they do not capture everything. The religious experiences themselves in all their specificity did act in history, were interventionist in a real sense. Maritain's inner life, trained and transformed under Christian disciplines of piety, transformed how she experienced the war and enabled her to bring something new into existing conversations with her newfound poetic voice. This poetic voice "put into circulation" (to stick with Certeau's language) a supernatural language that had once belonged only to the "sacred enclave" of her inner experiences. Such language could now describe war in Poland, give voice to grief over the unthinkable loss of a child, evoke compassion for the "wandering Jews" in 1939—it appeared as new words to be read, contemplated, debated by others.[78]

Finally, since Maritain's intellectual work in this period is primarily poetic in genre, and since her prose frequently takes up the themes of aesthetics and mysticism, she is invariably viewed by scholars as "the silent" or apolitical partner in her marriage who was "astonishingly sheltered from what was happening socially and politically in Europe."[79] According to Maritain, art and mystical practice, which are sometimes accused of enabling people to take an evasive detour around sorrow and horror, in fact do just the opposite. On examination, it becomes clear that her dark theological-poetic texts in the interwar years do not retreat from the political but access it from another angle. Aesthetic explorations of sufferers' pain and loss become political and religious reflections in Maritain's hands. Bringing to light Maritain's poetry and essays in the interwar period connecting the realms of faith, the arts, and history can do more than remedy the lack of scholarship on her work or enable a more capacious understanding of suffering in her writings. It can also help us rethink assumptions that view the realms of the aesthetic and imaginative as separate from the political.

CHAPTER 5

Holy Suffering, Memory,
and the Irredeemable Present

Raïssa Maritain in Exile (1940–1944)

From New York on July 6, 1940, just weeks after Germany started its occupation of France, Raïssa Maritain composed the preface to her famous two-volume memoir, *Les grandes amitiés*. She was explicit that the unbearable nature of the present had driven her into a recollection of her own past. "Life for me draws to a close," she wrote, "ended by the catastrophe that has plunged France into mourning [le deuil] and, with France, the world." She continued: "For the afflicted are not—cannot be consoled, the persecuted are not succored, God's truth is not spoken. . . . In the present, I do not feel that I am present. I turn my thoughts toward the past and toward the future; toward the future hidden in God; toward that past which God made for us and filled with so many sorrows and graces; toward our past life and toward our friends."[1] The catastrophe in the passage cited above refers to the war; Germany had invaded France two months earlier on May 10, 1940, and by June 14 had stormed Paris. On June 22, France had surrendered and signed an armistice with the Nazis, establishing the Vichy collaborationist government, which would last four years. When Maritain embarked on her largest writing project, she had been in exile for just six months.

In December 1939, the Maritains finally left France when Jacques's lecture tour led them to safety in North America. From their first stop, Toronto, the "flock of three" traveled to thirty cities in the first months of their arrival in North America before they finally settled in New York City in the summer of 1940. In this period, they learned that when the Gestapo had arrived in Paris, they had gone to the Institut catholique, looking for Jacques. Their Meudon home had been requisitioned, and Jacques's books had been confiscated from bookstores.[2] Such events made clear there was no longer any chance the Maritains could return to Meudon. Their exile would be long, and they never resided again in France as a couple.

Raïssa Maritain's memoirs were published in two volumes during the war, in 1941 and in 1944.[3] Throughout this period of intense writing, she primarily secluded herself in their New York apartment, going through letters and diaries and assembling the pieces of her past. Her own journals from this period are thin, but other New York intellectuals who knew her attest that she rarely left her apartment in these years.[4] With the exception of a small handful of chilling lamentation poems, nearly all of Maritain's wartime and early postwar writings have to do with her past. In addition to her memoirs, from her first *Commonweal* essay on Henri Bergson in 1941 to her edited English translation of Bloy's writings in 1947, she presented portraits of her early friends and mentors to French and American readers, just as the culture that had sustained them was disintegrating.[5]

Maritain was one among many European intellectuals to respond to the crises of 1940–44 by thinking intensely about memory and memorialization. In the spring of 1940, just as she embarked on *Les grandes amitiés*, Walter Benjamin wrote his posthumously famous "Theses on a Philosophy of History." "To articulate the past," Benjamin wrote, "does not mean to recognize it 'the way it really was.' It means to seize hold of a memory as it flashes up in a moment of danger."[6] For Benjamin, the past, including one's own, must be continually seized and salvaged, lest it be assimilated into the narratives of those in power. "In every era," Benjamin explained, "the attempt must be made anew to wrest tradition away from a conformism that is about to overpower it." Those who guard memories and history "can fan the spark of hope" in their firm conviction that "*even the dead* will not be safe from the enemy if he wins."[7] Memories do not merely report on the past but carefully shape it in response to the needs and dilemmas of the present.

Both Jews under Nazi law, Benjamin and Maritain lived in a shared moment of danger (although Maritain was safe in New York with other "aristocratic intellectuals," while Benjamin's despair drove him to suicide in September of 1940).[8] *Les grandes amitiés* can be read as an attempt to ward off the dangers that Benjamin articulated. All three of Maritain's beloved and, for her, overlapping traditions were gravely threatened at the time she began writing. While Judaism faced annihilation, both Catholicism and secular French institutions veered toward fascism, racism, and collaboration with the Nazis. Throughout *Les grandes amitiés* Maritain presented her Jewish and Catholic memories as vulnerable but fundamentally unassimilable into the narratives employed by what she called the "unchained storm of brutal forces" (l'ouragan déchaîné des forces brutales) bombarding Europe in 1940–44.[9] If Nazi propaganda claimed Jewish unassimilability and pollution, in *Les grandes amitiés*' carefully crafted depiction of her Russian Jewish childhood Maritain's nostalgic, even romantic memories enabled her to render Judaism as something valuable and beautiful. The warm glow she casts over this period in her life heightens the scandal of contemporary anti-Semitic violence. Although her memoirs were not written in a realistic or historicist manner (which would seem to align itself more easily with a voice of political protest), her wistful, melancholic prose struck a political note with her community of readers, as the letters she received from Catholics eager to communicate with Maritain about anti-Semitism illustrate.[10]

If humanizing Judaism to counter Nazi propaganda was one of Maritain's goals in *Les grandes amitiés,* presenting the image of the "suffering Jew" was equally important. For Maritain, to enter into the suffering-centered *imaginaire* of the French Catholicism of her memory was not a betrayal of the community of persecuted Jews but a way to recognize and garner compassion for their suffering. The Jewish community could be— even in the midst of the Shoah—assimilable in a fundamental way to Christianity. In *Les grandes amitiés* Maritain thus maintains her long-standing deep ambivalence about Jews and Judaism, praying for conversions while eliciting from readers horror toward anti-Semitic persecution and empathy with Jews' vulnerability. Her work during the war raises new questions: Does the evocation of an essentialist trope, like that of the suffering Jew, make a difference when it corresponds to a historical reality? What are the rhetorical effects of this symbol in this new setting of brutality? Does a woman's articulation of this scenario, in brutal, vivid detail, deepen the association between women and suffering and death?

Yet for all its continuity with the suffering-centered piety that had long been familiar to her, holy *souffrance* in Maritain's memories operated in a different register than in her earlier works. In her 1940–44 writings, redemptive, holy agony is associated almost exclusively with the past. As she puts it, the past was "a period in which everything—even anguish and suffering—now seems to me like a paradise lost."[11] In contrast to her previous willingness to think about present suffering as redemptive (although she always understood this in complex, changing ways), she explicitly refuses to link these notions to the present wartime violence and the horror of the Holocaust. The promises of the blessedness of those who have suffered—especially Jews—appear again and again in her memories, but in the rare moments that Maritain's later writings turn to the present she rejects this. Maritain depicts the war as a ghastly aberration to which "it is not possible to reconcile oneself in any shape or manner."[12] In short, earlier theologies of suffering come to a grinding halt when she writes explicitly about the terrors of 1940–44.

Maritain narrates the disintegrating present of 1940–44 primarily in her wartime and immediate postwar poems. Her chilling lamentation poems provide a stark glimpse into her spiritual life during the Shoah. She traverses a darker interior field in her poetic voice and puts her wartime poems to a completely different use than the prose of her memoirs. *Les grandes amitiés* speaks of the beauty of the pious Jewish home and the emotive hold that the Catholic idiom of redemptive suffering still has on her. In contrast, her wartime poems take a gritty, unwavering look at the present in a testimony of awestruck apprehension. Poetry is a genre that can in many instances be removed from the real, but through her poetry Maritain describes the grim realities of war in a way her prose never does directly: "Let me speak from the madness / that seizes my soul / Our days are evil, infested with hell" and "Four million Jews—and more—have suffered death / Without consolation. / Those who are left are promised to the slaughter."[13] Maritain's poetry during the war communicates her overpowering grief as she watched as the evanescent efforts to create a bond between Jews and Catholics at Meudon disintegrate in the face of unfolding violence. Her renunciation of holy *souffrance* as a paradigm for making meaning might suggest an evolutionary progress in which her earlier fascination with suffering gradually yielded to a modern capacity to be repelled by it.[14] Yet this is not the case; rather than abandoning themes of redemptive suffering, Maritain transferred them to a project of memory.

"THE ROOTS OF LIFE ARE CUT OFF": THE CONTEXT OF *LES GRANDES AMITIÉS*

Through news broadcasts and the stream of stories from émigré friends fleeing Europe for New York, Raïssa and Jacques learned quickly of the grim details of the new anti-Semitic decrees imposed by the Vichy government.[15] Several people close to the Maritains had been handed over to the Gestapo. Among them were Raïssa's goddaughter, Babette Jacob, Babette's eighty-year-old mother, and her younger brother. Babette and her mother later died in the gas chambers in Buchenwald, and her brother was shot. The elder brother of their close friends Jean and Suzanne Marx was also deported and killed.

For Raïssa, exile from France and the steady onslaught of atrocious news plunged her into a despair like no other. At first it was caused in large part by the exile; she did not have the work, friendships, and intellectual projects in the United States that Jacques had. She spoke almost no English. She wrote to her friend Charles Journet days after her arrival:

> The hardest to endure, even better that I don't think about it, is the distance. All our soul is there, close to everything we love. It seems that even the plenitude of life is there, there where they are suffering, but here we're breathing depleted air, insufficient for us to really live. I see myself as if in a dream; I cannot even think about the house I left, our little empty chapel gives me a vertigo of pain [me donne un

vertige de douleur]. But in this way at least I share in the suffering [je partage la souffrance] of all who had to abandon their homes.[16]

Maritain's June 1, 1941, journal entry echoes this despair: "I wept so much during Mass and after, thinking of my little chapel at Meudon. There, I had a place on earth. Now I feel as if I were nowhere."[17] She compares herself to Isaac on Mt. Moriah (Gen. 22) and adds on the next day: "I suffer indeed like someone for whom it is impossible to take any initiative whatsoever. I am bound hand and foot like a victim prepared for sacrifice. . . . I dare not move, I dare not will. . . . Yesterday I made the wish to die."[18] While working on the second volume of her memoirs, in February 1944, she wrote in her journal, "Terrible anguish on awakening. The tragic reality of Europe overwhelmed me, finding my heart defenseless, not yet armed for the daily struggle which begins when I get up."[19]

Even in the earliest days of their exile, Jacques remarked that the war had plunged Raïssa into a despair more profound than he had ever seen. He too wrote to Journet, "Since the beginning of the war, she suffers with great courage but with quiet anguish from every moment. Never have I seen her suffering like this as she is in exile; one would say all the roots of her life are cut off."[20] Yet Raïssa was not alone in this condition. In the relative privacy of his journals, Jacques echoed the grief that he normally allocated to his wife, always in connection with the war in Europe. In 1940 he wrote: "The German noose is tightening around Paris. This is mourning in its absolute form." He continued, "We can't even imagine the extent of our misfortune. We have been beaten to the ground." Later he added, "Horrible days of France's crucifixion. We weep, we wrack our brains, we understand nothing."[21] And on one day in 1940 he simply wrote, "Ghastly days."[22] Jacques, too, suffered to an unprecedented degree.

The Maritains describe their experiences of the war with the language of passive shock (*étonné* [stunned] was a word Raïssa returned to again and again), but both Jacques and Raïssa came to work actively in the resistance efforts of the exile community in New York. In the spring of 1942, along with forty other European Catholic exiles, Jacques and Raïssa signed and published the manifesto *Devant la crise mondiale: Manifeste de catholiques européens séjournant en Amérique,* denouncing totalitarianism, fascism, and anti-Semitism as incompatible with the Gospel.[23] Jacques's efforts are well documented. Early on he began arranging for the safe exile of Jewish friends by securing their entry permits to the United States. Later he worked in the creation of the École libre des hautes études, which gathered French and Belgian scholars under the roof of New York's New School for Social Research as a free French university outside Vichy censorship.[24] There Jacques lectured and served as president from 1942 to 1944.[25] In November 1940 he finished his book *À travers le désastre,* which became known as the first French Resistance book, both identifying causes of the rise of fascism in Europe and identifying alternatives. This book was reprinted clandestinely in France and, in 1942, with the help of Czeslaw Milosz, in Poland.[26] In March of 1941, Jacques began urging French resistance via the airwaves of Voice of America, and he was connected with the French Christian underground Resistance journal *Témoignage chrétien.*

Raïssa focused on her memoirs and lamentation poems, which, for reasons I describe below, also played a significant political role in the exile community. Jacques read the longest of her lamentation poems, "Deus excelsus terribilis" (1943), a despairing cry of grief over the annihilation of European Jewry, over the radio airwaves to the French Resistance community. *Les grandes amitiés* is by far Maritain's most famous work and can be considered among the classics of the twentieth-century French Catholic renaissance.[27] As letters poured in, it became clear that her memoirs had played an important role in wartime Catholic discussions of anti-Semitism.

The first volume appeared in French in 1941 with the Éditions de la Maison Française publishing house.[28] Julie Kernan helped Maritain translate the volume into English, and it appeared in 1942 as *We Have Been Friends Together.* The enthusiastic reception Maritain received from readers in both France and the United States encouraged her to persist. The second volume of *Les grandes amitiés* appeared in English and in French in 1944, under the new title *Les aventures de la grâce (Adventures in Grace).* New editions were issued throughout the 1950s, with both volumes under the shared *Les grandes amitiés* title, then posthumously in the 1960s, and again in 1974.[29] Throughout the 1940s and 1950s, chapters of *Les grandes amitiés* were published as excerpts in various theological and literary journals.

We can establish with some certainty precisely what Maritain knew about the mass destruction of European Jews during the time of her writing. By the time Maritain finished the first volume of her memoirs and began her second, she and Jacques knew about the horrors of the death camps. The Maritains knew many of the ghastly details at least by 1942. On July 2, the *New York Times* reported that the Nazis had killed over one million Jews.[30] That same year Jacques wrote the preface to the book *Racisme, antisémitisme et antichristianisme*, a collection of documents published in 1943 gathered by Fr. Johannes Oesterreicher (1904–93). Oesterreicher's documents laid bare the grim facts of the gas chambers and crematory furnaces.[31] The context comprised not only the horrors in Europe but also the frustration at how slow many Americans and exiles were to publicly acknowledge the unfolding events.[32] Compounding this was American government inaction. When the U.S. Congress finally convened hearings concerning the State Department's inaction regarding European Jews, many European exiles were stunned that even these hearings did not occur until late November 1943. President Roosevelt eventually created the War Refugee Board. But this came only in response to political pressure and not until January 24, 1944, a full year and a half after the *New York Times* reports. It would be March 24, 1944, before he issued a statement condemning German and Japanese ongoing "crimes against humanity."[33]

Four months after Roosevelt's statement of condemnation, Maritain finished the second volume of her memoir, *Les aventures de la grâce*. Just after, she wrote to a friend:

> You cannot imagine, and I do not even want to say, how deeply the events of the last six years have filled my soul with dust and ashes; events to which it is not possible to reconcile oneself in any shape or manner except by naked, arid faith in the divine Wisdom and Mercy, which not only surpass our feelings, which I thought I knew—but, as I know now, surpass them in going beyond any standard of measurement, even thought of as supernatural. Human madness and human cruelty have been given permission to go to all lengths, unchecked, and, speaking of the six million massacred of whom so little is said, we counted very close friends among them.[34]

Although Maritain insists here that it is not possible to reconcile oneself to the events of the Holocaust, her writings in the midst of these crises helped carry her through it. Maritain's exile, solitude, and sense of utter despair at the European violence and American silence furnished the material of her writing. However, her memoirs also enabled her to overcome, if only partially, her isolation. Maritain's memory and imagination brought her back into her community of the *renouveau catholique;* both volumes describe the people and ideas and her affective encounter with both that energized French Catholicism from roughly 1905 to 1935. Her practice of memorialization functioned to eulogize and revitalize her now-dead friends and the culture that had sustained them. The friendships were now in the past, but through her work she excavated them and brought them back to life. She seems to have taken the advice of her friend, the ever-encouraging Charles Journet, who suggested seeing her memoirs as letters to her now-dead friends, to new friends, and to those in the future.[35] Further, after the publication of *Les grandes amitiés,* she created a new community of readers in the present through the letters and reviews she received from all over the world.

Wartime and postwar audiences in France and the United States were ready for Maritain's memoirs for at least two reasons. First, as the wife of a leading Catholic intellectual with a reputation on both sides of the Atlantic, Maritain gave readers an intimate portrait of seemingly dazzling prewar intellectual and spiritual lives. Furthermore, the Catholic publishing house Sheed and Ward had opened in 1926 and had recently published for the first time English translations of many of the friends Maritain portrays, including Léon Bloy, Paul Claudel, François Mauriac, and G. K. Chesterton. American Catholic readers were enthusiastic to learn more.[36] The memoirs allowed Maritain to contribute to the American reception of French Catholic intellectual life by emphasizing what she considered to represent the best of the tradition. She had longed to do this since 1919, when she wrote in her journal: "Know your religion, Catholics, know your greatness!"[37] Finally, as a Jewish and Catholic writer, Maritain gave both French and American Catholics a way to think about Judaism within the framework of a French Catholic theological imagination, a continuation of her work at Meudon, crafting a unity of Catholicism with Judaism as in her 1939 "Chagall" poem and *Histoire d'Abraham.*

Much more than a narrative of her past, each chapter of *Les grandes amitiés* relates in complex ways to temporality; moving forward through time, her chapters also lead inward, tracking the development of Maritain's own spiritual and intellectual life. People and their ideas appear as memories that "flash up," and the pace of the first volume of *Les grandes amitiés* is one of gradual acceleration. The first volume begins with a slow portrait of her innocent Russian Jewish childhood and culminates with the intensity of her ravishing encounters with Léon Bloy's life and thought. The second volume does not move chronologically far beyond the first (both end in the years surrounding World War I), but each chapter provides Maritain with another opportunity to mine the religious and intellectual resources she found among her close circle of friends and mentors, including those thinkers she knew (and loved, she would add) only by their books, especially Thomas Aquinas. In the final pages of the first volume, Maritain explains the purpose of her book:

> The period covered by this narrative was, it seems to me, above all an epoch of great spiritual renewal at the brink of the decline of a world. That is why the mere thought of these things fills my heart with such inexpressible sweetness and melancholy, and, despite everything, with so much hope. Those who did not know these times cannot imagine what they were. But their abundant seed will later bear fruit in a form which we ourselves cannot imagine. . . . All these men [depicted in her memoirs] will have been in France the first workmen in the reconstruction which will perhaps be known to a world of the future.[38]

Maritain here blurs the past, present, and future. Like Jay Winter's romantics who "walk backwards into the future," she retrieves from the past to endure the present and to generate new possibilities on the other side of wartime chaos.[39]

NOSTALGIA, JUDAISM, AND SUFFERING IN *LES GRANDES AMITIÉS*

To begin with the issue of Judaism in Maritain's memoirs, it is helpful to recall how three decades earlier, in a 1909 essay, Maritain had claimed that she grew up learning very little about Judaism. As we have seen, she had gradually come to know it through the Christian and decadent *imaginaire* of Bloy, the Christian socialism of Péguy, and the experimental, largely Christian efforts to understand Judaism at Meudon, in the context of conversions. Maritain's astonishment and sense of discovery in a 1939 journal entry suggest that her previous invocations of Judaism had been superficial:

> Finished Shalom Asch's beautiful, astounding book: *Le Juif aux Psaumes,* on the morals and spirituality of Hassidism, in Poland in the middle of the nineteenth century.
> My maternal grandfather was a Hassid too.
> And my father's father was a great ascetic.
> I have all of that behind me [Il y a tout cela derrière moi].[40]

We see glimpses here that Maritain's most developed thinking on her own Jewish past was yet to come.

In *Les grandes amitiés,* written the following year in exile, long-buried memories of the piety of her Jewish household in Russia, where she lived until the age of nine, are suddenly awakened for the first time, at least in print. The first chapter of *Les grandes amitiés* begins with Maritain's childhood in Russia and includes a vivid depiction of her grandfather's Hasidism and the celebration of Jewish holidays in their home. Maritain's childhood memories come in richly detailed flashes, shrouded in an aura of nostalgia:

> After so many years I can still smell the exquisite odor of the Crimean apples, and taste the perfection of the Paschal wine, and indeed bring back all my childhood joys. On Friday all work stopped at sunset. My mother observed the principal Jewish rites; my father needed a little urging to do so. Friday evening when the first star appeared, mother placed a lace kerchief over her hair, lighted the candles, said the Sabbath prayers, and no other fire might be lit until the first star appeared on Saturday evening. On the Sabbath day no servile work was permitted; visits were received and made; we went to the synagogue. And when the Torah, covered with velvet, embroidered and stiff with gold and silver, was carried aloft in procession, I was allowed to touch it with the tips of my fingers, and I would kiss my

fingers afterwards. For the Feast of the Tabernacles all the floors were strewn with leaves and with field flowers; the house smelled of grass, like a sunny meadow. Then a tent was erected in the courtyard, wherein to eat our meals, and it was decorated with branches, grasses, and flowers.[41]

Maritain never presented specifics of Jewish doctrine. In another context, these offerings of everyday personal images of childhood awe and family life might have been banal. But given her context, they played a powerful role in humanizing Jewish culture and making it seem both beautiful and strangely recognizable to her largely Roman Catholic readership. Maritain's descriptions depict Jewish family life and Jewish observance in warm, highly sensual terms. Maritain's memories of Passover are perhaps the most vividly rendered:

But the most impressive feast was that of the Passover. The liturgical supper was eaten with the first vespers; the table, gleaming with its shining cloth and silver candlesticks, was laid with greatest care; the family's most beautiful possessions were used. My paternal grandfather presided over the meal, seated upon the highest chair, raised up even higher by cushions. Night was falling, and the bitter herbs were eaten; then prayer began. Filled with the mystery of this Passover, I was charged with asking, in Hebrew, questions to which my grandfather replied by the recitation of the Biblical narrative and the explanation of the rites of the Pascal night. It was a long discourse, also in Hebrew, but the meaning had been explained to us in advance, at the same time that I was taught my part in the dramatic dialogue. . . . I obscurely felt the immensity of those sorrowful mysteries without realizing, naturally, their significance and their content. Then came the climax of the sacred night: the passage of the Angel. All the cups were filled with red wine, strong and sweet, the almost liturgical savor of which I have never rediscovered in any wine, even in the wines of France. The Angel of the Lord was to drink from the largest cup, filled with this noble wine—the Angel of the Lord who on that night visited the homes of the Jews. All the lights were extinguished, and in a silence heavy with adoration and fear, the Angel was given time for his passage. Then the candles were all lighted again, the supper was quickly finished, and everyone went to rest, conscious of having taken part in a great action.[42]

Catholic readers could relate to Maritain's representations of the powerful ways the tastes, smells, and touches of a highly liturgical religious world imprint themselves on a child's imagination.

These efforts at contested memory extend to Maritain's recollections of her own family patriarchs in Russia. The varied styles of the religious practices of her grandfathers, for example, translate for Maritain into types that could easily be comprehensible to and even admired by Roman Catholics. She describes her maternal grandfather as a deeply pious Jewish peasant whom villagers called "Solomon the Wise" and who, despite his modest means, practiced hospitality to traveling strangers "as joyfully as if God Himself had come to visit them."[43] When she describes her paternal grandfather—a much more strictly observant Jew—she presents him as a great ascetic whose severity echoes Catholic stories of the saints: "He astonished us all by his mortifications; he ate only dry bread rubbed with a little onion and he drank only water. He slept in the courtyard, and indeed on the ground, until winter came; then, in the house he was willing to occupy the vestibule, where he slept upon a wooden chest. I do not remember that he ever spoke to me, except to read me marvelous stories from the Bible, like that of Joseph sold by his brethren, and to teach me to read Hebrew."[44]

These humanizing, even Christianizing, efforts were powerful stories for readers during the war. Her Catholic audience, Maritain surely hoped, could relate easily to these stories of ascetic sainthood and a rich liturgical sensorium. Her memoirs consisted of memories "seized," in Benjamin's sense, from the dominant narrative of anti-Jewish propaganda. Through these memories, Maritain critiqued prevalent counternarratives in 1940–44 about Jewish greed, polluted blood, and the Jewish pestilence. These stories revitalized her Meudon efforts at Catholic philo-Semitism and its spiritual solidarity with Judaism, and like Péguy's portrait of Bernard Lazare, reframed Judaism in the context of the personal. Maritain's childhood memories of Jewish piety gradually give way to the story of her conversion to Catholicism, but Judaism reappears continually in her memoirs as something from which she cannot ever fully veer away. By 1940, Maritain had moved beyond her 1909 evocation of spiritual Jew and carnal Jew, and even the transgressive decadent image of abjection and Judaism did not yet appear. Here was simply a depiction of Jewish Christian unity based on everyday piety in the context of the family, calling to mind a common humanity among Jews that her Christian audience could apprehend.

When this first volume reached readers in the United States and France, the earliest reviews picked up on Maritain's gesture toward a vision of cosmopolitan Catholicism that recognized, even admired, the familiar liturgical rhythms of the household piety of a Jewish family. Some even saw this as explicitly interventionist in context of the Shoah. The review article by Rev. James Gilles, C.S.P, that appeared in the *Catholic News* in 1943 makes a direct connection between these passages and the Holocaust. He opens with a note of bewilderment as to what the proper Catholic response should be in light of the "rumors" (his term) of the Jewish pogroms. "Ordinary argument is no avail," the priest wrote, adding, "appeals to authority, even the authority of the Pope who has said, 'spiritually we are all Semites,' and reminders that Our Saviour and His mother and all the apostles were Jews [don't] seem to produce the desired effect." He continued:

> Perhaps information may do what argument cannot. And the kind of information we need is that which shows the Jewish people at its best. Not argument; not expostulation but information. With that purpose in view I comment on the following passage in Raïssa Maritain's *We Have Been Friends Together*. It is in my judgment an exquisitely beautiful picture of religion behind the walls in a Jewish home. It reads like the story of the Last Supper in the Gospel. In fact the rite was the same. No good Catholic could possibly take part in hating or stimulating the hatred against a people who still observe the ritual performed by Our Lord and the Apostles. There can be no argument about that.[45]

Maritain's efforts had a way of humanizing Jews and Judaism, and the connection to what was in their midst in 1940–44 was not lost on readers.

Other Catholic writers had a similar response. In a 1944 review, Graham Greene commented on the implicit signaling of Jewish and Catholic unity in Maritain's depictions of Jewish liturgy: "In her narrative, we can feel all the time the texture of events and observe how Marioupol and Montmartre are cut from the same cloth; we remember a papal reminder that Christians are 'spiritual Semites.' The smell of the Crimean apples and the taste of the pascal wine merge into Montmartre incense."[46] Taken together, these wartime and early postwar reviews and letters express a shared sense that *Les grandes amitiés* provided ways to think about Judaism and Jewish people that had been unavailable in Catholic theology in the early 1940s. If anti-Semites would claim Jews as unambiguously other and defiled, Maritain showed Jews as similar to Catholics and just as human.

If humanizing Judaism as a response to Nazi propaganda was one of Maritain's goals in the first chapters of *Les grandes amitiés,* the image of the "suffering Jew" resurfaced in the latter half and is the culmination of the second volume. We know this idiom had long been familiar to her since the days of Péguy and Bloy, and in 1939 the "wandering Jew" had made a brief appearance in her poem on Chagall, recast to evoke sympathy and compassion from the reader. But Maritain's evocation of this familiar trope came to occupy the center of both her 1940 and her 1944 memoirs.

To do this discursive work, in both volumes Maritain's memories turn inexorably to Léon Bloy. In the first volume of *Les grandes amitiés* she draws freely, if chaotically, on Bloy's *Le salut par les juifs,* setting passages alongside selections from his later writings that are more explicit in their condemnations of anti-Semitism. Maritain piles these texts on top of one another to create an almost manic, stream-of-consciousness pastiche of her memories of Bloy's theology of Judaism. Maritain uses her memories of Bloy to connect the Holy Spirit, the suffering Jesus, and Jews in an "unspeakable community of suffering."[47] Drawing from Bloy's most intense imagery highlighting Israel's "groans," "moans," and "cries," she names Israel as the "outcast of outcasts." Recalling in 1940 a passage of Bloy that she loved in 1906, she revitalizes it for her contemporary readers: "[Jews] bled with Christ," she remembers Bloy's writing, quoting him in her own text, "they were stabbed with His wounds, they were parched with His thirst."[48] All of these memories of what her godfather taught her detail Jewish abjection and sorrow and frame it Christologically. Maritain offers very little of her own analysis in these sections on Jewish suffering save sparse lines like this one, in which she merely elaborates on the theme she has gleaned from her mentor: "Israel, in its misery, in its distress, in its tears the figure of the Holy Spirit."[49] Bearing the "misery of all the centuries," she writes, Israel "suffers infinitely."

In the 1940 volume, when Maritain's memories turn to Judaism, they dwell either on her own childhood or on Christological readings of Jewish suffering put forward by her early mentors. Her present circumstances are never directly mentioned in the text. There is an exception to this studied compartmentalization in the 1944 volume. Here she aims to make the image of the suffering Jew not merely an aesthetic trope to communicate a transgressive, abject God but a way to render visible what has been happening to Europe's Jews. In her final chapter, a lengthy meditation on the last years of Bloy's life, she claims that his crowning achievement was his writing filled with "pathos and sorrowful poetry," "springing from an emotion that lives in the very depths of Bloy's heart"—a cry "of all of those who have been abandoned."[50] Bloy's writings aimed to garner compassion for "the pitiable ones without number—women, old men, little children; the living and the dead." But above all, Maritain focuses on Bloy's writings on suffering Jews. She speaks of Bloy's admiration for Morris Rosenfeld, a nineteenth-century Russian-Pole whose poetry depicts the agonies of his people. Maritain cites Bloy's reading of one of Rosenfeld's poems on the issue of Jewish sorrow and wounds: "A Jewish tear / A tear of gall, of brain, and of blood / It tasted of persecution, misfortune, pogroms . . . / We had a home but they destroyed it; / They burned what was most sacred to us; / Of the most cherished and best they have made a pile of bones / Others have been led away with their hands tied / . . . We are Jews, disinherited Jews, / Without friends and without joy, without hope of happiness . . ."[51] For Maritain, the capacity of Rosenfeld's poem to resonate across time, first for Bloy in 1917 and then again in 1944, "proves that suffering for the Jews is a perpetual today [que la souffrance est pour les Juifs un perpétuel aujourd'hui]."[52]

According to Maritain's reading, Bloy saw Rosenfeld as nearer to God than most Christians, even though Rosenfeld "never converted" (a slight variation on his earlier claim that good Jews were abject, déjà Christian, and must convert?). Maritain continues to draw on Bloy's articulation of Jewish abjection: "The Jews," she remembers her godfather writing, "are the oldest of all, and when everything is in its right place, their proudest masters will be honored to lick their wandering feet [pieds de vagabonds]."[53] Here, as in her 1939 Chagall poem, Maritain draws on the valorized image of the wandering, vagabond Jew as she first apprehended it in 1905. So that the contemporary significance of Rosenfeld and Bloy in 1944 will not be lost on readers, Maritain adds a footnote, the only direct allusion to the Holocaust in the memoir, citing a *New York Post* article dated August 3, 1944: "Of the 9,300,000 Jews who lived in the various countries of Europe before this war, less than 5,000,000 remain. The Nazis have killed all the rest."[54] Elsewhere, her evocations of Bloy relate to present circumstances more indirectly: "The endless nightmare of this diabolical war weighs on me terribly. Since its beginnings I have been gripped by anguish," she remembers Bloy writing in his final days in 1917, referring to World War I.

On one level, by illustrating the centrality of Judaized suffering to the French Catholic *imaginaire* (the book is about the *renouveau catholique* after all), Maritain's memoirs spoke to the appeals increasingly heard among Jewish intellectuals to stand in solidarity with their fellow Jews amid the unthinkable suffering and persecution. In the late 1930s and during the war, earlier interwar experiments with conversion and assimilation were being seen in a new light as at best naive and at worst an utter betrayal of those who suffered. Henri Bergson, for example, wrote in 1937, "My thoughts have led me closer to Catholicism. I see in it the completion of Judaism. I would have converted had I not seen how the terrible wave of anti-Semitism had been getting ready to roll over the earth. I wanted to remain among those who will be persecuted tomorrow."[55] The notion of remaining a Jew to stay with those who suffer reiterates a long-standing concern that even the earliest converts to late modern Parisian Catholicism expressed: that conversion meant, above all, abandonment of the dead, of those who had suffered. In her memoirs, Maritain evokes this anxiety directly, recalling her parents' own initial misgivings about their daughter's conversion. Having lived through the Russian pogroms, they initially read their daughter's baptism as only "a horrible treachery regarding her great unfortunate family," something they could "not condone, or even explain."[56]

Within Maritain's elaboration of the theme of the "suffering Jew," however, was a claim that to enter into the Catholic imagination was not to deny Jewish persecution and agony but to actually encounter it, articulate it, break it down to its smallest parts, give it recognition, and generate compassion. As Maritain described her own past, the story was one in which conversion to Catholicism meant crossing a threshold into a symbolic world in which Jewish suffering predominated. The revivalist church therefore accommodated and Christianized what was seen between 1940 and 1944 as a crucial—the crucial—dimension of Jewish particularity. The particularity of Judaism can be seen within this framework as a marker, not of Jewish recalcitrance and separatism, but of a capacity for union with Catholicism through this essential feature of their identity—their suffering. Throughout both volumes of *Les grandes amitiés,* Judaism consistently yields to late modern French Catholicism, though a Catholicism that has become "Judaized," since, she writes, "the God we adore is a Jew. . . . It is the basis, the very basis of Christianity."[57] This suffering is seen through the lens of Christian salvation history, as when Maritain draws on memories of La Salette to frame her reflections on Judaism. She learned from the Virgin that "our God is a crucified God: the Beatitude of which He cannot be deprived did not prevent Him from fearing or mourning [ni de craindre ni de gémir], or from sweating blood in the unimaginable Agony [l'Agonie indicible], or from passing through the throes of death on the cross or from feeling abandoned."[58] In her narrative, Jewish suffering becomes narratively absorbed into the theological images of salvation and God's presence in the cross. That narrative enabled Maritain to maintain the deep ambivalence that had long marked her thinking on Jews, even during the Shoah: deep solidarity with persecuted Jews, hopes for the eradication of their suffering, and, simultaneously, advocacy for their conversion because French Catholicism, so saturated with suffering, could accommodate and recognize them. Within this powerful rhetoric there is both inherent compassion and potential violence. As Maritain articulates her memories, redemption could be found on the other side of this Judaized pain that stood at the center of her godfather's imagination and, in 1940–44, her own. In the first volume the relief from suffering is robust, even confidently hopeful in some places. Following Maritain's recollections of images of Bloy's *Salut par les juifs* in 1940, the well-known story of Ezekiel appears, in which the prophet's despairing cry is heard after Yahweh leads him to a valley full of bones named the House of Israel. Maritain's reflections focus on the divine words of Yahweh in response to Ezekiel's lamentation that "our bones are dried up, our hope is lost, we are cut off." Yahweh promises to redeem life and deliver the Israelites back to the land of Israel. She cites Ezekiel 37:12–14: "Thus speaks the Lord Yahwé: Behold I will open your graves, and I will bring you forth out of your sepulchers, O my people, and I will bring you into the land of Israel. And you shall know that I am Yahwé, when I shall open your tombs and I bring you forth from your graves, O my people. I shall put my spirit in you, and you shall live, and I shall give you rest on your soil."[59] The narrative placement of the divine promise to bring life into that which is most desolate—bones, graves, tombs—interrupts her graphic descriptions of sanctified Jewish sorrow and recasts Jewish suffering in the context of hope and new life.

In the 1944 volume, the redemption is much more muted: "We must pray," she remembers Bloy saying before he died in 1917. He wanted to pray, not for resurrection or redemption, but merely to "endure the horror of this world." "We must pray to *wait,*" she remembers learning from Bloy.[60] Deliverance on the other side of suffering in *Les aventures de la grâce* is modest, even meek: she remembers Bloy writing to her about "a tiny lizard the color of hope which can slip through the crevices of the wall of doves mentioned in the Canticle."[61]

Here and in the first volume the theological rhythm alternating graphically depicted grief with muted hope, divine presence, or even a robust redemption does not just occasionally appear in Maritain's memories but furnishes the pulse of the entire work. Indeed, her own life is understood through this Christian oscillation. For instance, on page 1 of *Les grandes amitiés,* Maritain's first memory is one of suffering. When she was two and a half years old, she saw her father crying outside a closed door while her mother gave birth to her younger sister, Véra. Maritain remembers, "standing against my father's knee as he sat before the closed door of my mother's room and wept. I leaned against him and tried to comfort him." She continues, "Thus the first image which remains in my memory is that of my father weeping; the second is that of my own desire to drive his pain away. Perhaps that is why I always had for my father an almost maternal feeling of protectiveness and compassion."[62] Maritain's early and unmediated contact with her father (a Jewish man, and she was alone with him) crying and presumably suffering promoted a concern for someone other than herself. The intense early anxiety brought on by the sight of her father inculcated compassion and can be seen as a remembered early experience with redemptive anguish.

Maritain remembers later fleeing Russia with her family because of the precarious situation of Russian Jews. This entailed an early separation from her father, who left before his daughters and wife; endless rounds of going from office to office with her mother and sister; and long train and boat lines. Of this separation from her father, exile from her homeland, and voyage to France, she wrote, "I have only a blurred memory of great fatigue, of anguish, and of melancholy [un souvenir confus de grande fatigue, d'angoisse et de mélancolie]."[63] This melancholy gives way to a sense that the pain was worth it, for the memories that follow are happy depictions of her early successes in school in Paris. The rest of her adolescence is similarly characterized by a series of sufferings that inevitably yielded intense rewards. Remembering her despair at the Sorbonne, in *Les grandes amitiés* Maritain explicitly contends that it was her suffering there that enabled her salvation and intellectual escape—an interpretation of her experience only vaguely present at the time but here more forcefully articulated. "We could resist this demoralization of the spirit only through our suffering. . . . What saved us then, what made our real despair still a conditional despair, was precisely our suffering."[64] The rhythm moves back and forth between tears, joy, weeping, and relief.

Throughout the war years, Maritain received letters from Catholics, both American and European, eager to discuss the issue of Judaism.[65] On the one hand, her story as a Jewish convert and godmother to countless others affirmed for some Christians the hope for continued Jewish conversions. One American reader wrote to her in 1944: "Well, I shall pray that a way may be shown to you how to help the great course of the conversion of the Jews in the United States. Never hesitate to write me if you think I can be of any help. The most beautiful description of your parents' conversion to the Church remains imprinted on my mind and may it become a symbol of our hope. It is most inspiring and touching."[66] Other letters reach for a way to think about the conversions and the unspeakable persecution. A French woman wrote to Maritain: "Like you, Madam, I have always thought that Catholicism is the completion [l'accomplissement] of the Jewish religion. All my efforts have been to convince those who are dear to me of this. And God has helped me and reassured me. But tell me, do you see an end to the persecutions? In these long years of suffering, I have stopped searching for a solution to this atrocious problem."[67] The letter reflects a widely held attitude in French Catholic philo-Semitic circles that seems paradoxical today, one that could simultaneously desire to eradicate Jews' suffering and desire their conversion.

Despite such ambivalent attitudes that her book both reflected and generated, Maritain received many more letters from French and American priests, nuns, and laypeople that described her memories of Judaism as putting an end to their prejudices against Jews. In 1941, a Canadian priest, the Rev. Maurice Pierquin, wrote:

> I have just read and enjoyed your great work, *Les grandes amitiés*. What an impression! What good will it do? I would like this work to be able to penetrate all the presbyteries and homilies, and stop the priests in their anti-Semitic campaigns. Today I am 61 years old and *voilà* your book, delivers salvation. . . . And above all you knew how to speak to my heart *and* open my intelligence. . . . I was not an anti-Semite, but there was in me a certain repulsion. I have overcome it, thanks to you, and for that I thank you. I can even confess to you that the blindfolds have been removed, I can see more clearly, the ardent light leads me to a haven, and eliminates all the garbage deposited in me since my childhood. [Je n'étais pas anti-sémite, mais il y avait en moi une certaine répulsion. Je suis vaincu grâce à vous et je vous en remercie. Même je peux vous l'avouer, les bandeaux étant ôtés, je vois plus clair, une lumière ardente me conduisant au port et éliminant toutes les scories déposées en moi depuis mon enfance.] Such is the Truth, I had to tell it to you and hope you will excuse me.[68]

Many Catholics from France, Canada, and the United States similarly described coming face to face, for the first time, with their own anti-Semitic feelings upon reading *Les grandes amitiés*. A French priest by the name of Père Pressoir wrote in 1947 to report that Maritain's book, especially her passages on Bloy, seemed to have "exorcised the anti-Semitism" out of him (exorciser cet antisémitisme) once and for all.[69] Now that he had learned from Maritain the "grande vocation d'Israël," he at last had an intellectually coherent understanding of why he had so deeply loved learning Hebrew and the Hebrew Bible in seminary.[70] Another Frenchman, Robert Leclercq, wrote to confide in her that reading Bloy earlier in his life had helped him see the error of anti-Semitism but that Maritain's exegesis of Bloy's position on the Jews had helped him understand Bloy more deeply. "Before knowing your godfather," he wrote to her, "I was in the sad state of Drumont [j'en étais au triste stade de Drumont]. By his *Salut,* Bloy had shown me my mistake, a mistake, which I understood it by reading him, was wretched." With "your help," he continued, "I truly penetrated his magnificent words, and through you I discovered the madness of my past aberrations [c'est par vous que j'ai découvert la folie de mes aberrations passées]."[71] Maritain's readers suggest that *Les grandes amitiés* provided (despite its problematic aspects) new ways for Catholics to think about Jews in this moment of danger. Her nostalgic rendering of her Jewish childhood made Judaism seem valuable, and even Maritain's emphasis on Jewish suffering could have been a powerful riposte to the thousands who refused to acknowledge what was happening in 1940–44.

While Maritain was in New York, she earned a reputation for being somewhat of an expert on Russian Judaism, mysticism, and Jewish-Christian relations. In 1943, between the publication of the first and second volumes of her memoirs, she published a book on Chagall. *Marc Chagall* traces the grave joy in Chagall's paintings—the cows, doves, brides, and swirling colors that can appear alongside devastating depictions of sorrow, murder, and despair—to his Jewish childhood.[72] Maritain cites passages from Chagall's own biography and interprets his Russian Jewish childhood in aesthetically rich, vivid details that echo her own memories. She cites a passage of Chagall's in which he remembers his childhood participation in the liturgy on the Day of the Atonement, or Yom Kippur. According to Maritain, Chagall describes Jewish high holidays as having made a powerful, intense impact on his religious imagination. She quotes him in full and adds, "Thus your paintings come into being. O Chagall! There is the form; there is the abstraction at the heart of Chagall's art. These are the roots. These are the beginnings. This is his essence."[73]

In 1944, the curator of the Museum of Modern Art considered asking Maritain to write an exposition on Chagall "with understanding and sympathy about the background of Russian-Jewish culture and mysticism" to accompany the museum's first Chagall exhibit. This idea was quickly rejected by partner museums, who were concerned about "stressing the Russian-Jewish culture and mysticism" of his art in 1944. One curator wrote, "All of us feel there is a danger of arousing a certain anti-Semitic feeling towards Chagall's art. . . . Perhaps Madame Maritain could develop the mysticism without the propagandizing element."[74] The idea was abandoned. In 1944 perhaps it seemed too early, too risky to think about the issue of Judaism in modern art, or perhaps curators feared that because of prevailing anti-Semitic sentiment the public would view Chagall's Judaism as a liability and they preferred instead to keep it hidden. On the other side, within the Jewish community, Maritain's take on the Jewish mysticism at the root of Chagall's paintings was not well received. She was accused (rightly) of framing Chagall's Judaism within a more general mysticism that could be accommodated by Christianity.[75] While favorably received in Catholic circles, her efforts encountered some obstacles elsewhere.

THE LIMITS OF REDEMPTIVE SUFFERING
AND MARITAIN'S WARTIME POETRY

In 1941, reflecting on her works of self-recollection in *Les grandes amitiés,* Maritain wrote, "However much all my memories well up in me, as I summon them before me, and come to life with the fresh colors of long ago, here I must admit that it is no longer possible for me to live over again with the same intensity the deep distress of my heart."[76] The field of memory is the field of intensity, distress, suffering, and, crucially, redemption (sometimes articulated through the image of holy, suffering Jews, suffering women like Mary, or Christ). "All this," she claims in her poems, "was *before.*"[77] Throughout her memoirs, suffering's attendant pleasures and its experiential possibilities with Christ are possible through an encounter with the vast field of memory.

Maritain's other intellectual labor during the war centered on her poems, in which she named the present as a caesura in time and a rupture in the theological possibilities at hand. In her poems, her turn to the wartime present is direct and sustained. Suffering is described as an atrocity that exceeds the theologies she developed and inherited in a less brutal past. In her poetic voice, the "today" of 1940–44 is exterior to La Salette's grief-stricken vision of the Beatitudes and the blessed misery of the Jewish Christ. Maritain describes this temporal disconnect between her past and the present in terms of the felt presence or absence of redemption within the suffering. She opens her long lamentation poem "Deus excelsus terribilis," written in New York on November 28, 1943, during a period between her writing the two volumes of her memoirs:

When long ago we received Your Word
We suffered [nous avons souffert], it is true,
In body and in soul—in senses and in spirit,
And we have known anguish.

But always we could assign a place to our pain
And know that elsewhere existed happiness.
Always some answer could be found
From heaven or from earth,
The assuagement that light diffuses
The refreshment of tears, prayer,
The memory, at least, of hope
And friendship equal to sorrow.

All this is abolished,
All this, which was before
We walk among the dead
And weep bitterly
The God of our faith has abandoned us,
He leaves us alone to ourselves.

All this is swallowed up in the eternal past
All this which was *before*.
Before God surrounded Himself with terrors
Before he let go His weighty arm
And made His justice shine forth
In the black sun of His mysterious decrees.[78]

God was present in the tears of the Jewish Christ; La Salette promised an ecstatic merging of beatitude and suffering; Léon Bloy saw holiness in distressed and repulsive places; and Yahweh promised to open graves and restore life to dry bones. But "all this is abolished" today. Jacques read fragments of this poem on January 12, 1944, during one of his radio messages to the French Resistance. It was published in *Commonweal* in French and in English in 1944.[79] The timing of the poem's composition and release signals that the text's refusal to find suffering pleasurable, redemptive, or meaningful should not be read as an evolution or maturation out of an earlier naïveté. In Maritain's concurrent memoirs she was excavating the voices of her past just as her poems refused them. In the present, the God of "Deus excelsus terribilis" has forsaken those who now "walk among the dead and weep bitterly."

In the stanzas that follow, Maritain situates her grief unambiguously in the present context of the annihilation of European Jewry. Her poetic works speak in a voice rarely heard in her prose:

> Before the martyrdom of the Nations,
> France—crucified between her thieves—
> And Poland and their sisters of distress.

> Before the innumerable massacre of the Jews,
> The lament of Israel immolated by slaves,
> *Salus ex Judaeis!*

> Before God veiled His face
> With that veil of blood,
> Before He turned away from innocence.[80]

In *Les grandes amitiés,* the suffering is sanctified and promises redemption. Ezekiel speaks in her memoirs, but here Israel's lament is left chillingly unrequited. God veils his face with blood and turns away.

The third section of Maritain's poem changes to a direct plea to God, "*Vous,*" a prayer. The transcendent breaks into the poem—not to offer comfort or even suggest God's intimacy with suffering humanity, as her memoirs would have it, but to point to the eschatological distance between the divine and human:

If we cry Abba! Father!
You do not harken to our cry.
It bounds back to us as an arrow
Striking a brazen target,
You plunge us back into the night.

It is as though we had lost our Father
Who is in Heaven
An abyss yawns between loving-kindness and want
And You will not cross it.[81]

The mood of the poem turns into shocked disbelief in a God who plunges disciples back into the darkness. This God is a Father secluded in heaven. Those below are incapable of bridging the chasm that divides them from God, "and You," she accuses God, "will not cross it." This is not a rejection of the theological; rather, it taps into an exegetical tradition of protest, drawing on the Psalms, such as Psalm 88, with its cry, "Why, Lord, do you reject me and turn your face from me?"

Maritain begins in the next stanza to articulate an eschatological notion of memory. Elsewhere her early sufferings have been remembered and articulated, but here she claims that memory cannot bear to recall the dead of today: they will be remembered only "in life eternal." She writes:

We shall never forget our dying
We shall remember it in life eternal.
What the soul cannot support,
What cannot be imagined, and cannot be told,
What we suffer, what we shall have suffered,
We will keep forever in memory.[82]

Memories of those now dead are unsupportable, unimaginable, and unutterable today. One sees here a remainder of faith in something transcendent, but it can be experienced only in eternal life after death. The present is intractable and irredeemable.

Her poem then shifts its tone again, returning to a description of wartime horrors in gritty, realistic detail:

France, shattered, fouled, ravaged,
Famine there, wasting bodies,
The children who will not grow up,
Adolescents who are in slavery
In prison in captivity
The young French men
Women at hard labor
And the hostages of hate
Put to death by thousands.
What cannot be told
What the mind refuses to bear.[83]

Maritain faces the present in graphic detail but refuses to overlay it with meaning or immediate redemption. In the next stanza, she emphasizes that the deaths are not simply women, men, and children, but Jewish men, women, and children. This becomes an accusation of God and a call for God to remember God's own lineage:

Four million Jews—and more—have suffered death
Without consolation.
Those who are left are promised to the slaughter.
. . . .
It is Your lineage, Lord, which is exterminated!
Israel was led to the butchery,
Flock without shepherd without fold,
They were tracked down like game,
In the streets of towns and villages,
The Gardens of France
Women with their children they would not give up
Hurled themselves from the windows.
Others espoused death to flee ignominy,
Old men shortened their days
Because they saw their hope condemned.[84]

These graphic images of women jumping out of windows with their children, or Israel hunted down in the streets, are like photographs or paintings of the horror: they resist explanation or easy theological narrativization.

In the next stanza, Maritain faces her resistance to providing a theological reading of redemptive suffering in her understanding of the present. She acknowledges that "faith assures us that all is well," but faith has changed, she writes, because it is "carried in a murk of blood." She accuses God: "You Yourself, our God, You have forsaken us." This rupture in her understanding of faith and of God is described as violent and foreign, something that overwhelms her as if from without, like a madness seizing her, infesting time with hell, ensnaring her:

> Let me then speak from the madness that seizes my soul.
> Our days are evil, infested with hell,
> Despair sets its traps.
> No one will be saved if You do not shorten the days
> Given over to the Prince of this World.
> Faith assures us that all is well on Your side,
> You Who rule the universe by Wisdom
> But we carry our faith in a murk of blood
> Because cruelty and hatred have flooded the earth
> With their unrepressed torrents.[85]

Maritain then moves to cite the source of cruelty and hatred, and her prayer to God is again one of accusation. She leaves no question as to who is at fault for the "unrepressed torrents" of violence in 1940–44.

> It is because You Yourself, our God,
> You have forsaken us.
> And the Angel of Truth keeps silent—
> The mirror of Your indifference—
> Because You have abandoned us to ourselves.[86]

In indifference and abandonment God forsakes his own Jewish lineage. In the midst of Jewish agony, there is absolutely no sense of divine intimacy, only callous neglect. Suffering is exterior to divine life.

As Maritain shifts to the last stanza, the mood changes from accusatory to hortatory. The pace quickens, and there is a new sense of urgency in what is an exhortation, a plea, a prayer to the God she has accused of abandonment. Her addressee shifts from God to Jesus. She begs him:

> It is time, awaken, Lord Jesus, come!
> Oh Thou Who hast taken a heart like our hearts
> To share in our pain and pity.
> Send us a world of light and peace,
> Grant us to understand in the ways of Thy wisdom,
> To speak in the ways of Thine intelligence,
> To console in the ways of Thy compassion. Make the crimes cease.
> Remember innocence.
> Have mercy on Thy people,
> The people of misery and affliction,
> The humiliated and oppressed of all Nations,
> And the Jews, the oppressed of all the world.
> Send the Apostles who will enchant our pain
> In the efficacy of Thy love
> And the sweetness of the Holy Ghost
> As once Thou hadst raised up Thy psalmists
> And given divine frenzy and knowledge
> To the Prophets
> For our salvation.[87]

The last stanza creates a caesura in historical time and transports the reader, finally, from 1943—"What the soul cannot support / What cannot be imagined, and cannot be told"—into the realm of the eternal. Transcendence for the first time breaks into the poem. But this rupture in the present is not descriptive, it is only a plea or a wish. She begs Jesus to "make the crimes cease." The pain of the present is irredeemable, but she begs for apostles who will "enchant our pain" (as they did in the past?). Throughout *Les grandes amitiés,* God is remembered as sharing in pain, present in sorrow, but here his presence is begged for rather than presumed or described. Maritain reaches for the symbols that have been central to her intellectual and religious life since 1905: symbols of frenzy, blood, death, anguish, and despair, here put into the service of a realistic depiction of the unfolding chaos of 1944.

A similar sense of despair in the face of a hellish world gone mad is visible in Maritain's first postwar poem "Portes de l'horizon" (Doors of the Horizon) (1947):

> Doors of the horizon trembling in the shadow,
> Endless devastations at the margin of the skies,
> Wrecks of broken worlds—derelicts,
> Sounds fallen into hellish labyrinth of madness!
> O despair, whither shall we run
> In the storm where everything is burning
> Under the thrust of murderous desires.
> All the happiness of life perishes,
> Nothing any longer to sustain any hope,
> Fire takes what man has betrayed,
> And the heavens in flames give birth to new stars
> Haughty luminaries to brighten disaster
> And silent death.[88]

As in "Deus excelsus terribilis," there is nothing to animate hope, and Maritain describes the world's beauty and light—new stars—as gaudy, too much, mocking the silent death below.

In another wartime poem, "Le prisonnier," dated December 22, 1943, just three weeks after "Deus excelsus terribilis," Maritain evokes a similar unwavering engagement with the present. She focuses her words on the intimate detail of a prisoner behind bars awaiting his death:

> Thy servant is in irons
> In the shadow of death
> Lord deliver him
> I see his face behind bars
> Like a saint's face in holy pictures
> His wide face protruding eyes
> Fringe of black hair on his brow
> Streaked with white wool
> He looks like the Christ

Of Quentin Matsys.
He gazes straight in front
Stunned at his misfortune
He sees God's sky
And that all will go well

No he is not yet painted
In the holy pictures
He sits on his bed
His head in his arms
He weeps
Alone among enemies
Who hate all he loves
For whom his kindness his intelligence
Are objects of contempt
Prisoner of his innocence
He keeps patience
Like his master Jesus Christ
Like Him sorrowful unto death
He has so loved justice
He is like the Christ
Of Quentin Matsys
He is learning
The language of heaven.[89]

This 1943 poem shares *Les grandes amitiés'* Christological comparison between this wartime sufferer, perhaps a Jew, and Christ. But here there is no ecstasy or the hope and fulfillment of the Beatitudes. The "language of heaven" in the concluding line is chilling. The prisoner, like the narrator of "Deus excelsus terribilis," is simply "étonné," stunned. Quentin Matsys (1466–1530), to whose paintings she likens this prisoner, was a Flemish painter whose work is known for its intense depiction of feelings. His portraits capture ugliness (*The Ugly Duchess* his most famous), human grimaces, pain, and sorrow.

The atrocities recounted in "Le prisonnier" and "Deus excelsus terribilis" take place on an intimate, personal level. The highly concrete image—of a face behind bars, black hair, wide face, head fallen onto his arms, alone, crying—both personalizes and concretizes unimaginable wartime horror and contains universal claims, reminding Maritain's readers that the terrifying politics of the war is felt most acutely on the personal level. The atrocities in Maritain's poems are never abstract; they map the lives of individual sufferers affected by the dreadfulness of 1940–44. Just after the war, Maritain wrote to a friend describing how the image of a single face generates a broader, more public and political understanding of atrocious events. Thinking of the individual friends she knew who had died in the camps, she wrote, "When one can put a name to a few of those who died in Auschwitz, in Belsen or in Dachau, and call up a face among them, the vast sorrow one feels for all the other victims itself assumes a face which haunts you with unspeakable horror and compassion."[90] Arguably, the face of the prisoner, the mothers she describes as hunted in the streets of France, and the friends killed in the death camps were images she hoped could serve readers as objects of "seeing," specific instances they could fixate on that could evoke their compassion, or at least their acknowledgment of the millions of victims in their midst.

It is striking that the memories described in Maritain's prose rarely, if ever, speak of the present the way her poems do. But when Maritain's prose focuses on the present in something approximating realistic description, she voices frustration that poetic language can never adequately describe what is happening. She wrote cryptically in 1945:

> Time of hatred, time of sorrow [la douleur]. Haggard hope does not know what to cling to. . . . Our time of blood and death; of tortures, of despair, of chaos, of disconsolation, of misery, of famine, of anguish [d'angoisse], of accursed discoveries; time of irremediable and boundless calamity; drowning every heart which cruelty has not yet devoured. . . . Then, poetry! let poetry do penance, let her be silent, because she has not words for the reality of our time; let her veil her face; let her stop flirting with our sorrow; let her forget flowers, games, graces, rhetoric and eloquence; let her strip herself and humble herself if she wishes to survive the unimaginable, the indescribable, the moral darkness of our time.[91]

Though her poems come closer to describing wartime horror than her prose, Maritain here expresses doubt that her poetry can ever be the communicative vehicle for the unthinkable events of 1940–44. She echoes Theodor Adorno's famous statement, "To write poetry after Auschwitz is barbaric," but she subverts it with her own poetic voice. For Maritain, the reality of the war simply eluded poetic language, and presumably, theological language; she once posed the question, "Did not Boccaccio say long ago that 'poetry is theology'?"[92]

Although Maritain's earlier theological vision of redemptive suffering seems to have been entirely unable to accommodate her experiences of World War II, why did she choose to articulate precisely this theological vision during the war itself in her memoirs? Why would she put the suffering-centered prose of her memoirs to such a redemptive use? Even beyond *Les grandes amitiés,* during the war and postwar years another of Maritain's intellectual projects was introducing the works of Léon Bloy to English-speaking readers. She wrote elegies in *Commonweal* and edited a translated edition of several passages from Bloy's corpus (*Pilgrim of the Absolute,* 1947). She wanted to hear Bloy's voice speak at his most radical, transgressive, and graphic. Her edition of Bloy's writings, *Pilgrim of the Absolute,* refuses any narrative coherence—it is a chaotic, manic pastiche of selected paragraphs, passages, sometimes even isolated sentences from his corpus. The extracts appear in her book just as flashes of pain that leave the reader shocked and awestruck. She selected the following passage from Bloy's *Le sang du pauvre,* when he tries to describe the reality of the cross, with no other narrative explanation:

> the cross of absolute renunciation, the cross of eternal abandonment and denial for all of these, whoever they be, who want none of it; the cross of wholly wearying fast, of total sacrifice of the sense, of mourning for anything which can console, the cross of the stake, of boiling oil, of molten lead, stoning, drowning, of flaying alive, of quartering, of being hacked to bits, of being devoured by wild beasts, the cross of all the torments devised by the bastard sons of devils . . . the terrifying Cross of Dereliction of the Son of God, the Cross of utter Misery and Destitution![93]

This passage is from the first book of Bloy's that Maritain encountered, and what is striking here is that the wild violence of the cross is deeply *desired,* explicitly internalized and yearned for, again and again. Such writings were for her "like a torrent which drags the rocks and trees from its banks and carries them headlong with the mud and the pebbles from its bed."[94] She singled out Bloy's passages about Judaism, and those that animated the familiar trope of suffering, abject women endowed with power. Maritain turned to this language for the images to contend with her present, but in her poems she refused to explicitly connect the wartime chaos with the redemptive longing and joyous encounter with suffering that she remembered from Bloy.

THE USES OF MEMORY AND IRRECONCILABLE THEOLOGIES OF SUFFERING

Turning from the theological vision of Maritain's wartime poems and considering again the recesses of her memories in 1940–44, I find a term suggested by Dipesh Chakrabarty to be helpful. He says that all cultures have a "dark side," which he means less in a pathological sense than in a sense of opacity. The worlds we study are never fully transparent and entirely available to the scholar; there are places over which the scholar must merely puzzle, inspect from all sides, knowing there are horizons she cannot trespass and will never fully penetrate.[95] If there is a dark side in Maritain's world, I see it in the terrain of memory, especially the memories of ecstatic *souffrance* that she turned to, again and again, in the face of the Holocaust. For Chakrabarty, recognition of this opacity enables the scholar to acknowledge that her speculative ventures into interpretation of these opaque places are always incomplete and remain tentative. This seems more true here than anywhere else in Maritain's life and writing.

Yet opacity does not preclude attempts to understand it, and it is helpful to begin with Maritain's mentors and friends, many of whom had much to say on the notion of memory and the function it fulfills in our experiences of the world. Henri Bergson, in his *Matière et mémoire,* a text Maritain knew well, interrogates the relation between incoming new sense data and the images from the past that are called up to interpret it. Our consciousness, according to Bergson, links perception with memory and enables us to anticipate the future. Thus there is no "pure perception" of the present, he argues, but the past becomes available to consciousness only when it is necessary and useful for understanding the present and integrating it with action. If memories of the past survive, "It is with a view to utility; at every moment they complete our present experience, enriching it with experience already acquired."[96] He suggests that remembrances are constructive rather than just repositories of a "bygone era."[97] This helps us understand that Maritain's memories of the French Catholic renaissance—even memories of the pleasurable *souffrance* she rejects in her poetry—may have been functional and necessary for her to survive her present. How might this have worked?

In the beginning of the chapter, I drew on Walter Benjamin's notion of memory in order to read *Les grandes amitiés* as, at least in part, a political rejoinder to prevailing anti-Semitic narratives, and I tried to show how this was an effective, if problematic, project by pointing to the countless letters Maritain received from Catholics revising their attitudes and ideas about Judaism. Here I would like to consider how these memories may have been not only outwardly useful for her readers but inwardly meaningful and useful to Maritain as a Jew, as a Catholic, as a woman, and as an exile and witness to the Shoah. Bergson's notion of the usefulness of recollected images from the past suggests that the memory flashes in *Les grandes amitiés* did not need to directly, or even consciously, link to the events of 1940–44. They may have been called up to subconsciously enrich her experiences and integrate her past into the present, which was otherwise nonintegrable.

It makes sense to turn again to Bloy. In one of his early works that Maritain also knew well, he describes how memory, particularly memories of suffering, can engender both healing and an experience of God. By calling up images of past anguish, Bloy claimed, these recollections could reverberate in an experience of intimacy with God in the present. In his writings on La Salette for example, which I discussed in chapter 2, he describes a character, Marchenoir (based closely on himself), who has undergone a severely traumatic experience—the death of his own child. Bloy describes the character as grief-stricken but hardened against any emotion. When Marchenoir went on a pilgrimage to La Salette, the sight of the Virgin in anguish, mourning over the death of the Son so long ago, suddenly "unwound his despair." Bloy writes that the grief about his son, stored deep in his memory, came to the surface when he saw the Virgin in tears for Christ. As Marchenoir "threw himself down in tears and sobs" before her, his grief intensified, but as he looked on her, he no longer suffered ("je ne souffrais plus"). "An angel," Bloy writes, in the voice of Marchenoir, "had unwound from me, strand by strand, the whole tangle of my despair, and I was exulting in the intoxication of the sacred Madness."[98] Therefore, contact with the weeping, grief-stricken Virgin led to a kind of emotive healing and experience of the divine. It evoked memories of his own suffering, the pleasurable healing of consolation, and possibly the relief of purging his grief.

Through the character of Marchenoir, Bloy seems to suggest that it is difficult—even impossible—to move through grief without the aid of external images of suffering. One can (even *should* for Bloy?) displace one's own despair in the present onto images of others' sufferings, or even one's own sufferings from the past, images that can then serve as vehicles for intensifying grief and affliction, evoking "tears and sobs." This oddly can become "useful" in Bergson's sense. Although Maritain resisted overlaying the Holocaust with the holy weeping of La Salette or the promise of the Beatitudes for those who suffer, such images of holy *souffrance* were precisely those that seem to have carried her through the war. Alternatively, perhaps it was her refusal to redeem the suffering, pathos, and violence expressed in her poetry that enabled her.

There is still another explanation. If we take Maritain at her word in her poetry, she experienced 1940–44 as a time in which God was veiled, Jesus hidden ("Il en est temps, réveillez-vous Seigneur Jésus, venez!"). Perhaps Maritain, to find God at all in her midst, had to draw from the archives of her memories. Self-recollection may have been the only way to access God during the Shoah. Maritain had by this time long been immersed in traditional Christian theological resources. Augustine, whose words Maritain had once called "ineffable," famously said that the search for God "must be carried out in the fields and broad meadows of memory, where there are treasure chests of innumerable images brought in from things of all sorts experienced by the senses."[99] When God was seen as absent, perhaps God existed only in the memories of a safer past, a past when suffering engendered intimacy with the divine. Maritain's memoirs show the arduous efforts of one Jewish-Catholic woman to keep alive an image of God when God seemed to have fled and "surrounded Himself with terrors."

Maritain had to bring that world back to life with the powers of emotion and imagination. She believed that all work describing the past—both memory and history—should entail the affections of the scholar. "History must ever take into account—contrary to the conviction of the critical school—*feeling* and *emotion,* which is to say the human soul," she wrote in one postwar essay.[100] She saw possibilities for transcendence embedded in this genre. In 1951, Maritain wrote a memorial essay about Bloy in English for *Commonweal* magazine. In it, she quoted her godfather, who had written that books about the past "can be truly holy because if done well, the writers make miracles. It is absolutely necessary that they raise the dead and cause the dead to walk before them and before us." She continued, "They must light once more those lamps that are extinguished in the catacombs of the past into which they lead us. To accomplish such a task . . . what is needed is the intuitive heart. It is necessary to love what you are telling and to love it madly. . . . Like the prophet one must lie down against the dead child, breast against breast, mouth against mouth, and infuse into him one's own life."[101] Memorial work of the sort Maritain described entailed a set of emotions (an intuitive heart), psychic states, and bodily feelings. She imagined the past as a community of dead whom the scholar must resuscitate, "mouth against mouth." For her, Bloy had been dead nearly twenty-five years and Péguy thirty, and by the time she finished the second volume of her memoirs the Jews she spoke about so generally, even ahistorically, in her text had died in the millions. Could she have imagined herself with this eclectic community in ruins, mouth against mouth, infusing into them her own life?

We can best understand Maritain's deliberately inner, affective encounter with the past by thinking about the place of and practices of memory in Christian piety, all of which would have been well known by her. Mnemonic techniques of internalization, which are crucial to Christian piety, typically concentrate on rendering the life, death, and resurrection of Jesus contemporary with one's own experience.[102] Maritain's affectively and even erotically charged image of breathing new life into the dead "breast against breast, mouth against mouth," echoes long-standing practices in the history of Christian mysticism in which the goal is to mnemonically encounter Christ. Take for instance, the words of the hagiographer of the thirteenth-century mystic Angela of Foligno, whom Maritain read with great devotion: Angela claimed she had had a vision of herself in Christ's tomb on Holy Saturday, kissing the closed eyes of her dead beloved. Maritain redeploys these erotic images of awakening Christ from the past and recasts them to imagine breathing life back into a more proximate past in the midst of its ruin.

Therefore, we have to understand the past portrayed in *Les grandes amitiés* with such agony and such redemption, not as a proposition for the wartime present, or as a generalized statement of the essence of Catholicism, but as a spiritual and theological strategy for contending with the horror and violence of the war. This is also true for darkness and rage in her wartime poetry. It may then seem less as an "unwitting exposure of the neurotic streak in French Catholicism" than as something more elusive, subtle, even humane. Interestingly, some French Catholic readers of *Les grandes amitiés,* possibly more accustomed to thinking about the range of ways that vivid depictions of suffering, even without any suggestion of redemptive solace, can be healing, wrote to Maritain to this effect. One French reader wrote to her in 1941, "What perhaps has struck me the most was what you said at the end about suffering in beatitude, of 'the kind of glory of suffering.' The small ray of light in our night of suffering we see all around us is a great relief [la souffrance dans la béatitude, de cette sorte de gloire de la souffrance. Ce petit rayon de lumière dans une nuit de souffrance comme nous la voyons tout autour de nous est un grand soulagement]."[103] A reviewer in New York expressed a similar sentiment: "It is small wonder that this book should open and close with a note on misfortune and suffering. There rises behind it always the wounded figure of France, having its own mystery and meaning. Hoping for better and more blessed days, one may trace their desired outline in the effort and ecstasy of the past."[104] The graphic depictions of the Crucifixion, La Salette, her godfather's death, and his *imaginaire* centered on suffering Jews may have enabled Maritain, and some readers, to articulate an affective response to 1940–44, which otherwise left them aghast.

The political importance of urging readers to face the Jewish suffering in their midst—in this case suffering communicated through memories—should not be underestimated. If we see Maritain's texts outside the social, political, and biographical context from which they emerge, the remembered theology of suffering from Maritain's past sounds bizarre, incomprehensible, or cruel, even if we can admit that there is something ultimately not fully penetrable or transparent about it. A certain opacity remains in the story of Maritain's memories of redemptive suffering, simply because such a theology of her past clashes with her theology of the 1940–44 present as seen in her poems. The two bodies of work display two notions of God, history, and suffering that are starkly irreducible to one another. One vision gains theological traction with suffering and frames it in terms of redemption, and another refuses this. The tension inherent in these two visions that Maritain offers in 1940–44 is not easily resolved. Maritain always said that the mind refused to bear the present, but her poems may have given her a more indirect way to access and articulate it. Even so, the possibilities for poetry to communicate effectively during the war were never fully satisfactory for her.

Working on two different temporal planes, Maritain's wartime writings refuse to convey only one understanding of the theological or the political. Dipesh Chakrabarty's work helps us consider Maritain's different modes of theologizing and witnessing during the war less as a failure to integrate her thoughts into a singular narrative than as what he calls "heterogeneous practices of seeing." He writes, "To breathe heterogeneity into the word 'imagination' is to allow for the possibility that the field of the political is constitutively not singular."[105] The heterogeneous ways Maritain saw her present and engaged her past enabled her to resist a singular theological and political vision. There was no singular vision in 1940–44 to which she could easily reconcile herself. I think her texts, her prose and poetry, enable her to be counted among the very few truly rich voices of Catholic theological lamentation and resistance during the Holocaust, precisely because they *were* so multivalent in genre, tone, and theological vision.

Jacques was also one of the few who unambiguously expressed Catholic resistance during the war. In his most effective speeches and essays, Jacques included excerpts of Raïssa's grief-stricken poems to give his readers a different way of seeing the political reality he was describing in his more rational language of Thomism and natural law. In one of his important English-language essays, "On Anti-Semitism" (1941), he quoted from Raïssa's poem "Marc Chagall." In one of his 1944 speeches urging resistance, he read from "Deus excelsus terribilis." In 1947, Jacques printed one of Raïssa's previously unpublished poems, "Le nom d'Israël," as an epigraph to his book *Le mystère d'Israël,* reflecting on the Holocaust from the perspective of a Christian.[106] Raïssa's concrete meditative reflections offered two theological visions, the one irreducible to the other in a crucial way. In doing so, they offered readers, both Jacques and others, the means to practice variegated ways of seeing what could not be singularly described within existing theological frames.

Conclusion

Raïssa Maritain's Posthumous Presence and the Allure
of Suffering Reconsidered

Raïssa Maritain witnessed *Les grandes amitiés* on its way toward becoming a classic: twenty thousand copies were sold in the first three years, forty thousand in the 1950s, fifty thousand in 1960. After she died, new editions came out in 1962, 1963, 1966, and 1974. The book was published not only in French but in English, Spanish, Italian, Polish, Hungarian, and Chinese.[1] The accolades Maritain received for *Les grandes amitiés* meant a lot to her. She collected every review printed from around the world, meticulously preserved each one in a huge scrapbook, and underlined parts of the reviews that seemed noteworthy, typically when a reviewer mentioned themes of suffering, Judaism, or her godfather Léon Bloy.[2]

While still in New York at the close of the war, the Maritains learned that their exile would not be permanent. In December 1944, Jacques was appointed French ambassador to the Vatican, a position requiring relocation to Rome that he accepted with great reluctance. It meant another uprooting in a time when his life, and that of Véra and Raïssa, was "a wandering one, pressured and jostled by external events, burdened with heavy duties and anxieties."[3] The move took all three of them to an entirely new country, immersed them in a yet another new language, and required endless social obligations. All of this meant further delays to the extensive, sustained intellectual work Jacques and Raïssa were longing to return to after the war.

Just before they departed New York for Rome, on March 15, 1945, the French-American Club (a group Jacques had helped launch that had been active in war resistance efforts) hosted an honorary luncheon at the Waldorf-Astoria to bid the Maritains formal farewell. Most of the speeches praised Jacques, thanking him for the guidance he had given to so many Americans and Europeans when, as one speaker said, "the terrible thing happened in France. The terrible evidence was there in the face of the world and the world looked at France not knowing whether she was alive or dead or whether if alive she could not, in utter misery and exhaustion, consent to die."[4] But many also spoke about and to Raïssa, thanking her for what she showed them in *Les grandes amitiés*. People claimed that through this book they had learned about the *renouveau catholique* but had also learned what it was like for the thousands of exiles like her who found themselves having to suddenly flee. C. G. Paulding, an editor at *Common-weal* magazine, described realizing through her writing what it meant to leave "everything in France, all at once, the living and the dead, every road, every village . . . the wars, the revolutions, the music, the philosophy, the debate with Bergson, the music of Satie, all the painting, Rouault, Chagall, the poetry."[5] It is not clear that Raïssa ever really recovered from the exile and loss the speaker described, or from learning of the monstrous crimes that had subsequently occurred on the European continent.

Once the Maritains arrived in Rome, Raïssa abandoned her plan to continue a third volume of her memoirs and returned to two earlier works that dealt most directly with Judaism, republishing her original book on Chagall under a new title, *Chagall ou l'orage enchanté,* and revising her book on Abraham, *Histoire d'Abraham.* Maritain never let her thoughts veer too far from her godfather, and she spent the summer of 1947 selecting more portions of Bloy's work to present to English-speaking readers. During his ambassadorship, Jacques made attempts to direct the Vatican toward a more forthright condemnation of anti-Semitism and an acknowledg-ment of the atrocities of the Shoah, but the pope toward whom Jacques felt "heart-rending ambivalence" was slow to act.[6] In 1948 Jacques's am-bassadorship term was completed, and the president of Princeton Uni-versity offered him an emeritus appointment in philosophy. On June 16, 1948, Jacques, Raïssa, and Véra sailed from Naples back to New York.

Before they arrived at their new house in Princeton, their good friend the French artist André Girard prepared the walls of the house with colorful murals of the French countryside to lift the spirits of the Maritains, who were still homesick for their native country. But when they walked in, Raïssa, still reeling from the war, told Jacques, "I cannot live here. It is impossible for me to live in this abundance of flowers and butterflies. I cannot."[7]

For much of their time at Princeton, Raïssa, Véra, and Jacques struggled with illnesses that accompany old age. In 1954 Jacques suffered a heart attack, from which he eventually recovered, and in 1957 Véra was diagnosed with breast cancer. During her first years at Princeton, Raïssa struggled off and on with various health scares but managed to produce two more volumes of poetry, *Portes de l'horizon* (1953) and *Au creux du rocher* (1954). In 1959, she and Jacques coauthored a book of reflections on the liturgical movement, *Liturgie et contemplation*. In one of her postwar poems written at Princeton, entitled "Comme on meurt" ("As One Dies"), she offered a reflection on mortality in the twilight years of her own life:

> O painful repose, O pure unknowing
> God present but concealed
> Under the dazzling veil of your Essence and Mysteries.
>
> Magnet of all creatures,
> In the soul your spirit attracts
> Your hidden God whose Name
> No one can spell.
>
> To speak to You she has only her breath and moan.
> She suffers with sacred dread
> The word You carry forward in the depths
> Where she knows herself not.
> She wails as does a tree about to fall,
> As one dies.[8]

Maritain evokes here long-standing, familiar idioms—a woman facing the abyss of death, moaning ("sa plainte"), suffering/feeling ("elle éprouve") the intensity of both human mortality and God—experienced as a kind of "sacred dread" (crainte sacré). The dying one is here at rest, but it is a painful ("douloureux") rest where God here is "present but concealed" (présent mais voilé). This is a subtle shift from Maritain's God in 1944, who was only concealed, absent, hidden behind a veil of blood ("Dieu ait voilé son visage / De ce voile de sang").[9] The presence of the divine in the midst of death and loss perhaps returned, for a time.

Two years after a long and difficult struggle, in 1959, Véra died. She was buried in Princeton. Jacques said later that Raïssa had been "physically broken" by losing her sister. She and Jacques made plans to spend the summer in Paris to recover from this loss. They checked into their hotel in Paris on July 7, 1960, but as they entered the room Raïssa had a stroke and was hospitalized for several months. It was 1960 in Paris, and many of her friends from days of the *renouveau catholique* had long died—taken by old age, illness, the two world wars. But still there were some who had survived it all. Jean Cocteau, for instance, who had years ago lost contact with Jacques and Raïssa, had heard from Jacques's niece that the Maritains were back in Paris and that Raïssa was ill. Cocteau came to the hospital to pray over his bedridden friend and fellow poet on November 2 and 3, 1960. Finally, around twelve noon on November 4, 1960, Raïssa Maritain died.

Later that night Jacques and Cocteau prayed together over her body. Cocteau wrote Jacques a condolence letter afterwards: "I am so happy for the memories I have, that fate allowed me to be with you in the room where Raïssa was in the difficult transition from the quotidian to the eternal. I saw her internal struggle, and I saw her victorious, smiling, young, closed eyes—and even in her physical shell she reflected ecstasy [dont même son enveloppe physique reflétait l'extase]. . . . So little has changed. I love you and I embrace you Jacques."[10] In Cocteau's tender perception of his departed friend, Raïssa, even at the moment of her death, was enclosed in ecstatic *souffrance,* that familiar and beloved idiom of the French Catholic revival.

Jacques too would reach for this symbol as he established Raïssa's posthumous legacy. Grief-stricken, he went through his late wife's papers, diaries, notes, and fragments of essays, and what he found left him "égaré" (lost, bewildered).[11] He had always known about Raïssa's commitment to the practice of contemplation, but these private writings showed him the depth and extent of what she had undergone in her fifty-four years as a contemplative Christian. These writings became "precious" to him; he felt they contained wisdom that could "enlighten many souls" and "renew and vivify our approach to certain eternal truths, and enlarge our horizons."[12] He also said he wanted to do justice to Raïssa by telling the world how much his philosophical works had their source in her contemplative prayer and what he called her "oblation" of herself to God.[13]

Jacques collected these disparate writings, gathered those he deemed most important, and sent copies to a small group of close friends, asking them to guard the documents with secrecy. He sought advice as to whether they should be made public. Most encouraged him, and the *Journal de Raïssa* appeared in French in 1963, published by Desclée de Brower. When Jacques asked his good friend Thomas Merton for advice about an English translation, Merton wondered if Americans would understand her words, which might be not only too searing but even incomprehensible in the late 1960s climate of the "ecumenism-liturgy" movement and what he called "LSD spirituality."[14] Nevertheless the English translation appeared in 1971. Raïssa's posthumous *Journal* never achieved the fame of her memoirs, but many who encounter it describe being moved, shocked, awestruck by the intensity of her inner life. In 1999, Harper-Collins listed it in the top 100 Spiritual Books of the Century.

With his *petit troupeau* now gone, Jacques was weighed down by sorrow and fatigue. At age seventy-eight he began a new, but final, chapter of his life. He joined the Little Brothers of Jesus as a lay member of their religious order, devoted to prayer and a life among the poor. He moved to their hermitage in Toulouse, where he spent his remaining years and drafted his final book, *The Peasant of the Garonne*. Among the many striking features of this text is the depth of his continued grief over Raïssa that he makes explicit in the book and his profound sense that she worked through him, prayed over him, led him through this project. As he completed this text, in June of 1967, he wrote a moving letter to Charles Journet:

> I am a man in pieces, held up entirely by the hands of Raïssa. I no
> longer am in control of anything, there remains nothing of *me* in my
> agency [in n'y a plus de moi agent] *[sic];* if anything good remains in

the work for which people want me to survive, it is owed, every time, to what I receive from her, and it passes through me as water through a sieve, I remain empty [je reste vide]. . . . Truly, it is a little like a death that continues on for a little while. I remember saying to Jean-Marie de Menasce a long time ago: "What will become of the little flock the day one of the three leaves the earth?" And he answered me, "Do not worry, the two others will die right after." Raïssa did not wait long to join Véra. And me, I'm still here, and it's not just the pain [la douleur] but . . . I have almost lost entirely any integrated memory of the life of the three of us, the events of our life together, which is so painful [pénible], and I see it is (almost all my past escapes me, and there remains nothing of the continuity of memories, with the interior coherence that such memories produce) like a sort of psychological death, waiting for the other.[15]

Jacques was eighty-five years old when he wrote these poignant words; he was a man in the evening of his life for whom any coherent memories of his past life had already faded. He claimed that since Raïssa's death he did not so much recall her as feel her presence: he felt Raïssa "passing through him, like water through a sieve." All his past "escape[d] him," yet she was there with him every day "guiding his hand"—so much so, he confessed to Journet, "that it is not I who made this [The Peasant of the Garonne], but Raïssa."[16] Jacques wove passages of Raïssa's writing throughout the book, which he dedicated to her as "the one who instructed my poor philosopher's head in the things of God."[17] He echoed, even fifty years later, his earliest claim made in 1907 that Raïssa was his "earthly intermediary" to the realm of the divine.[18]

Although Jacques's fascination with his contemplative wife immersed in *souffrance* remained a fact throughout their marriage, by this late stage in his life he had come to cherish not just her suffering but also her theological and philosophical vision, which he felt guiding his hand, line by line, as he penned his final book. So much had changed since their earliest days as a young married couple. One thinks back, for example, to how in Raïssa's early 1909 essay Jacques crossed out her use of *je,* replacing it to include him with a *nous,* and how she then defiantly crossed out the *nous* again and reasserted the singular pronoun. Jacques's support of Raïssa's intellectual work came gradually. In *Peasant of the Garonne*, he used Raïssa's life and intellectual legacy as a symbol to critique some of the modernizing impulses of the Second Vatican Council. The target of his complaints was mainly the conciliar notion that ritual practice should be something consciously performed, active, understood, spoken, and sung. He worried that the strange ways the self could be transformed in silence—what he claimed he had learned about from Raïssa—were in danger of being eclipsed. For Jacques, what Raïssa gave was a model of transfiguration of the self before God, one that required suffering and pain, something he feared was unintelligible to the modernizing church. It was also crucial for Jacques that Raïssa's commitment to the dark night of the soul was made, not from the cloister, but from an immersion in the everyday traumas of humanity and history. Jacques highlighted an old letter Raïssa had written to Pieter van der Meer de Walcheren in 1933, which was later published in the *Journal:* "I have the feeling that what is asked of us is to live in the storm of life," she wrote her friend, "without keeping back any of our substance, without keeping back anything for ourselves, neither rest nor friendships nor health nor leisure—to pray without ceasing—in fact to let ourselves pitch and toss in the waves of the divine will till the day when it will say: 'It is enough.'"[19] As Jacques saw it from a perspective *in the world,* the fundamental lesson from his late wife was the familiar theme of *souffrance.* In many ways, he was right about her commitment to suffering in the midst of history's chaos: "We do not 'curl ourselves up in a ball' . . . so as to offer as little surface as possible for suffering to get a grip on," Raïssa wrote in a 1925 notebook, adding, "Christians stretch themselves out on the Cross and expose themselves to all the blows."[20] Indeed, Raïssa's corpus is steeped in sorrow, beginning with the inner *anéantissement* (annihilation, shattering) that she described in the earliest entries of her spiritual journal, her 1905 promotion of Bloy's *Le salut par les juifs,* in which he identifies Jewish abjection as a marker of divine election, and her dedication to the afflicted, weeping Virgin of La Salette, whose tears, she explained to the pope in 1914, "correspond to the state of the world."[21] This continues with her intense, vivid descriptions in the 1930s of feeling "assimilated" into Christ's passion and hearing frightening promises of being "espoused in blood" to the bridegroom Christ, as well as with her contemporaneous writings on the dark, anguished faith of the patriarch

Abraham, who "died to happiness" and "consented to the destruction of all hope."[22] Her poems too offer dramatic snapshots of grief: Mary wiping the blood from the face of her Son, a row of coffins in Poland, women hurling themselves out of windows with their babies, a Jewish prisoner behind bars. In her private correspondence there are moments of light and beauty, but even here she steers the discourse inevitably toward the darkness: her struggles with illness, the exhaustion from social obligations, the pain engendered by spiritual practice, a sense of shock over the traumas of the mid-twentieth century.

Curiously, to make sense of all of this, Jacques, like many contemporary scholars, turns to the doctrine of vicarious suffering, drawing on a 1947 study of co-redemption that revitalizes this late medieval theology for the twentieth century.[23] And though I would claim that this doctrine cannot serve as the sole analytic frame for understanding Maritain's thought, Jacques's attempt, in a time of profound grief and loss, to understand her legacy in terms of "making up *what is lacking* in the Passion of Christ" (Raïssa's words quoted by Jacques) is actually very moving and tender. As he describes it, Raïssa's alleged commitment to co-redemption testifies to how deeply she was committed to both Christ and the world. Jacques's long, grief-stricken excursus on his late wife's writing draws extensively on her own *Journal* to show how Raïssa understood her spiritual suffering as participating in Christ's unfinished passion and his work of redeeming humankind in its most needy and sinful moment. For Jacques, the mystery of co-redemption thrusts the suffering Christian (particularly the mystic who willingly undergoes the pain of self-annihilation) into the deepest forms of solidarity and love. His view humanizes Raïssa's preoccupation with affliction and makes the concept of vicarious suffering understandable as something other than a pathological mandate that the Christian passively accept the pain in her life, even desire it, as a means to atone for others' sins.

To be sure, there are moments when the doctrine of vicarious suffering *does* seem to animate Maritain's life and thought. However, as tempting as it is to group all of Maritain's flashes of darkness under one unifying concept, like vicarious suffering, and assign to it one normative evaluation, like "pathological," "alienating," or even "compassionate" or "sympathetic," her corpus resists such simple appraisal. As moving as

Jacques's final testimony to Raïssa is, it is nonetheless incomplete. In the messy realities of life, a doctrine like co-redemption merges with other social, theological, biographical, and historical forces in ways that are impossible to fully disentangle. Maritain's writings, spanning the entire first five decades of the twentieth century, are inseparable from her personal history and the intersection of that personal history with the theological, cultural, and political currents of late modern Europe. To flatten her experience and reflections on suffering is to deprive ourselves of a chance to gain a sharper picture of the opportunities and agonies of this moment of extraordinary creativity and pathos in late modern Catholicism.[24]

When Raïssa Maritain moved toward baptism in the early 1900s she entered a robust French intellectual tradition based on the ongoing critique of positivism. Men and women across the ideological spectrum—from students of Bergson's radical spiritualism, to the decadent poets of crime and degeneracy, to the intransigent monarchists of the Far Right—severed ties with the republicanism of previous generations, rejecting its scientism and anticlericalism. Critics indicted positivism for its alleged naïveté and optimism and, most importantly for people like Maritain, for its refusal to confront suffering as a central aspect of the human condition. Reflecting on her 1906 conversion three years later, Maritain claimed that the positivist unwillingness to "believe in" suffering and death exhibited "a strange blindness, a type of madness." Anyone, she wrote then, who lived without worrying about mortality and pain was "completely crazy."[25] For a generation of French thinkers yearning for alternative horizons, there was no tradition more deeply immersed in reflections on *souffrance* than French Catholicism. For many, this was what Catholicism had gotten right, and what was so alluring about it was precisely the potency of its symbols as a *countercultural* force against secular, bourgeois republicanism. We hear this celebration of Catholicism's dissimilarity echoed by a huge range of twentieth-century French writers. Remembering her more youthful days in Paris in the 1920s, Simone de Beauvoir recalled that she "had no difficulty in amalgamating [Paul] Claudel and [André] Gide; in both of them, God was defined, in relationship to the bourgeois world, as the *other,* and everything that was other was a manifestation of something divine."[26] Entering this countercultural set of religious symbols and practices centered on suffering, Maritain, as a writer and charismatic leader, re-energized and transformed them.

Over thirty years after her conversion, in a vastly different context, the issue of "a strange blindness" concerning suffering and death resurfaced, but this time with a new moral and political urgency. Raïssa and Jacques Maritain were exiles in New York during the Holocaust in 1940–44. Jacques drew on Raïssa's prescient metaphor to as a way to indict the countless men and women who refused to see and name the attempted annihilation of European Jewry as it occurred. In 1940, Jacques blamed the public unwillingness to acknowledge these atrocities and react with urgency on "a philosophy which refuses to see death and which hides away in funeral homes everything which might bring to mind the eternal destiny of man."[27] Such a philosophy not only exhibited the "strange blindness" Raïssa had noted so long ago but had "no power to make us struggle affectively with death."[28] Jacques was appalled that so many could "witness such a spectacle *without seeing it*."[29] Writing in 1944, in the final pages of *Les grandes amitiés'* second volume, Raïssa similarly called to mind her early notion of a crazy "blindness" among those who averted their eyes from the atrocious crimes committed against Europe's Jews. In 1944, she quoted in *Les grandes amitiés* a passage of Bloy's written during the First World War, revitalized here during the Shoah with a painful foresight about humans' tragic refusal to see the agony of others: "I see people going about their business as if nothing were happening," Bloy wrote in 1917, "entertaining themselves as much as they can, while each day thousands of men are being massacred. There's a total indifference among all those whom the war does not threaten. Supernatural blindness [Aveuglement surnaturel]."[30] Raïssa and Jacques both found this refusal to see, name, and struggle against the suffering of 1940–44 to be among the most shocking of the atrocities. Of the six million massacred, Raïssa wrote in 1945, "so little is said."[31]

Such experiences of contending with affliction, and even willing it, reflecting on it, dissecting it, writing about it, and naming it as holy, gave Maritain—perhaps unpredictably—a unique ability to communicate the theological implications of the horrors that unfolded and a unique method to combat prejudice through her memoirs. This is just one of the many reasons to avoid quick dismissal of suffering-centered theologies like those of Maritain and her French Catholic revival colleagues. When suffering, death, and agony are ignored or glossed over within a system of thinking and practice, they can too easily lose their social, psychological, and political urgency and even their reality. Interpretations that describe this tradition as masochistic, neurotic, or obsessive shut out the political and moral insights that a focus on human suffering can provide.

Yet it must be emphasized that there was no predictable trajectory from Maritain's immersion into this religious world to the stance she took during World War II. French Catholic theologies of *souffrance* did not align themselves with any one particular moral or political posture in history. For one thing, Maritain's engagements with anguish did not always map onto the political landscape in a direct, causal way. Sometimes her devotional, highly imaginative interior world existed at a step removed from social and political history and should be understood in terms other than the political.[32] Categories such as imagination and fantasy are useful analytic tools. Moreover, mapping the relationship between her politics and a devotional and theological world saturated with suffering is difficult because, as with so many of the French Catholic revivalists, both Raïssa's and Jacques's careers veered politically between the Right and the Left. Scholars have shown, for example, how French Catholic revivalists between the wars deployed images of blood, sacrifice, and subjugation not only to awaken recognition and compassion but to mobilize French nationalism and a vengeful victimhood, in a rhetoric that would be taken up by later French fascists.[33] Maritain herself could shift from a compassionate focus on war's victims to a more belligerent focus on political adversaries, as in *Les grandes amities,* where she quotes a polemical passage from Bloy on German aggression in World War I and applies it to World War II: "In the nineteenth and twentieth centuries a nation was found to undertake something that has never been seen since the beginning of History: THE EXTINCTION OF SOULS. This was called *German Culture.* To enslave and abase souls was no longer enough for the Prince of Darkness. He wanted to extinguish them and he succeeded. Germany ceased to belong to the human race. It became a monstrous, ferocious brute threatening the world. . . . I await the Cossacks and the Holy Ghost." Maritain adds, "The Cossacks have come. Today they are sweeping down on the Germany that Hitler took pains to conform to the most frightful visions of Léon Bloy."[34] These essentializations illustrate the range of ways French Catholic revivalists' discourses of suffering mapped onto the political. Their *souffrance* entailed more than simply grief for those persecuted under state violence. It played a role within the dynamics of militarism and nationalism, in thrall to absolutes.

We must also be attuned to other risks entailed in the suffering-centered *imaginaire* of the revival and its potential rhetorical violence. When Maritain reached for the symbols of suffering in 1906, she did not choose from an infinite variety of discourses and cultural forms. They came to her ready-made. Symbols of suffering and grief were closely tied to femininity and to Judaism because, like Catholicism itself, both women and Jewish particularity were seen as "other" to the rational, secular, masculine sphere of *laïcité*. And as a woman and a Jew whose writings took up themes of Catholic affliction, Maritain strengthened these associations. But she also transformed them.

On the issue of gender and suffering, Maritain's story must be understood in relation to the long tradition in Western thought that aligns subjectivity, action, and rationality with masculinity, and the body, passivity, suffering, and death with femininity. Some exegetical and theological traditions in Christianity keep these associations intact but reverse the valuations, idealizing and normalizing the suffering and passivity assigned to women so that women become the best vessels for a Christian God who chooses the weak and lowly.[35] In her own lifetime, Maritain was "held in the grip of available meanings" associated with this tradition—in this case, the woman who loves suffering, the vanquished but resilient *femme juive*, the mystical, supernatural sick woman in the throes of death.[36] These "bore down hard" on her, to use Robert Orsi's provocative phrase, and did not just make suffering that was already there more meaningful, more stable.[37] They energized parts of her life more than others and steered it in certain directions. For example, we know that Maritain abandoned her plans for university studies and merged her career ambitions with those of Jacques sometime shortly after her marriage. Furthermore, if her agonized poetry and grief-imbued memoirs were well received, her forays into neo-Thomism were less welcome (recall Gilson's claims).[38] Perhaps *souffrance* was the primary discourse through which she could speak and write (and moan and weep) so as to be heard in the French Catholic revival.[39]

These constraints, of course, were also generative. Available meanings about *souffrance,* women, and Judaism galvanized a genuine fascination with Raïssa. Consider the assessment of the priest Dom Miège, an advisor to Jacques, who claimed in 1931 that Raïssa's illness and discomfort and the social demands placed on her were not real distractions for her because she was "wholly supernatural."[40] Likewise, available meanings enabled Maurice Sachs to see within Raïssa a spirit containing "centuries of oppression."[41] Bloy saw frailty in her, and Jacques remained in awe over his wife's intimacy with a God whose love for her was, as he saw it, like "blows of an ax."[42] Even in death Raïssa's body radiated ecstasy.[43]

Despite the power of these projections, I would diverge from interpreters like Richard Burton, for whom Maritain's world was so saturated with suffering that it was essentially masochistic, inherently alienating, and thoroughly tragic for her. As Amy Hollywood has shown us, we must take care not to conflate the gaze of hagiographers, confessors, husbands, and friends with the writings of the women themselves: "We cannot make male-authored texts our primary source of information for women's relations to cultural representations and discourse, particularly when writings by women are available to us."[44] Caught as she was in the web of available meanings, Raïssa Maritain was also an intellectual, a woman whose legacy was more than her affliction. She wrote; she spoke; she consoled and advised; and she made significant interventions in the wartime and postwar Catholic conversation about anti-Semitism. At Meudon, pilgrims came to see her as well as Jacques; she served as mentor and godmother to many; her essays, poems, and books were published, read, even translated. Michel de Certeau once described another female spiritual figure in Christian history in a way I find useful: "She is the beneficiary of the roles suggested to her by her circumstances, and by which she is not entirely duped, fragile, cornered."[45] Maritain was entangled in discourses of suffering femininity and suffering Jews, but these entanglements were not entirely confining; she also loosened them. She saw the role of the intellect as central to both men and women and as a needed counterweight to the traditions of suffering-centered mysticism. Maritain highlighted the tears of Thomas Aquinas alongside those of the Virgin: she claimed that intellectual and affective mysticism belonged together and that both should be available spiritual paths for men and women.

It is also not the case that the suffering in her writing is merely a reflection of larger social structures whereas its subversion is the "real" Maritain. As I have tried to show, just as her story represents a challenge to the tradition of suffering femininity, it also presents a willed, deeply sought-after elaboration of that tradition. In 1947, for example, when Maritain selected portions of her godfather's writings to be made available to the English-speaking world, she chose this: "There is, above all for women, only one way of being in contact with God, and that way, that whole unique way, is Poverty. . . . Woman really *exists* only on condition of being without bread, without abode, without friends, without husband and without children . . . [and] linked with every form of wretchedness."[46] Maritain worked hard to promote Bloy, even his most outrageous, over-the-top essentializations of Jews and women; she insisted that his rhetoric was meant to provoke the experiences of pity, compassion, and sanctity. But there is no way to predict the affective responses of readers as they encounter Bloy's brutal descriptions of embodied agony. Along with pity, one could imagine feelings of relief that women bear the brunt of human anxieties about suffering, or, more perniciously, perhaps feelings of repulsion or even hatred toward those who symbolize those things that arouse such intense anxiety for people: vulnerability, mortality, and death.

The symbol of the suffering Jew provokes similar dilemmas of interpretation. Trafficking in essentialism and ahistoricism, this symbol was at the same time a rejoinder to the stereotype of the wealthy merchant and a provocation to reimagine the boundaries between Christianity and Judaism. At the time of Maritain's writing, Jewish abjection was not only a symbol; it also reflected history. Bloy always insisted that most moderns wore a "frightful mask" to avert their eyes from darker truths, and Maritain's use of the suffering Jew in her 1940–44 memoirs worked to similar ends. Yet the very symbol of the suffering Jew is a reifying image of Jews and Judaism, one that evokes and recasts powerful anti-Semitic tropes for philo-Semitic ends.[47] Robert Jay Lifton, for example, challenges those who designate European Jews as perpetual victims who embody for others what he calls "the death instinct, the death taint."[48] To see others as tainted with death is one way we can reclaim our own vitality and power over and against them. They become the "'designated victims,' the people off whom we live not only economically but psychologically."[49]

In a similar vein, Michael Weingrad has shown how the "abject Jew" has remained an uncanny placeholder for many major postwar French theorists.[50] Weingrad points to the connection Jean-François Lyotard makes between "the jews" and the radicalized Other in the Modern West. For Lyotard, he claims, "the jews" are the embodiment of alterity, "the Other, scorned as such, murdered as such, exterminated."[51] While attention to Jewish suffering is not necessarily troubling in itself, Weingrad is right to worry that theorists such as Lyotard have little concern for the details of Jewish thought and history. He finds the work of Lyotard and others to veer toward the ahistorical and to remain unconcerned with Jews who do not fit the model of abjection and alterity.[52]

The same worry arises in reflections on Bloy and Maritain—both of whom claimed that Jewish suffering was "un perpétuel aujourd'hui." Despite the accuracy of Maritain's appraisal of the political and historical moment in which she wrote, it is hard to see how Jews, or women, who are not suffering or not converted could fit within the theological imagination. In addition, though the position of ignoring suffering has its dangers, so does the continual reiteration of suffering, which can produce the kind of "fatigue" described recently by Tony Judt. "There is another kind of banality," he writes, "the banality of overuse—the flattening, desensitizing effect of saying or thinking the same thing too many times until we have numbed our audience and rendered them immune to the evil we are describing. And that is the banality—or banalization—we face today."[53] One might think of the banalization of suffering, particularly the suffering of these two communities, as one of the risks of the French Catholic *imaginaire*. The antidote to these tendencies is to acknowledge not only the ways in which communities have been victims but also the ways they have thrived, which would entail greater attentiveness to the differences and complexities of women's and Jews' (and even Christians') histories. But this necessary act of historicizing would undermine the highly aesthetic, theological symbols that have been used to ground unity, possibly draining them of their imaginative power. Perhaps for this reason, Catholic revivalists never historically analyzed affliction with any real precision or interest.

Their experiments may seem ephemeral, or grim, even somehow anachronistic to contemporary readers. But by valorizing affliction and

presenting it vividly, Raïssa Maritain and this disparate group of intellectuals, artists, mystics, and activists did much to counteract the aversion
and studied indifference to suffering and mortality, and to marginal persons, that they felt was the predominant attitude of the society in which
they lived. That attitude, though taking new forms, has continued into our
own time, and even if we do not wish to sanctify suffering as they did, we
are not exempt from the tendency of drifting into indifference toward it.
Their challenging work offers a stark reminder of this risk, and an urgent
invocation of the possibilities beyond it.

NOTES

Throughout the notes and bibliography, the following abbreviations are used:

JRMA   Jacques and Raïssa Maritain Archives, Kolbsheim, France
OCJRM   Jacques Maritain and Raïssa Maritain, *Oeuvres complètes de Jacques et Raïssa Maritain,* 17 vols. (Freiburg: Éditions Universitaires, 1993)

Introduction

   1. Raïssa Maritain, *Journal de Raïssa, OCJRM* 15:361. All translations of French sources are my own unless otherwise noted.

   2. This quote and the succeeding ones in the paragraph are from Raïssa Maritain, "Récit de ma conversion," *OCJRM* 15:837. Although most of the secondary literature on Raïssa Maritain refers to her as "Raïssa," I have decided to adhere to standard academic protocol unless otherwise noted and refer to her by her last name, Maritain. When her famous husband Jacques appears in the text (the more well-known "Maritain"), I refer to him as "Jacques" and use "Raïssa" in the surrounding sentences to avoid confusion. "Maritain" in the singular refers to Raïssa.

   3. Charles Péguy, "Les suppliants parallèles" [1905], in *Oeuvres en prose complètes,* vol. 2 (Paris: Gallimard, 1988), 869–935.

   4. René Bazin, *Charles de Foucauld: Explorateur du Maroc, ermite au Sahara* (Paris: Plon, 1921), 242.

   5. Simone Weil distinguishes *souffrance* and *malheur* in her classic essay on this theme, "L'amour de Dieu et le malheur," in *Simone Weil: Oeuvres complètes,* vol. 4 (Paris: Gallimard, 2007), 754–69, translated into English by

Emma Craufurd as "The Love of God and Affliction," in *Waiting for God* (London: Fount, 1977), 67–82.

6. Quoted in John Hellman, *Emmanuel Mounier and the New Catholic Left, 1930–1950* (Toronto: Toronto University Press, 1981), 135.

7. Léon Bloy, *Dans les ténèbres* (Paris: Mercure de France, 1918), 104–5.

8. Ibid., 47–49.

9. For use of the term *imaginaire* and its social and cultural function in French Catholicism, see the essays in the excellent volume edited by Laurence van Ypersele and Anne-Dolorès Marcélis, *Rêves de chrétienté, réalités du monde: Imaginaires catholiques* (Louvain: Actes du Colloque, 1999).

10. There are several very useful studies on the French Catholic revival in French and English. See, for example, Stephen Schloesser, *Jazz Age Catholicism: Mystic Modernism in Postwar Paris, 1919–1933* (Toronto: University of Toronto Press, 2005); Philip Nord, "Catholic Culture in Interwar France," *French Politics, Culture and Society* 21, no. 3 (Fall 2003): 1–20; Stephen Schloesser, "Mounier and Maritain: A French Catholic Understanding of the Modern World," *Theological Studies* 65 (2004): 676–77; Philippe Chenaux, *Entre Maurras et Maritain: Une génération intellectuelle catholique, 1920–1930* (Paris: Éditions du Cerf, 1999); Étienne Fouilloux, *Une église en quête de liberté: La pensée catholique française entre modernisme et Vatican II, 1914–1962* (Paris: Desclée de Brouwer, 1998); Frédéric Gugelot, *La conversion des intellectuels au catholicisme en France, 1885–1935* (Paris: CNRS, 1998); Frédéric Gugelot, "Le temps des convertis: Signe et trace de la modernité religieuse au début du XXe siècle," *Archives de Sciences Sociales des Religions* 47, no. 119 (July–September 2002): 45–64.

11. Gugelot, "Temps des convertis," 62–63.

12. I distinguish this cluster of interests from the somewhat related question about the bodily practices that religious devotees pursue that cause physical pain and discomfort, such as fasting and self-flagellation, in order to deepen their experience of God. For a helpful analysis of this topic, see Ariel Glucklich, *Sacred Pain: Hurting the Body for the Sake of the Soul* (Oxford: Oxford University Press, 2001).

13. For a comparison of these three thinkers' relation to Judaism and their attraction to Christian mysticism, see Sylvie Courtine-Denamy, "Rejet identitaire et quête de 'spiritualité': Raïssa Maritain, Edith Stein, Simone Weil," in *L'Europe et les juifs*, ed. Esther Benbassa and Pierre Gisel (Geneva: Labor et Fides, 2002), 141–66.

14. Ivan Strenski, *Contesting Sacrifice: Religion, Nationalism, and Social Thought in France* (Chicago: University of Chicago Press, 2002), 47. Strenski focuses on the theme of sacrifice in French Catholicism, which he in part situates within the doctrine of vicarious suffering. See also Richard D. E.

Burton, *Holy Tears, Holy Blood: Women, Catholicism, and the Culture of Suffering in France, 1840–1970* (Ithaca: Cornell University Press, 2004), 15; Richard Griffiths, *The Reactionary Revolution: The Catholic Revival in French Literature* (London: Constable, 1966), 167. For one helpful problematization of Burton's thesis, see Stephen Schloesser, "No Pain, No Gain," *Commonweal* 131, no. 16 (September 24, 2004): 24.

15. "A 'Revival' in France," *Nation* 15, no. 379 (October 3, 1872): 215–16.

16. "Sensitive Plants," *Church Times,* February 1, 1946, JRMA.

17. Griffiths, *Reactionary Revolution;* Burton, *Holy Tears;* Giovanni Dotoli, *Autobiographie de la douleur: Léon Bloy, écrivain et critique* (Paris: Klincksieck, 1998). For an excellent analysis of this doctrine and its gendered dimensions within the broader field of Catholicism, see Paula M. Kane, "'She Offered Herself Up': The Victim Soul and Victim Spirituality in Catholicism," *Church History* 71, no. 1 (2002): 80–119.

18. Griffiths, *Reactionary Revolution,* 157.

19. I am grateful for correspondence with Thomas Ryan, S.M., to help me clarify this point.

20. See Marcel Denis, *La spiritualité victimale en France* (Rome: Centre Générale d'Études, 1981); Giuseppe Manzoni, "Victimale (spiritualité)," in *Dictionnaire de spiritualité* (Paris: Beauchesne et ses fils, 1932–95), 16:531–45; Édouard Glotin, "Réparation," in *Dictionnaire de spiritualité* (Paris: Beauchesne et ses fils, 1932–95), 13:369–413.

21. Henri Bremond, *Histoire littéraire du sentiment religieux en France depuis la fin des guerres de religion jusqu'à nos jours* (Paris: Bloud et Gay, 1916–36), 3: 575–81; Joseph Komonchak, "Modernity and the Construction of Roman Catholicism," *Cristianesimo nella Storia* 18 (1997): 353–85; Raymond Jonas, *France and the Cult of the Sacred Heart* (Berkeley: University of California Press, 2000), 56.

22. For an excellent discussion on the devotional and the political convergences around the infant Jesus, see Sandra La Rocca, "Le Petit Roi d'Amour: Entre dévotion privée et politique," *Archives de Sciences Sociales des Religions* 113 (January–March 2001): 5–26.

23. Antoine Blanc de Saint-Bonnet, *De la douleur* (Lyon: Giberton et Brun, 1849); Sylvain-Marie Giraud, *De l'esprit et de la vie de sacrifice dans l'état religieux* (Paris: Beauchesne, 1929). For the friendship between Saint-Bonnet and Léon Bloy, see Dotoli, *Autobiographie de la douleur,* 29–30.

24. Burton, *Holy Tears,* 73.

25. Ibid., 15. See similar sentiments expressed in Strenski, *Contesting Sacrifice,* 47; Griffiths, *Reactionary Revolution,* 167.

26. R. Maritain, *Journal de Raïssa, OCJRM* 15:337.

27. Charles Baudelaire, "The Widows," in *The Poems and Prose of Charles Baudelaire*, ed. James Huneker (New York: Bretanos, 1919), 125.

28. On this intellectual movement, see Stephen Schloesser, "From 'Spiritual Naturalism' to 'Psychical Naturalism': Catholic Decadence, Lutheran Munch, *Madone Mysterique*," in *Edvard Munch: Psyche, Symbol, and Expression*, ed. Jeffrey Howe (Boston: Boston College, McMullen Museum of Art, 2001); Ellis Hanson, *Decadence and Catholicism* (Cambridge, MA: Harvard University Press, 1997).

29. Valerie A. Lesniak situates Maritain's thought on suffering within the framework of the Christian mystical tradition: "'Suffering the Divine': An Interpretation of the Journal of Raïssa Maritain" (PhD diss., Graduate Theological Union, 1991*)*.

30. William M. Thompson, introduction to *Bérulle and the French School: Selected Writings*, ed. William M. Thompson, trans. Lowell M. Glendon (Mahweh, NJ: Paulist Press, 1989), 32–76.

31. Thomas Merton to Joseph Cuneen, November 21, 1966, Archives of International Thomas Merton Center, www.mertoncenter.org/Research /Correspondence/z.asp?id=427. This is also mentioned in John Howard Griffin, *Jacques Maritain: Homage in Words and Pictures* (New York: Magi Books, 1974), 69.

32. Eugene Weber, *The Hollow Years* (New York: Norton, 1994), 11. For more on World War I and French Catholicism, see Annette Becker, *War and Faith: The Religious Imagination in France, 1914–1930*, trans. Catherine Temerson (Oxford: Berg, 1998); Joseph Byrnes, *Catholic and French Forever: Religious and National Identity in Modern France* (University Park: Pennsylvania State Press, 2005), 155–76.

33. Hannah Arendt, *Between Past and Future* (New York: Penguin, 1968), 3. My thanks to Mara Willard for pointing out this line in Arendt.

34. The first two quoted passages are from Raïssa Maritain, "Léon Bloy et le révélateur du globe," *OCJRM* 14:1110; the third passage is from Raïssa Maritain, "Deus excelsus terribilis," *Commonweal* 40, no. 24 (September 29, 1944), 565 (for a revised, slightly condensed version of this poem, see *OCJRM* 15:625–31).

35. Tony Judt, "From the House of the Dead: An Essay on European Memory," in *Postwar: A History of Europe since 1945* (New York: Penguin, 2005), 803–34.

36. Michel de Certeau's theoretical reflections on the uses and limits of both historical and theological methods for examining religious texts have influenced my thinking. See Michel de Certeau, "History and Mysticism," in *Histories: French Constructions of the Past*, ed. Jacques Revel and Lynn

Hunt (1973; repr., New York: New Press, 1998), 421, and *The Writing of History* (New York: Columbia University Press, 1988), esp. 19–39. See also his methodology in the wonderful *The Possession at Loudun* (Chicago: University of Chicago Press, 1996). For a similar discussion in relation to the field of feminist history, see Joan Wallach Scott, *The Fantasies of Feminist History* (Durham: Duke University Press, 2011), 1–22, 48–67.

37. For a useful discussion of the epistemological issues of historical causation in religious studies (focused on human interiority especially), see Robert Orsi, *Thank You, St. Jude: Women's Devotion to the Patron Saint of Hopeless Causes* (New Haven: Yale University Press, 1998), 203–11; Robert Orsi, *Between Heaven and Earth: The Religious Worlds People Make and the Scholars Who Study Them* (Princeton: Princeton University Press, 2005), 110–45; Robert Orsi, "When 2 + 2 = 5," *American Scholar* 76, no. 2 (Spring 2007): 34–43; Tyler Roberts, "Between the Lines: Exceeding Historicism in the Study of Religion," *Journal of the American Academy of Religion* 74, no. 3 (September 2006): 697–719. For a discussion of historical causation, religious experience, and feminist analysis, see Amy Hollywood, "Gender, Agency, and the Divine in Religious Historiography," *Journal of Religion* 84, no. 4 (October 2004): 514–24. See also Cynthia Marshall, *The Shattering of the Self: Violence, Subjectivity, and Early Modern Texts* (Baltimore: Johns Hopkins University Press, 2002).

38. R. Maritain, *Journal de Raïssa, OCJRM* 15:379.

39. For more on the unstable space between religious symbols, history, and inner life, see Caroline Bynum, Stevan Harrell, and Paula Richman, eds., *Gender and Religion: On the Complexity of Symbols* (Boston: Beacon Press, 1986); Marshall, *Shattering of the Self.*

40. Yvonne Turin, *Femmes et religieuses au XIXe siècle: Le féminisme "en religion"* (Paris: Nouvelle Cité, 1989), 148–51; Barbara Corrado Pope, "Immaculate and Powerful: The Marian Revival in the Nineteenth Century," in *Immaculate and Powerful: The Female in Sacred Image and Social Reality,* ed. Clarissa W. Atkinson, Constance H. Buchanan, and Margaret R. Miles (Boston: Aquarian Press, 1986), 173–200; Cristina Mazzoni, *Saint Hysteria: Neurosis, Mysticism, and Gender in European Culture* (Ithaca: Cornell University Press, 1994).

41. Jacques Maritain, *Carnet de notes, OCJRM* 12:139–40.

42. Amanda Anderson, "The Temptations of Aggrandized Agency: Feminist Histories and the Horizon of Modernity," *Victorian Studies* 43, no. 1 (Autumn 2000): 43–65.

43. For more on agency and religion beyond the categories of oppression and resistance, see the excellent discussion in Saba Mahmood, *Politics*

of Piety: The Islamic Revival and the Feminist Subject (Princeton: Princeton University Press, 2005), 14–25, 153–89.

44. One excellent exception is Judith D. Suther's *Raïssa Maritain: Pilgrim, Poet, Exile* (New York: Fordham University Press, 1990), particularly her insightful analysis of Maritain's poetry. See also the tributes and essays in "Le Centenaire de Raïssa," special issue of *Cahiers Jacques Maritain* 78 (September 1983). For more on gender in relation to the category of the intellectual in the history of Christianity, see Constance Furey, "'Intellects Inflamed in Christ': Women and Spiritualized Scholarship in Renaissance Christianity," *Journal of Religion* 84, no. 1 (January 2004): 1–22; on this theme in the context of twentieth-century France, see Toril Moi, *Simone de Beauvoir: The Making of an Intellectual Woman* (Oxford: Oxford University Press, 2008), ch. 2.

45. Raïssa Maritain [R.M., pseud.], trans., *Des moeurs divines: Opuscule attribué à Saint Thomas d'Aquin* (Paris: Pouart, 1921), *OCJRM* 14:206–15; Raïssa Maritain [R.M., pseud.], trans., *Les dons du Saint-Esprit: Traité de Jean de Saint-Thomas* (Juvisy: Éditions du Cerf, 1930), originally published as a series of articles in 1926–29, *OCJRM* 14:217–481; Raïssa Maritain [R.M., pseud.], ed. and trans., "Est-il pour nous 'de la plus grand utilité de connaître les grâces dont nous sommes favorisés'?" *La Vie Spirituelle* 65, no. 11 (February 5, 1925), *OCJRM* 14:1087–96.

46. Raïssa Maritain [R.M., pseud.], *Le prince de ce monde* (Paris: Desclée de Brouwer, 1929), *OCJRM* 14:206–15.

47. Henri de Lubac discusses this in "Annexes," his appended commentary to Étienne Gilson's *Lettres de M. Étienne Gilson adressées au P. Henri de Lubac et commentées par celui-ci,* ed. Étienne Gilson (Paris: Éditions du Cerf, 1986), 195–96.

48. Susan Santon, *Great Women of Faith* (Mahweh, NJ: Paulist Press, 2003), 50.

49. Madeline Marget, "Too Much Ado about Raïssa," *Commonweal* 117, no. 17 (October 12, 1991): 586–87. See also Florence Montrevaud, "Raïssa Maritain," *Le XXe siècle des femmes* (Paris: Nathan, 1989), 473.

50. My thinking about the range of literary genres that can be related to the political imagination draws on Dipesh Chakrabarty, particularly "Nation and Imagination," in *Provincializing Europe: Postcolonial Thought and Historical Difference* (Princeton: Princeton University Press, 2000), 149–79, as well as his later essay "Memories of Displacement: The Poetry and Prejudice of Dwelling," in *Habitations of Modernity: Essays in the Wake of Subaltern Studies* (Chicago: University of Chicago Press, 2002), 115–37.

51. Charles Hirschkind, "The Ethics of Listening: Cassette-Sermon Audition in Contemporary Egypt," *American Ethnologist* 28, no. 3 (2001): 623–49.

52. Mahmood, *Politics of Piety,* 32–34, 192–99.

53. Roger Aubert, *La théologie catholique au milieu du XXe siècle* (Tournai: Casterman, 1954); Brian Daley, "The *Nouvelle Théologie* and the Patristic Revival: Sources, Symbols, and the Science of Theology," *International Journal of Systematic Theology* 7, no. 4 (October 2005): 362–82; R. C. Grogin, *The Bergsonian Controversy in France, 1900–1914* (Calgary: University of Calgary Press, 1988).

54. Bruce W. Holsinger, *The Premodern Condition: Medievalism and the Making of Theory* (Chicago: University of Chicago Press, 2005). For roots in late nineteenth-century French culture, see Elizabeth Nicole Emery and Laura Morowitz, *Consuming the Past: The Medieval Revival in Fin-de-Siècle France* (Burlington, VT: Ashgate, 2003).

55. Léon Bloy, *La femme pauvre* (1897; repr., Paris: Mercure de France, 1932), 121.

56. R. Maritian, "Léon Bloy et le révélateur," *OCJRM* 14:110.

57. Étienne Fouilloux explores the ambivalence of the French philo-Semitic current in *Les chrétiens français entre crise et libération, 1937–1947* (Paris: Seuil, 1997). For a broader survey of Jewish-Catholic relations, see Pierre Pierrard, *Juifs et catholiques français, d'Édouard Drumont à Jacob Kaplan, 1886–1994* (Paris: Cerf, 1997).

58. Charles Péguy, preface to *Cahiers de la Quinzaine,* March 1, 1904.

59. Yves Congar, *The Meaning of Tradition,* trans. A. Woodrow (San Francisco: Ignatius Press, 2004), 6–11; Henri de Lubac, *Catholicism: Christ and the Common Destiny of Man,* trans. Lancelot Sheppard and Elizabeth Englund, O.C.D. (San Francisco: Ignatius Press, 1988), 31, 144, 321, 347.

60. See Thomas Merton, *The Seven Storey Mountain* (New York: Doubleday, 1989), 60; Sarah Gordon, "Flannery O'Connor and the French Catholic Renaissance," in *Flannery O'Connor's Radical Reality,* ed. J. Gretlund (Columbia: University of South Carolina Press, 2006), 68–84; Mark Bosco, S.J., *Graham Greene's Catholic Imagination* (New York: Oxford University Press, 2005); William Bush, *Georges Bernanos* (New York: Twayne, 1969), 55; Dorothy Day, "There Is No Time with God," *Catholic Worker,* November 1953, 1, 7.

61. For a further exploration of the convergences between Catholic and (non-Christian) critical theorists in mid-twentieth-century France, see Michael Weingrad, "Parisian Messianism: Catholicism, Decadence, and the Transgressions of Georges Bataille," *History and Memory* 13, no. 2 (Fall/Winter 2001): 113–33; Holsinger, *Premodern Condition;* Stefanos Geroulanos, *An Atheism That Is Not Humanist Emerges in French Thought* (Stanford: Stanford University Press, 2010), 103–27, 251–67.

62. Walter Benjamin, *The Correspondence of Walter Benjamin, 1910–1940,* ed. Gershom Scholem and Theodor Adorno, trans. Manfred R. Jacobson

(Chicago: University of Chicago Press, 1994), 250; Emmanuel Levinas, "From Existence to Ethics," in *The Levinas Reader,* ed. Sean Hand (Oxford: Blackwell, 1989), 49.

63. See Weingrad, "Parisian Messianism"; Amy Hollywood, *Sensible Ecstasy: Mysticism, Sexual Difference, and the Demands of History* (Chicago: University of Chicago Press, 2002).

64. The literature revising the secularization narrative in Europe is vast and continually expanding. For an overview of the more recent literature, see Hugh McLeod, "New Perspectives on the Religious History of Western and Northern Europe 1850–1960," in *Kyrkohistorisk årsskrift* 100, no. 1 (2000): 135–45. See also Tom Kselman, "Challenging Dechristianization: The Historiography of Religion in Modern France," *Church History* 75 (2006): 130–39; Michael Saler, "Modernity and Enchantment: A Historiographic Review," *American Historical Review* 111, no. 3 (September 2006): 692–716.

65. For a more recent discussion of how some of these French thinkers defy old stereotypes of traditional/modern, Left/Right, see the discussion of Charles Péguy's conversion to Catholicism in Charles Taylor, *A Secular Age* (Cambridge, MA: Harvard University Press, 2007), 746–47.

66. R. Maritain, "Deus excelsus terribilis," *OCJRM* 15:628.

67. For two convincing works illustrating why the antagonism model should not be abandoned completely, see Joseph Komanchak, "Modernity and the Construction of Roman Catholicism," *Cristianesimo nella Storia* 18 (1997): 353–85, and Darrin McMahon, *Enemies of the Enlightenment: The French Counter-Enlightenment and the Making of Modernity, 1778–1830* (Oxford: Oxford University Press, 2001).

68. Talal Asad, "Trying to Understand French Secularism," in *Political Theologies: Public Religions in a Postsecular World,* ed. Hent de Vries and Lawrence E. Sullivan (New York: Fordham University Press, 2006), 494–526.

69. For a set of different useful discussions of the dangers posed to communities who idealize abjection and suffering, see Beverly Kienzle and Nancy Nienhuis, "Battered Women and the Construction of Sanctity," *Journal of Feminist Studies in Religion* 17 (Spring 2001): 33–62; Michael Weingrad, "Jews (in Theory): Representations of Judaism, Antisemitism, and the Holocaust in Postmodern French Thought," *Judaism* 45 (Winter 1996): 79–98; Amy Hollywood, "Acute Melancholia," *Harvard Theological Review* 99 (2006): 381–406.

70. Theodor Adorno, "Commitment," in *Aesthetics and Politics: Key Texts of the Classic Debate within German Marxism,* ed. Ernst Bloch (London: Verso, 2002), 182.

Chapter 1. That "Strange Thing, So Unknown to Us—Catholicism"

1. Raïssa Maritain to Jacques Maritain, 1902, in J. Maritain, *Carnet de notes, OCJRM* 12:139–40.

2. Raïssa Maritain, *Les grandes amitiés, OCJRM* 14:718.

3. Raïssa Maritain's "Récit de ma conversion" is now included in *OCJRM* 15:827–34.

4. Since this handwriting change is not visible in the printed format, I thank René Mougel from the archives of the Cercle d'Études Jacques et Raïssa Maritain for pointing it out on the original. To help me think about how to read women's writings in the history of Christianity within the presentations and authorizations of their priests, husbands, or confessors, I found the work of scholars of medieval Christian women to be very helpful, especially *Gendered Voices: Medieval Saints and Their Interpreters,* ed. Catherine Mooney (Philadelphia: University of Pennsylvania Press, 1999), and John W. Coakley, *Women, Men, and Spiritual Power: Female Saints and Their Male Collaborators* (New York: Columbia University Press, 2006).

5. Gugelot, *Conversion des intellectuels;* see also his essay "Temps des convertis."

6. Gugelot, "Temps des convertis," 58–61.

7. Ibid., 58. For a useful discussion of friendship, letter writing, and Christian spirituality, see Constance Furey, *Erasmus, Contarini, and the Religious Republic of Letters* (Cambridge: Cambridge University Press, 2006).

8. For more on intimacy and emotion in the context of conversion, and particularly for his intriguing discussion of homosexuality, see Stephen Schloesser, "'What of That Curious Craving?' Catholicism, Conversion, and Inversion *au Temps du Boeuf sur le Toit*," *Historical Reflections / Réflexions Historiques* 30, no. 2 (2004): 221–53.

9. An excellent recent discussion of Pieter van der Meer de Walcheren and the Maritains can be found in Mathijs Sanders, "Maritain in the Netherlands: Pieter van der Meer de Walcheren and the Cult of Youth," in *The Maritain Factor: Taking Religion into Interwar Modernism,* ed. Rajesh Heynickx and Jan De Maeyer (Leuven: Leuven University Press, 2010), 83–99.

10. Pieter van der Meer de Walcheren, *Rencontres: Léon Bloy, Raïssa Maritain, Christine et Pieterke* (Paris: Cerf, 1998), 33.

11. Pieter van der Meer de Walcheren, *Journal d'un converti* (Paris: Téqui, 1921). For more on the impact of this book in the revival, see Gugelot, "Temps des convertis," 59–62.

12. R. Maritain, *Grandes amitiés, OCJRM* 14:755.

13. Ibid., 710.

14. Ibid., 631.

15. Ibid., 633.

16. Ibid., 646.

17. Ibid., 658.

18. Paula E. Hyman, *The Jews of Modern France* (Berkeley: University of California Press, 1998), 119–23.

19. R. Maritain, "Récit de ma conversion," *OCJRM* 15:827.

20. Emile Poulat, "La laïcité en France au vingtième siècle," in *Catholicism, Politics and Society in Twentieth-Century France,* ed. Kay Chadwick (Liverpool: Liverpool University Press, 2000), 18–25; Philip Nord, *The Republican Moment: Struggles for Democracy in Nineteenth-Century France* (Cambridge, MA: Harvard University Press, 1998), 106–10; Caroline Ford, *Divided Houses: Religion and Gender in Modern France* (Ithaca: Cornell University Press, 2005), 7–10, 139–47.

21. Ruth Harris, "How the Dreyfus Affair Explains Sarkozy's Burqua Ban," *Foreign Policy,* May 12, 2010; Nord, *Republican Moment,* 106–10; Asad, "Trying to Understand."

22. Michael Weingrad, "Juifs imaginaires," *Prooftexts: A Journal of Jewish Literary History* 21, no. 2 (Spring 2001): 260.

23. R. Maritain, "Récit de ma conversion," *OCJRM* 15:828.

24. Ibid.

25. The literature dealing with the reign of positivism in France and the backlash against it is vast. I have found the following sources most helpful: Owen Chadwick, *The Secularization of the European Mind in the Nineteenth Century* (New York: Cambridge University Press, 1990), and H. Stuart Hughes's somewhat dated though still very useful text *Consciousness and Society: The Reorientation of European Social Thought, 1890–1930* (New York: Knopf, 1961).

26. Auguste Comte, *The Positivist Philosophy of Auguste Comte,* trans. Harriet Martineau (Bristol: Themmes, 2001), 2–6. For the impacts of Comte on French intellectual life, see Part II of Henri de Lubac's *The Drama of Atheist Humanism,* trans. Edith Riley (San Francisco: Ignatius Press, 1983); O. Chadwick, *Secularization,* 248–79; Grogin, *Bergsonian Controversy in France,* 12–33.

27. Phyllis Stock, "Students versus the University in Pre–World War Paris," *French Historical Studies* 7, no. 1 (Spring 1971): 93–101.

28. R. Maritain, "Récit de ma conversion," *OCJRM* 14:828.

29. Ibid.

30. Ibid. The original full paragraph is vivid in its articulation of her frustration, and well worth quoting at length: "L'homme n'est qu'un accident

comme un autre dans la nature, il n'en est pas le centre comme le prétendent quelques esprits arriérés, mais pourtant il est la mesure de toutes choses. Il y a milles vérités particulières et variables. Tout change, tout évolue. L'homme descend du singe, en tout cas la pensée n'est peut-être qu'une manifestation de la matière comme l'électricité, et l'intelligence est un corps mou qui vit à 38° (Bonnier). La conscience n'est qu'un épiphénomène. Le libre arbitre est une illusion, il mettrait en défaut la loi de conservation de l'énergie. La notion du devoir doit disparaître avec les nuages de la métaphysique et les ténèbres des religions."

31. R. Maritain, *Grandes amitiés, OCJRM* 14:688–91.

32. R. Maritain, "Récit de ma conversion," *OCJRM* 15:829.

33. Ibid.

34. Henri Massis and Alfred de Tarde, *L'esprit de la nouvelle Sorbonne: La crise de la culture classique, la crise du français* (Paris: Mercure de France, 1911), 71.

35. Henri Massis, *Évocations* (Paris: Plon, 1931), 137.

36. Stock, "Students versus the University," 102.

37. This is not to downplay the aggressive aspects of the critiques. Throughout Agathon's texts, for example, the assault on the Sorbonne is frequently couched in nationalist terms critiquing the spirit of the Sorbonne as an intrinsically foreign, German spirit corrupting the French literary and humanistic tradition.

38. Gugelot, "Temps des convertis," 45–47.

39. Poulat, "Laïcité en France," 20–29.

40. Charles Péguy, quoted in Hughes, *Consciousness and Society*, 342.

41. R. Maritain, "Récit de ma conversion," *OCJRM* 15:830.

42. R. Maritain, *Grandes amitiés, OCJRM* 14:762–63.

43. Ibid., *OCJRM* 14:759.

44. R. Maritain, "Récit de ma conversion," *OCJRM* 15:833.

45. Ibid., 829.

46. Grogin, *Bergsonian Controversy in France;* Hughes, *Consciousness and Society*, 115.

47. R. Maritain, "Récit de ma conversion," *OCJRM* 15:829.

48. Henri Bergson, *Time and Free Will: An Essay on the Data of Immediate Consciousness,* trans. F. L. Pogson (New York: Dover, 2001), 90–121.

49. R. Maritain, "Récit de ma conversion," *OCJRM* 15:830.

50. R. Maritain, *Grandes amitiés, OCJRM* 14:705–6.

51. For a fascinating analysis of the debates between Bergson and Alfred Loisy about the relationship between inner experience and history, see Harvey Hill, "Henri Bergson and Alfred Loisy: On Mysticism and the

Religious Life," in *Modernists and Mystics,* ed. C. J. T. Talar (Washington, DC: Catholic University of America Press, 2009), 104–36.

52. R. Maritain, "Récit de ma conversion," *OCJRM* 15:831.

53. R. Maritain, *Grandes amitiés, OCJRM* 14:692.

54. Grogin, *Bergsonian Controversy in France,* chs. 1–3, 6. For an analysis of the broader continental reach of Bergson's interest in mysticism and the occult, see Alex Owen, *The Place of Enchantment: British Occultism and the Culture of Modernism* (Chicago: University of Chicago Press, 2004), 135–44.

55. R. Maritain, *Grandes amitiés, OCJRM* 14:710.

56. Aubert, *Théologie catholique;* Talar, *Modernists and Mystics,* 13–15.

57. Dom Prosper Guéranger, *L'année liturgique* (Paris: H. Oudin, 1868).

58. Ernest Hello, *Le livre des visions et instructions de la bienheureuse Angèle de Foligno* (Paris: Poussielgue frères, 1868).

59. Auguste Poulain, *Des grâces d'oraison: Traité de théologie mystique* (Paris: V. Retaux, 1901). For more on Poulain and this broader movement, see Talar, *Modernists and Mystics,* 40–47.

60. Grogin, *Bergsonian Controversy in France,* 41.

61. Ibid., 33.

62. Ibid., 41. For the gendered dimensions of this interest in female mystics in early twentieth-century France, especially the fascination with Teresa of Ávila, see Mazzoni, *Saint Hysteria.* The work of Jacques Maître offers an intriguing psychoanalytic rather than historical interpretation of the presence of female mystics in French thought in *Mystique et féminité: Essai de psychanalyse sociohistorique* (Paris: Éditions du Cerf, 1997). For a similar discussion referring to later French atheistic writers and their interest in female saints and mystics, see Hollywood, *Sensible Ecstasy.*

63. For an excellent discussion of the controversies surrounding this theological movement, see Étienne Fouilloux, "Dialogue théologique? 1946–1948," in *Saint Thomas au XXe siècle,* ed. S.-T. Bonino, O.P. (Paris: Saint-Paul, 1995), 153–95. See also Jürgen Mettepenningen, *Nouvelle Théologie— New Theology: Inheritor of Modernism, Precursor of Vatican II* (New York: T & T Clark, 2010).

64. For overviews of neoscholasticism and ultramontane Catholicism, see Francis Schüssler Fiorenza, "Neo-Scholasticism: Its Distinctive Characteristics," in *Systematic Theology: Roman Catholic Perspectives,* vol. 1, ed. Francis Schüssler Fiorenza and John Galvin (Minneapolis: Fortress Press, 1991); Joseph Fitzer, ed., *Romance and the Rock: Nineteenth-Century Catholics on Faith and Reason* (Minneapolis: Fortress Press, 1989).

65. Many theologians noted how neoscholastic theology shared many of the assumptions of scientific positivism. Henri de Lubac wrote,

"Just when it [neoscholastic theology] imagined that it was most successfully opposing the negations of naturalism, [it] was most strongly influenced by it, and the transcendence in which it hoped to preserve the supernatural with such jealous care was, in fact, a banishment. The most confirmed secularists found in it, in spite of itself, an ally." Lubac, *Catholicism,* 313–14.

66. This interest played into her first encounter with Jacques, who helped lead a campaign against the oppression of students in Russia.

67. Daniel Halévy, *Charles Péguy and Les Cahiers de la Quinzaine,* trans. Ruth Bethell (New York: Longmans, 1947), 108.

68. Péguy, "Suppliants parallèles," 890.

69. Ibid.

70. R. Maritain, "Récit de ma conversion," *OCJRM* 15:836.

71. Ibid. The passage in the original is worth quoting in full: "La seule considération de la mort nous découvre une réalité absolument indéniable et puissant, d'un ordre supérieur à la puissance comme au savoir de tout ce qui est humain, et celui qui vit sans se soucier de cette réalité est vraiment fou. Là, la science n'est rien et ne sert à rien. Je me rappelle que la fin sinistre de Curie, avec l'inepte indignation du public et des journalistes contre la 'mort stupide' me fit très vivement sentir. Je vis aussi que ceux qui ne croient pas en Dieu parce qu'ils ne le voient pas, ne croient pas plus à la mort, alors que chaque jour ils voient la mort autour d'eux: elle les surprend toujours, ils en ont une idée qui ne les touche pas, et n'agit pas sur eux: et c'est un aveuglement étrange, une sorte de folie."

72. For excellent discussions of Péguy on Dreyfus and Judaism, see Harris, *Dreyfus;* Annette Aronowicz, *Jews and Christians on Time and Eternity: Charles Péguy's Portrait of Bernard-Lazare* (Palo Alto: Stanford University Press, 1998); Sarah Hammerschlag, *The Figural Jew: Politics and Identity in French Postwar Thought* (Chicago: University of Chicago Press, 2010), 25–66.

73. Charles Péguy, "Notre jeunesse," in *Oeuvres en prose, 1909–1914* (Paris: Gallimard, 1957), 628–29.

74. Ibid., 630.

75. Ibid.

76. Ibid., 632.

77. Ibid., 640.

78. Hammerschlag, *Figural Jew,* 7.

79. Mark Antliff, *Avant-Garde Fascism: The Mobilization of Myth, Art, and Culture in France, 1909–1939* (Durham: Duke University Press, 2007), 63–110.

80. Péguy, "Notre jeunesse," 690.

81. Aronowicz's *Jews and Christians* gets to the heart of the ambivalence of Péguy's philo-Semitism and ultimately sees him as a prescient thinker worth, in parts, retrieving. See also Hammerschlag, *Figural Jew,* 62–63.

82. Lazare Prajs, *Péguy et Israël* (Paris: Nizet, 1970), 36, quoted in Aronowicz, *Jews and Christians,* 150.

83. Maritain discovered Bloy through Maurice Maeterlinck, who had written a review of Bloy's novel *La femme pauvre* that intrigued her. Maeterlinck had also written in praise of Bergson and had contributed to the revival of medieval mysticism with his 1891 French translation of the Flemish mystic Ruysbroeck, which Maritain read in 1902. In so doing he brought together for Maritain the writings of Bergson, Bloy, and the mystics that would constitute the nexus of Maritain's intellectual world between 1900 and 1906.

84. R. Maritain, *Grandes amitiés, OCJRM* 14:718.

85. Ibid., 729.

86. Bloy to Jacques and Raïssa, June 23, 1905, in Léon Bloy, *Lettres à ses filleuls, Jacques Maritain et Pierre van der Meer de Walcheren* (Paris: Librairie Stock, 1928), 5–6.

87. R. Maritain, "Récit de ma conversion," *OCJRM* 15:832.

88. Léon Bloy, *Mon journal,* vol. 2, *1905–1907* (Paris: Mercure de France, 1956), 273, 283, 286, 296, 342.

89. Bloy, *Lettres à ses filleuls,* 7–8.

90. R. Maritain, "Récit de ma conversion," *OCJRM* 15:831.

91. Léon Bloy to Jeanne Molbech, November 21, 1889, in *Letters to His Fiancée,* trans. Barbara Wall (New York: Sheed and Ward, 1937), 76–77, originally published as *Lettres à sa fiancée* (Paris: Stock, 1922).

92. Bloy, *Mon journal,* 212.

93. Léon Bloy, *Le sang du pauvre* (Paris: Librairie Stock, 1932), 10.

94. Bloy, *Letters to His Fiancée,* 91.

95. Léon Bloy, *La femme pauvre* (1897; repr., Paris: Mercure de France, 1932), 121.

96. R. Maritain, "Récit de ma conversion," *OCJRM* 15:834. "Mais alors je voulus savoir la place que le catholicisme fait à la religion juive."

97. Ibid., 834.

98. Bloy, *Mon journal,* 267; Bloy, *Lettres à ses filleuls,* 15–16.

99. Bloy, *Lettres à ses filleuls,* 11–13. This letter echoes his journal entry of the same period in which he writes, "Il faut donc, Raïssa, que vous soyez vraiment ma soeur, pour m'avoir fait cette charité. Quand on aime le *salut,* on n'est pas seulement mon ami, on est, par force, quelque chose de plus." Bloy, *Mon journal,* 272.

100. "C'est avec autant d'orgueil que d'amour que je le dédie à ma petite juive Raïssa (Rachel) que son *frère* Jésus saura bien récompenser." Bloy, *Mon journal,* 286. Emphasis in original.

101. R. Maritain, *Grandes amitiés, OCJRM* 14:732.

102. For an excellent overview of both the philo-Semitic and anti-Semitic impulses in Bloy and the Maritains (along with Jacques's interwar activities on behalf of Jews), see Michel Fourcade, "Maritain face au réveil de l'antisémitisme, 1933–1939," *Cahiers Jacques Maritain* 41 (2001): 3–51; and Pierre Vidal-Naquet, "Jacques Maritain et les juifs: Réflections sur un parcours," in *L'impossible antisémitisme* [by Jacques Maritain], *précédé de "Jacques Maritain et les juifs," par Pierre Vidal-Naquet* (Paris: Desclée de Brouwer, 2003). For two competing interpretations of Bloy on anti-Semitism, see Philippe Chenaux, "Léon Bloy et sa postérité," in *Juifs et chrétiens: Entre ignorance, hostilité et rapprochement, 1898–1998,* ed. Annette Becker, Danielle Delmaire, and Frédéric Gugelot (Lille: Université Charles-de-Gaulle-Lille, 2002); Fourcade, "Maritain face au réveil." Other useful texts on this issue include Richard Crane's discussion of Bloy in *The Passion of Israel: Jacques Maritain, Catholic Conscience, and the Holocaust* (Scranton: University of Scranton Press, 2010), and Bernard Doering, "The Jewish Question," in *Jacques Maritain and the French Catholic Intellectuals* (Notre Dame: University of Notre Dame Press, 1983), 126–67; Jeffrey Mehlman, "The Suture of an Allusion: Lacan with Léon Bloy," in his *Legacies of Anti-Semitism in France* (Minneapolis: University of Minnesota Press, 1983).

103. Léon Bloy, *Le salut par les juifs* (Paris: Libraire Adrien Demay, 1892).

104. Ibid., 4.

105. Ibid., 19.

106. Ibid., 20.

107. Ibid., 26, 14.

108. Hammerschlag, *Figural Jew,* 31–35.

109. Bloy, *Salut par les juifs,* 20.

110. Samuel Moyn, "Antisemitism, Philosemitism, and the Rise of Holocaust Memory," *Patterns of Prejudice* 43, no. 1 (2009): 1–16.

111. Bloy, *Salut par les juifs,* 9.

112. Bloy became increasingly interested in Judaism's debt to Christianity in later publications (*Le vieux de la montagne* [1911], *La porte des humbles* [1920]), where he reveled in Nietzsche's accusations of Christianity as the religion of the Jewish underclass: "People forget, or rather do not want to know, that our God made man is a Jew, the Jew of Jews by nature, the Lion of Judah; that His Mother is a Jewess, the flower of the Jewish Race; that all His Ancestors were Jews; that the Apostles were Jews, as well as the

Prophets; finally that our holy Liturgy is entirely drawn from the Jewish books." *Vieux de la montagne,* 303.

113. Bloy, *Salut par les juifs,* 21.

114. Bloy, *Vieux de la montagne,* 303.

115. Quoted in Henri de Lubac, "A New Religious 'Front,'" in *Theology in History,* trans. Anne Englund Nash (San Francisco: Ignatius Press, 1996), 475.

116. Bloy, *Vieux de la montagne,* 299.

117. Bloy, *Salut par les juifs,* 89.

118. Ibid.

119. Quotes from Léon Bloy, *Le désespéré* (Paris: A. Soirat, 1886), 310.

120. Ibid., 146.

121. Bloy, *Salut par les juifs,* 128.

122. Ellis Hanson, *Decadence and Catholicism* (Cambridge: Cambridge University Press, 1997); Stephen Schloesser, "From 'Spiritual Naturalism' to 'Psychical Naturalism': Catholic Decadence, Lutheran Munch, *Madone Mysterique,*" in *Edvard Munch: Psyche, Symbol, and Expression,* ed. Jeffrey Howe (Boston: McMullen Museum of Art, Boston College, 2001), 75–110.

123. Bloy, *Salut par les juifs,* 129.

124. Ibid., 20. For more on Bloy and Dreyfus, see Richard Griffiths, *The Use of Abuse: The Polemics of the Dreyfus Affair and Its Aftermath* (New York: 1991), ch. 9.

125. "Chère petite samaritaine qui avez eu compassion du voyageur percé de coups, soyez guérie à votre tour par cet autre voyageur que vos ancêtres ont crucifié." *Mon journal,* 267.

126. Ibid., 166.

127. *Lettres à ses filleuls,* 13–14.

128. Bloy, *Mon journal,* 267.

129. R. Maritain, "Récit de ma conversion," *OCJRM* 15:834.

130. Ibid.

131. Ibid., 830.

132. Noted in Hammerschlag, *Figural Jew,* 141.

133. Weingrad, "Juifs imaginaires," 260.

134. R. Maritain, *Grandes amitiés, OCJRM* 14:720.

135. Maritain writes this as an editorial footnote to her selection of Bloy's works entitled *Pilgrim of the Absolute,* trans. John Coleman (New York: Pantheon Books, 1947), 339 n.

136. Ibid., 730.

137. Benjamin, *Correspondence,* 250.

138. Levinas, "From Existence to Ethics," 49.

139. Franz Kafka to a friend, quoted in Alberto Manguel, *Black Water: The Book of Fantastic Literature* (New York: Three Rivers Press, 1984), 90.

140. Constance Furey, "Body, Society, and Subjectivity in Religious Studies," *Journal of the American Academy of Religion* 80, no. 1 (2012): 7–33; Orsi, *Between Heaven and Earth*, 2–18.

Chapter 2. *"She Who Weeps"*

1. For good general studies on La Salette, see the essays in *La Salette: Apocalypse, pèlerinage et littérature (1856–1996)*, ed. François Angelier and Claude Langlois (Grenoble: Editions Jérôme Millon, 2000); Sandra L. Zimdars-Swartz, *Encountering Mary: From La Salette to Medjugorje* (Princeton: Princeton University Press, 1991); Burton, *Holy Tears*, 1–19. For the most thorough treatments of La Salette and the Maritains, see René Mougel, "Les Maritain et La Salette," *Cahiers Jacques Maritain* 52 (June 2006): 53–71; Philippe Chenaux, "Maritain et La Salette," in Angelier and Langlois, *La Salette*, 107–19.

2. For a full text of the Virgin's message in French translated from the local *patois*, see the appendix to Griffiths, *Reactionary Revolution*, 363–69.

3. There are several excellent studies on the proliferation of Marian apparitions in nineteenth-century Europe. See Blackbourn, *Marpingen*; Harris, *Lourdes*. For a provocative analysis of the interpretive challenges such events present to modern scholars, see Orsi, "When 2 + 2 = 5."

4. Bloy, *Mon journal*, 296; Léon Bloy to Pierre Termier, quoted in Mougel, "Maritain et La Salette," 59.

5. Mougel, "Maritain et La Salette," 54–60.

6. For analyses that differ from my own, see Burton, *Holy Tears*, and Mazzoni, *Saint Hysteria*; see also the essays in David Evans and Kate Griffiths, eds., *Pleasure and Pain in Nineteenth-Century French Literature and Culture* (London: Whitford and Hughes, 2009), 31–52, 141–158.

7. Glotin, "Réparation"; Henri Mitterand, "Jouir/souffrir: Le sensible et la fiction," in Evans and Griffiths, *Pleasure and Pain*, 31–44.

8. My thinking here draws from Caroline Walker Bynum's now-classic "Introduction: The Complexity of Symbols," in *Gender and Religion: On the Complexity of Symbols*, ed. Caroline Walker Bynum, Stevan Harrell, and Paula Richman (Boston: Beacon Press, 1986), 1–20. Bynum uses the term *polysemic* in order to complicate the claims that gender-related symbols always simply proscribe or describe reality: "Gender-related symbols, in their full complexity, may refer to gender in ways that affirm or reverse it, support or

question it; or they may, in their basic meaning, have little at all to do with female and male roles. Thus our analysis admits that gender-related symbols are sometimes 'about' values other than gender. . . . It is not possible to ask *How* does a symbol—any symbol—mean? without asking For whom does it mean?" (2–3). For another useful discussion of the multivalence of gendered symbolism in modern Catholicism, see the chapter entitled "The Many Names of the Mother of God" in Orsi, *Between Heaven and Earth,* 48–72.

    9. For helpful ways to think of Maritain as occupying a space beyond resisting or reproducing her own oppression, I have relied on Anderson, "Temptations of Aggrandized Agency."

    10. Bloy, *Le sang du pauvre,* 43.

    11. Léon Bloy, *The Woman Who Was Poor,* trans. I. J. Collins (New York: Sheed and Ward, 1947), 295, originally published in 1897 as *La femme pauvre.*

    12. Ibid., 298.

    13. León Bloy, *Le désespéré* (Paris: A. Soirat, 1886), 286.

    14. Ibid., 260.

    15. Ibid., 204.

    16. Bloy, *Letters to His Fiancée,* 76–77.

    17. Bloy, *Pilgrim of the Absolute,* 121.

    18. Bloy, *Letters to His Fiancée,* 48.

    19. Bloy, *Pilgrim of the Absolute,* 144.

    20. Bloy, *Woman Who Was Poor,* 73–88.

    21. Ibid., 78.

    22. Ibid., 79.

    23. For a survey of eros in Christian theological language, see Bernard McGinn, "God as Eros: Metaphysical Foundations of Christian Mysticism," in *New Perspectives on Historical Theology,* ed. Bradley Nassif (Grand Rapids, MI: Eerdmans, 1996).

    24. This phrase first appeared in Bloy's *Letters to His Fiancée* and was re-produced in *The Woman Who Was Poor,* 131.

    25. To help me think about why readers encountering suffering in Bloy's texts could experience this encounter as healing or pleasurable, I have benefited from Marshall's *Shattering of the Self.*

    26. Bynum, "Introduction," 1–20.

    27. Ford, *Divided Houses,* 7–23.

    28. Ibid., 19–22.

    29. Ibid., 17.

    30. Claude Langlois, *Le catholicisme au féminin: Les congrégations françaises à supérieure générale au XIXe siècle* (Paris: Éditions du Cerf, 1994), 306. For a useful analysis of eighteenth-century precedents, see Olwin H. Hufton,

"Women in Revolution, 1789–1796," *Past and Present* 53 (1971): 90–108; Nicholas Atkin, *Priests, Prelates, People: A History of European Catholicism since 1750* (Cambridge: Oxford University Press, 2004), ch. 2.

31. Langlois, *Catholicisme au féminin*, 300–312. Évelyne Diébolt analyzes how this trend continued through most of the twentieth century, when the vast majority of church staff were women. According to Diébolt, many yearned for more official recognition for their roles and were disappointed with the lack of changes for women after Vatican II. She cites a mass exodus from the church on the part of Catholic women after the 1960s. Évelyne Diébolt, "Les femmes catholiques: Entre église et société," in K. Chadwick, *Catholicism, Politics,* 219–43.

32. For a helpful overview of the concept of French *laïcité* and the struggles between the clergy and the state over the concept of religious neutrality as a way to make sense of their mutual antagonism, see Poulat, "Laïcité en France," 18–25.

33. For more on the historical precedents for this theme, see McMahon, *Enemies of the Enlightenment.*

34. Pius IX, "Address to the Constituency: Timeliness of the Definition" [December 9, 1854], in *Papal Teachings: Our Lady* (Boston: St. Paul Editions, 1961), 83, quoted in Barbara Corrado Pope, "Immaculate and Powerful: The Marian Revival in the Nineteenth Century," in *Immaculate and Powerful: The Female in Sacred Image and Social Reality,* ed. Clarissa W. Atkinson, Constance H. Buchanan, and Margaret R. Miles (Boston: Aquarian Press, 1986), 180.

35. In addition to Caroline Ford's work, see Komonchak, "Modernity"; Jonas, *France and the Cult,* 54–90.

36. André Rayez, "France: XIXe siècle," in *Dictionnaire de spiritualité* (Beauchesne et ses fils, 1932–95), 5:970–94.

37. Sylvain-Marie Giraud, *The Spirit of Sacrifice and the Life of Sacrifice in the Religious State,* trans. Herbert Thurston (New York: Benziger, 1905).

38. Blanc de Saint-Bonnet, *De la douleur.* For the friendship between Saint-Bonnet and Bloy, see Dotoli, *Autobiographie de la douleur,* 29–30.

39. Schloesser, "From 'Spiritual Naturalism'"; Hanson, *Decadence and Catholicism;* see also the essays in Evans and Griffiths, *Pleasure and Pain.* For an exploration of the legacy of this nineteenth-century movement in the twentieth, see Weingrad, "Parisian Messianism."

40. Kathleen Ann Comfort, "Divine Images of Hysteria in Émile Zola's Lourdes," *Nineteenth-Century French Studies* 30, nos. 3 and 4 (Spring–Summer 2002): 330–46. Cristina Mazzoni has argued that in the late nineteenth century *l'hystérique* was a medical designation used in anticlerical scientific and psychological discourse that discredited Catholic claims of

the supernatural and debunked women's claims to religious experience. Seeing women as "hysterical" rather than mystical secularized and naturalized claims of the church. Mazzoni sees a continuity between psychological discourses of hysteria and naturalist literature's representation of femininity, neurosis, and religion. Mazzoni, *Saint Hysteria,* ix.

41. Schloesser, *Jazz Age Catholicism,* 3–47.

42. Evans and Griffiths, *Pleasure and Pain,* 9–28.

43. Hello, *Livre des visions.*

44. For an analysis of French intellectuals' later, twentieth-century fascination with suffering-centered medieval mysticism (particularly Bataille's fascination with Angela of Foligno), see Hollywood, *Sensible Ecstasy,* 72–73.

45. Hannah Arendt, "Christianity and Revolution," *Nation,* September 22, 1945, 288–89.

46. Léon Bloy, *Celle qui pleure: Notre Dame de La Salette* (Paris: Société du Mercure de France, 1908), 222. On January 23, 1907, Bloy wrote to Raïssa detailing the parallels he found between his own life and that of Mélanie. Bloy, *Lettres à ses filleuls,* 58.

47. Bloy, *Lettres à ses filleuls,* 19.

48. For more on this theme in gender and women's writings in the history of Christianity, see Amy Hollywood, "Inside Out: Beatrice of Nazareth and Her Hagiographer," in Mooney, *Gendered Voices,* 79–81.

49. For an excellent study of Véra's role in the household of the Maritains, see Nora Possenti, *Les trois Maritain: La présence de Véra dans le monde de Jacques et Raïssa Maritain,* trans. René Mougel (Paris: Parole et Silence, 2006).

50. Raïssa Maritain to Véronique Bloy, n.d., JRMA.

51. Quoted in J. Maritain, *Carnet de notes, OCJRM* 12:172. For Jacques's full report, see Jacques Maritain to Léon Bloy, January 20, 1907, JRMA.

52. J. Maritain, *Carnet de notes, OCJRM* 12:172.

53. Ibid.

54. Ibid., 173.

55. Ibid., 172.

56. Ibid., 186.

57. Ibid., 166.

58. Ibid., 202.

59. Jacques Maritain, "Avertissement," introduction to *Journal de Raïssa,* by R. Maritain, *OCJRM* 15:160.

60. Caroline Walker Bynum, *Fragmentation and Redemption: Essays on Gender and the Human Body in Medieval Religion* (New York: Zone Books, 2002), 27–52, 181–238; Dyan Elliott, "The Physiology of Rapture and Female Spirituality," in *Medieval Theology and the Natural Body,* ed. Peter Biller and A. J. Minnis (Woodbridge, Suffolk: York Medieval, 1997), 141.

61. Amy Hollywood, *The Soul as Virgin Wife: Mechthild of Magdeburg, Marguerite Porete, and Meister Eckhart* (Notre Dame: University of Notre Dame Press, 2001), 19–37.

62. Coakley, *Women, Men.*

63. Bynum, *Fragmentation and Redemption,* 33–50.

64. Ibid., 37; for teachings of specific medieval women, see Coakley, *Women, Men.*

65. J. Maritain, "Avertissement," *OCJRM* 15:160.

66. Mougel, "Maritain et La Salette," 68–71.

67. Ibid.

68. Ibid., 70.

69. Quoted in J. Maritain, *Carnet de notes, OCJRM* 12:173.

70. Bynum, *Fragmentation and Redemption,* 131.

71. Quoted in J. Maritain, *Carnet de notes, OCJRM* 12:172.

72. R. Maritain, *Journal de Raïssa, OCJRM* 15:121.

73. For antecedents of similar relationships in the medieval period, see Coakley, *Women, Men,* and Mooney, *Gendered Voices.*

74. Catherine Pozzi to Raïssa Maritain, 1931, in *L'élégance et le chaos: Correspondance de Catherine Pozzi avec Raïssa et Jacques Maritain, Hélène Kiener et Audrey Deacon,* ed. Nicolas Cavaillès (Paris: Editions Non Lieu, 2011), 84–85.

75. Ibid., 85.

76. Raïssa Maritain, *Les aventures de la grâce, OCJRM* 14:824.

77. Ibid.

78. Ibid., 830.

79. Scholars continue to debate the extent to which neo-Thomism was either Catholicism's capitulation to or alternative to liberal modernity. For a persuasive account of the rationalist style of some neo-Thomism mimicking the rationalism of the Enlightenment, see Lubac, *Catholicism,* 306–7. For a thorough treatment of Leo XIII's neo-Thomism as a *counter* to modern liberal ideologies, particularly liberal notions of freedom, see John T. McGreevy, *Catholicism and American Freedom: A History* (New York: Norton, 2003), 37–38.

80. R. Maritain, *Aventures de la grâce, OCJRM* 14:829.

81. Hollywood, *Sensible Ecstasy,* 5–12.

82. R. Maritain, *Journal de Raïssa, OCJRM* 15:275.

83. Raïssa Maritain, "Trois Lettres de Raïssa," *Cahiers Jacques Maritain* 7–8 (September 1983): 13.

84. To help me understand the conversations around the relationship between the affections and the intellect in Thomas Aquinas, I relied on Thomas Ryan, "Revisiting Affective Knowing and Connaturality in Aquinas," *Theological Studies* 66, no. 1 (March 2005): 49–68.

85. Jacques Maritain and Raïssa Maritain, *De la vie d'oraison, OCJRM* 14:37.

86. Ibid., 36.

87. Ibid.

88. Ibid.

89. Ibid., 18.

90. R. Maritain, *Moeurs divines;* R. Maritain, *Dons du Saint-Esprit.*

91. R. Maritain, "Est-il pour nous."

92. Raïssa Maritain, *L'ange de l'école: Vie de Saint Thomas d'Aquin racontée aux enfants* [1934], *OCJRM* 14:333–413, translated by Julie Kernan as *Saint Thomas Aquinas, the Angel of the Schools* (New York: Longmans), 1955.

93. R. Maritain, *Journal de Raïssa, OCJRM* 15:181–82.

94. Ibid., 178.

95. Ibid., 232–33.

96. Ibid., 231.

97. Ibid., 265.

98. Ibid., 200.

99. To help me think about the importance of somatic language as metaphors for interior mystical writing, I have relied on Hollywood, *Soul as Virgin Wife,* 19–37.

100. R. Maritain, *Journal de Raïssa, OCJRM* 15:225.

101. Ibid., 194, 184.

102. Caroline Walker Bynum, *Wonderful Blood: Theology and Practice in Late Medieval Northern Germany and Beyond* (Philadelphia: University of Pennsylvania Press, 2007), 3–12.

103. R. Maritain, *Journal de Raïssa, OCJRM* 15:276.

104. Ibid., 200.

105. Ibid., 383.

106. Ibid., 366.

107. Ibid.

108. Ibid., 366.

109. Ibid., 347.

110. Ibid., 376.

111. Ibid., 380.

112. For an analysis of the practice of internalizing Christ's passion in Christian medieval piety, see Hollywood, "Acute Melancholia."

113. Scott E. Pincikowski, *Bodies in Pain: Suffering in the Works of Hartman von Aue* (New York: Routledge, 2002), esp. 62–80.

114. Thompson, introduction to *Bérulle and the French School.*

115. Joan Wallach Scott, *The Fantasy of Feminist History* (Durham: Duke University Press, 2009), 48–52.

116. Denise Riley, *The Words of Selves: Identification, Solidarity, Irony* (Stanford: Stanford University Press, 2000), 13.

117. Ibid.; Scott, *Fantasy of Feminist History,* 49.

118. R. Maritain, *Journal de Raïssa, OCJRM* 15:181–82.

119. Ibid., 188.

120. Ibid., 123.

121. J. Maritain, "Avertissement," *OCJRM* 15:158–59.

122. For two excellent studies that carefully attend to the complexity of the relationship between religious symbols of suffering femininity and the women who encounter them, see the chapter "Two Aspects of One Life: Saint Gemma Galgani and My Grandmother in the Wound between Devotion and History, the Natural and the Supernatural," in Orsi, *Between Heaven and Earth,* 110–45; Kienzle and Nienhuis, "Battered Women."

123. For a fascinating analysis of how new medical discoveries led people to relinquish the old fatalism and the religious acceptance of suffering, see Michael Bliss, *The Making of Modern Medicine: Turning Points in the Treatment of Disease* (Chicago: University of Chicago Press, 2011). The buoyant faith in health care and the assumption that doctors will help, so integral to life in the contemporary First World, were simply not a robust part of Maritain's world, even in the twentieth century.

124. Stephen Schloesser makes a similar point in "No Pain, No Gain," 24.

125. Maurice Sachs, *Witches' Sabbath,* trans. Richard Howard (New York: Stein and Day, 1964), 33.

126. R. Maritain, *Journal de Raïssa, OCJRM* 15:347.

127. An interesting exception seems to have been the intellectual Léontine Zanta (1872–1942). Zanta was the first woman *docteur d'État* in philosophy in France and defended her dissertation on Renaissance Stoicism in 1914. Never awarded an academic position in higher education, Zanta made her way as a well-known tutor, journalist, and writer. She published widely in the fields of feminism, philosophy, and religion. Information on Zanta is scant, but see Moi, *Simone de Beauvoir,* ch. 2.

Chapter 3. Building a New Tribe in the Gathering Storm

1. There are many excellent accounts of the Meudon salon. See Nora Possenti, "Au foyer de Meudon," *Cahiers Jacques Maritain* 51 (December 2005): 11–31; Jean-Luc Barré, *Jacques and Raïssa Maritain: Beggars for Heaven,* trans. Bernard Doering (Notre Dame: University of Notre Dame Press, 1999), 147–79.

2. Sachs, *Witches' Sabbath,* 109.

3. Such Jewish converts, often émigrés, were typically part of the Maritains' salon and that of the Catholic writer Stanislas Fumet (1896–1983). Like Jacques, Fumet was married to a Jewish convert to Catholicism, and Madame Fumet's home hosted men and women similar to those who came to the Maritains. Philippe Chenaux, "Fumet éditeur," in *Stanislas Fumet ou La présence au temps,* ed. E. Germain (Paris: Cerf, 1999), 41. Esther Benbassa has shown that, from 1917 through 1939 in Paris, 769 Jews converted to Catholicism: *The Jews of France: A History from Antiquity to the Present,* trans. M. B. DeBevoise (Princeton: Princeton University Press, 1999), 157.

4. Gugelot, "Temps des convertis," 54.

5. J. Maritain, "Avertissement," *OCJRM* 15:164.

6. Sachs, *Witches' Sabbath,* 111.

7. Hélène Iswolsky, *Light before Dusk: A Russian Catholic in France* (New York: Longmans, Green, 1942), 179.

8. For an example of an article that makes Jewish self-loathing the interpretive framing for these interwar conversions, see Judith Morganroth Schneider, "Max Jacob juif," *French Review* 63, no. 1 (October 1989): 78–87.

9. Crane, *Passion of Israel.* Étienne Fouilloux also provides an excellent overview of the paradoxes in interwar philo-Semitism (prayers for conversion of Jews combined with critiques of anti-Semitism) and the legacy of such paradoxes in the Vichy years and beyond. See Fouilloux, *Chrétiens français,* 33–35, 100–103.

10. For a useful overview of the Catholic discourses energizing anti-Semitism, see Ralph Schor, *L'antisémitisme en France pendant les années trente* (Bruxelles: Editions Complexe, 1992).

11. John Hellman, "Bernanos, Drumont, and the Rise of French Fascism," *Review of Politics* 52, no. 3 (Summer 1990): 441–59.

12. For a good historical precedent, see Thomas Kselman, "The Bautain Circle and Catholic-Jewish Relations in Modern France," *Catholic Historical Review* 92, no. 3 (July 2006): 177–96.

13. Julie Kalman, *Rethinking Anti-Semitism in Nineteenth-Century France* (Cambridge: Cambridge University Press, 2010).

14. For more on the little-known but fascinating Marek Szwarc, see Jean-Louis Andral and Sophie Krebs, *L'école de Paris, 1904–1929: La part de l'autre* (Paris: Gallimard, 2000), 363.

15. A full bibliography of Jean de Menasce's writings has been compiled in P. Gignoux and A. Tafazzoli, eds., *Mémorial Jean de Menasce* (Louvain: Fondation culturelle iranienne, 1974). Menasce went on as a Dominican to study Judaism, Christianity, and Islam in ancient Egypt. For a wonderful

story of the work in the history of religion by the Dominican order in the twentieth century, see Dominique Avon, *Les frères prêcheurs en Orient: Les dominicains du Caire (années 1910–années 1960)* (Paris: Éditions du Cerf, 2005).

16. Esther Benbassa makes this point well in *The Jews of France: A History from Antiquity to the Present,* trans. M. B. DeBevoise (Princeton: Princeton University Press, 1999), 157.

17. See Weingrad's important discussion, in "Juifs imaginaires," of the strange scholarly practice of seeing very secularized Jews as emblematic of French Judaism *tout court.*

18. Emmanuel Levinas, "Fraterniser sans convertir," *Paix et Droit* 16, no. 8 (October 1936): 12. I first became aware of this essay through the excellent article by French historian Joël Sebban, whose work I only recently discovered. His "Être juif et chrétien: La question juive et les intellectuels catholiques français issus du judaïsme (1898–1940)," *Archives Juives* 44, no. 1 (2011): 102–22, accords very well with my research in this chapter and led me to a new set of sources.

19. Pietre van der Meer de Walcheren, *Rencontres: Léon Bloy, Raïssa Maritain, Christine et Pieterke* (Paris: Desclée de Brouwer, 1961), 110.

20. Georges Cattaui, "Raïssa Maritain," *Preuves,* January 1961, 68–69.

21. Iswolsky, *Light before Dusk,* 179.

22. Jan Kott, *Still Alive: An Autobiographical Essay,* trans. Jadwiga Kosicka (New Haven: Yale University Press, 1994), 20.

23. Sachs, *Witches' Sabbath,* 33.

24. For more on the theme of gender, orientalism, and philo-Semitism, see Nadia Valman, "Bad Jew/Good Jewess," in *Philosemitism in History,* ed. Jonathan Karp (Cambridge: Cambridge University Press, 2011), 149–69.

25. Marc Raeff, *Russia Abroad: A Cultural History of the Russian Immigration, 1919–1939* (Oxford: Oxford University Press, 1990), 140–41. See also Dennis Dunn, *The Catholic Church in Russia: Popes, Patriarchs, Tsars and Commissars* (Burlington, VT: Ashgate, 2004), 80.

26. Benbassa, *Jews of France,* 148–49.

27. R. Maritain, "Récit de ma conversion," *OCJRM* 15:827.

28. Phyllis Cohen Albert, *The Modernization of French Jewry* (Hanover: University Press of New England, 2007), 36–37.

29. Hyman, *Jews of Modern France,* 190.

30. Quoted in Sebban, "Être juif et chrétien," 107. Frédéric Gugelot makes a similar argument in "De Ratisbonne à Lustiger: Les convertis à l'époque contemporaine," *Les Belles Lettres: Archives Juives* 1, no. 35 (2002): 8–26.

31. Gugelot, "De Ratisbonne à Lustiger," 13.

32. Quoted in Gugelot, *Conversion des intellectuels,* 180.

33. Maurice Sachs, Jacques Maritain, and Raïssa Maritain, *Correspondance: Maurice Sachs / Jacques et Raïssa Maritain, 1925–1938,* ed. Maurice Sachs (Paris: Éditions Gallimard, 2004).

34. Ibid., 39–40.

35. Sachs, *Witches' Sabbath,* 24.

36. Sachs, J. Maritain, and R. Maritain, *Correspondance,* 40–42.

37. Ibid.

38. Ibid., 60.

39. R. Maritain, *Journal de Raïssa, OCJRM* 15:342.

40. Elizabeth Ezra, *The Colonial Unconscious: Race and Culture in Interwar France* (Ithaca: Cornell University Press, 2000).

41. Michel Bressolette also makes this point in his preface to Sachs, J. Maritain, and R. Maritain, *Correspondance,* 9–11. John Hellman similarly raises issues about exoticism at Meudon in terms of the widespread fascination of the medieval as radically "other" in relation to modernity. See John Hellman, "The Humanism of Jacques Maritain," in *Understanding Maritain: Philosopher and Friend,* ed. Deal W. Hudson and Matthew J. Mancini (Macon, GA: Mercer University Press, 1987), 117–32.

42. But like Cocteau's, Sachs's religious fervor was short-lived. Sachs's image of Catholicism's "sanctification of extreme passions" was in part a fantasy that would come to a grinding halt less than a year after his conversion. Sachs was kicked out of the seminary for his homosexuality and a widely publicized summer affair with an American teenager. This event precipitated the slow decline of Sachs's religious career. This episode is discussed at length in the Sachs-Maritain correspondence. For a good chronicle of the chaotic life of Sachs, see Henri Raczymow's *Maurice Sachs ou Les travaux forcés de la frivolité* (Paris: Gallimard, 1988). For a helpful analysis of Sachs's relationship with Judaism, see David J. Jacobson, "Jews for Genius: The Unholy Disorders of Maurice Sachs," *Yale French Studies* 85 (1994): 181–200.

43. Catherine Pozzi to Raïssa Maritain, 1931, in Pozzi et al., *Élégance et le chaos,* 36.

44. These phrases come from Michel Bressolette's excellent preface to the French edition of the Jacques Maritain–Jean Cocteau correspondence: Jean Cocteau and Jacques Maritain, *Correspondance, 1923–1963,* ed. Michel Bressolette and Michel Glaudes (Paris: Gallimard, 1998). On this larger issue of *rapprochement,* see Harry W. Paul, *The Second Ralliement: The Rapprochment between Church and State in France in the Twentieth Century* (Washington, DC: Catholic University of America Press, 1967).

45. Joseph Roth, *Report from a Parisian Paradise: Essays from France, 1925–1939,* trans. Michael Hofmann (New York: Norton, 2004), 99.

46. Michael Hofmann, introduction to Roth, *Report,* 4.

47. Roth, *Report,* 109.

48. Joseph Roth, "The Leviathan," in *The German-Jewish Dialogue: An Anthology of Literary Texts, 1794–1993,* ed. Richie Robertson (Oxford: Oxford University Press, 1999), 265.

49. Dunn, *Catholic Church in Russia,* 80.

50. Tereska Torres, *Le choix* (Paris: Desclée de Brouwer, 2002); Tereska Torres, *The Converts* (New York: Knopf, 1970).

51. Torres, *Choix,* 78.

52. Ibid., 109.

53. Dunn, *Catholic Church in Russia,* 80.

54. Quoted in Gugelot, "De Ratisbonne à Lustiger," 18.

55. Quoted in ibid.

56. Raïssa Maritain, "Á propos du Christianisme de Henri Bergson," *OCJRM* 14:1146.

57. Raïssa Maritain, "Élisabeth-Marie," reprinted in *Aventures de la grâce, OCJRM* 14:910–11.

58. Schor, *Antisémitisme en France.*

59. Barré, *Jacques and Raïssa Maritain,* 145.

60. Benbassa, *Jews of France,* 179.

61. Ibid., 88.

62. Susan Zuccotti, *Under His Very Windows: The Vatican and the Holocaust in Italy* (New Haven: Yale University Press, 2005), 16.

63. This lecture was published as Henri de Lubac, "Le fondement theologique des missions," *Bibliotheque de l'Union mission du clerge de France* (1941): 3–29, and was partially reproduced and translated in Henri de Lubac, *Theology in History* (San Francisco: Ignatius Press, 1996), 367–427.

64. Ibid., 466.

65. See the excellent article by Fourcade, "Maritain face au réveil."

66. Benbassa, *Jews of France,* 155.

67. Ibid., 155–56. This paragraph refers only to Christian anti-Nazi work in the years preceding the war. For an helpful analysis of Catholics during the war years, see Henri de Lubac, *Mémoire sur l'occasion de mes écrits* (Namur: Culture et verité, 1989); and Henri de Lubac, *Résistance chrétienne à l'antisémitisme: Souvenirs, 1940–1944* (Paris: Fayard, 1988); Renée Bédarida, *Les armes de l'esprit: Témoignage chrétien* (Paris: Ouvrières, 1977). For the mixed Catholic responses, particularly the tensions between the laity and largely conformist clergy, see Fouilloux, *Chrétiens français.*

68. Lubac did insist that "the explanation of Judaism is not to be found within itself. . . . It achieves its full meaning at the very moment when, as such, it ceases to be" (*Catholicism,* 59). But later, during the Occupation, he veered away from the language of Christian displacement or replacement of Judaism: in 1946 he asserted the "indissoluble bond between our two Testaments" and the importance of "always, in the final analysis, interpreting the Old by the New, but also always basing the New in the Old" so as to "remain faithful to the teaching of Saint Ireneaus, which was that of all our Doctors: the writings of Moses are Words of Christ" (Henri de Lubac, *Le fondement théologique des missions* [Paris: Éditions de Seuil, 1946], 27). Similarly, Lubac's fellow priest, theologian, and Lyon Resistance member Joseph Chaine wrote: The New Testament "does not destroy the Old, but there is the most perfect synthesis. . . . Between the two Testaments there is only continuity" (Joseph Chaine, "La Révélation de dieu en Israël," in *Israël et la foi chrétienne,* by Henri de Lubac, Joseph Chaine, Louis Richard, and Joseph Bonsirven [Fribourg: Éditions de la Librairie de l'Université, 1942], 80).

69. Doering, "Jewish Question," 147. Maritain's and Bernano's complete correspondence can be viewed at JRMA.

70. Roth, *Report,* 207.

71. Charles Journet and Jacques Maritain, *Correspondance,* ed. René Mougel (Freiburg: Éditions Universitaires, 1996–2008), 2:468–69.

72. Raïssa Maritain, *Histoire d'Abraham ou La sainteté dans l'état de nature* [1935], *OCJRM* 14:568–617.

73. Ibid., 569.

74. Ibid., 597.

75. Ibid., 596.

76. Ibid., 583 n. 8.

77. Ibid.

78. Quoted in Sebban, "Être juif et chrétien," 115.

79. R. Maritain, *Histoire d'Abraham, OCJRM* 14:617.

80. Richard Levy, ed. *Antisemitism: An Encyclopedia History* (Santa Barbara, CA: ABC Clio, 2005), 229.

81. According to Michael Phayer, the Catholic resistance community had very little in terms of pastoral guidance or words from the Vatican beyond this crucial phrase; see Michael Phayer's sobering *The Catholic Church and the Holocaust, 1930–1965* (Bloomington: Indiana University Press, 2000), 2–3, 52, 128.

82. See especially the essays "L'impossible antisémitisme," "Le mystère d'Israël," and "Les juifs parmi les nations," in Jacques Maritain's *L'impossible antisémitisme,* in *L'impossible antisémitisme, précédé de "Jacques Maritain et les juifs,"* par Pierre Vidal-Naquet (Paris: Desclée de Brouwer, 2003); Jacques Maritain,

"On Anti-Semitism" [1941], *OCJRM* 8:564. For more on Jacques Maritain and the Jewish question, see Crane, *Passion of Israel;* Robert Royal, ed., *Jacques Maritain and the Jews* (Notre Dame: Notre Dame University Press, 1994); Vidal-Naquet, "Jacques Maritain."

83. J. Maritain, *Carnet de notes, OCJRM* 12:402.

84. Réginald Garrigou-Lagrange, *Le judaïsme avant Jésus-Christ* (Paris: Gabalda et fils, 1931).

85. Raïssa Maritain to Pieter and Christine van der Meer de Walcheren, April 9, 1938, in *Le repentir: Déclaration de l'Église de France* (Paris: Desclée de Brouwer, 1997), 38–41.

86. Raïssa Maritain to Charles Journet, April 23, 1938, in Journet and Maritain, *Correspondance,* 2:702. See also, in the same volume, Jacques Maritain to Charles Journet, March 11, 1939, saying he feels "too disgusted, physically nauseated" (trop de dégoût, d'écoeurement physique) to write to Father Garrigou-Lagrange and saying it is not possible for him to reconnect with Garrigou-Lagrange, who has done far too much harm (811–14).

87. R. Maritain, *Journal de Raïssa, OCJRM* 15:398.

88. Ibid., 413.

89. Ibid.

90. Quoted in Sebban, "Être juif et chrétien," 116.

91. For the importance of the papacy in shaping people's beliefs, see Frank Coppa, *The Papacy, the Jews, and the Holocaust* (Washington, DC: Catholic University of America Press, 2006).

92. James Bernauer, "The Holocaust and the Catholic Church's Search for Forgiveness," paper presented at the Boisi Center for Religion and American Public Life, Boston College, October 30, 2002, www.bc.edu/dam/files /research_sites/cjl/texts/cjrelations/resources/articles/bernauer.htm.

93. On the pernicious underpinnings of philo-Semitic efforts, see Courtine-Denamy, "Rejet identitaire"; Berlinerblau, "On Philo-Semitism"; Moyn, "Antisemitism, Philosemitism."

94. See Schneider, "Max Jacob juif."

95. Gauri Viswanathan, *Outside the Fold: Conversion, Modernity, and Belief* (Princeton: Princeton University Press, 1998).

96. Sachs, *Witches' Sabbath,* 113.

Chapter 4. Poetry "in the Storm of Life"

1. Raïssa Maritain, "La couronne d'épines," *OCJRM* 15:544–45.

2. Denis Pelletier discusses the role of *Vigile* in his extensive review of Gugelot's *Conversion des intellectuels* in *Vingtième Siècle: Revue d'Histoire* 63

(July 1999): 167–69. For an analysis of the collapse of *Vigile,* see Edward Welch, *François Mauriac: The Making of an Intellectual* (New York: Éditions Rodopi, 2006), 38–41.

3. The table of contents of this issue reads: "'Dialogue spirituel,' par R. P. Surin; 'Le mariage dans la littérature religieuse du XVIIe siècle,' par H. Bremond; 'La tradition française et la chrétienté,' par E. Gilson; 'Préface à "Bonheur et souffrances du chrétien,"' par François Mauriac; 'La couronne d'épines,' par R. Maritain; 'L'enfant Mozart,' par H. Ghéon; 'De la connaissance métaphysique et des noms divins,' par J. Maritain."

4. Schloesser, *Jazz Age Catholicism.*

5. For a discussion of the concept of counterspaces making up "multiple modernities" alongside one another, see Charles Taylor, *Modern Social Imaginaries* (Durham: Duke University Press, 2004).

6. Thomas Munro and Leo Balet, "Detailed Communications," *Journal of Aesthetics and Art Criticism* 1, no. 4 (Winter 1941–42): 73–81.

7. For one example of this perspective, see Marget, "Too Much Ado."

8. Thomas Merton, *Literary Essays of Thomas Merton,* ed. Patrick Hart (New York: New Directions, 1984), 308.

9. Czeslaw Milosz, *The Witness of Poetry* (Cambridge, MA: Harvard University Press, 1983), 4.

10. Ibid., 31.

11. Raïssa Maritain, "La poésie est-elle un mensonge?" *OCJRM* 14:1135–37; "Le poème en prose," *OCJRM* 14:1133–35; "Le poète et son temps," *OCJRM* 15:699–700; "Sens et non-sens en poésie," *OCJRM* 15: 659–82; "Magie, poésie, et mystique," *OCJRM* 15:683–98; and "Message aux poètes qui sont à la guerre," *OCJRM* 14:1136–37.

12. The phrase and concept of "religious sensorium" come from Hirschkind, "Ethics of Listening."

13. R. Maritain, *Journal de Raïssa, OCJRM* 15:413.

14. Milosz, *Witness of Poetry,* 84; R. Maritain, "Deus excelsus terribilis," *OCJRM* 15:628.

15. Although his Catholicism could never have been that far away; Cocteau lived for most of his adult life with his mother, a devout Catholic who attended Mass daily. Jean Cocteau and Jacques Maritain, *Lettre à Jacques Maritain et la réponse à Jean Cocteau* (Paris: Delamain, 1926).

16. Bressolette, preface to Sachs, J. Maritain, and R. Maritain, *Correspondance: Maurice Sachs,* 10.

17. For more on Maritain and Cocteau's friendship, see Stephen Schloesser, "Maritain on Music: His Debt to Cocteau," in *Beauty, Art, and the Polis,* ed. Alice Ramos (Washington, DC: Catholic University Press, 2000).

18. Cocteau and Maritain, *Lettre;* Cocteau and Maritain, *Correspondance,* 87. While most of the correspondence between Raïssa and Cocteau is included in Cocteau and Maritain, *Correspondance,* I would like to thank René Mougel of JRMA for showing me the remainder of their unpublished exchanges.

19. In Cocteau's poem "Le feu du feu," the line now reads, "entre la Vierge et moi les anges vont et viennent." Cocteau and Maritain, *Correspondance,* 90.

20. Ibid.

21. Ibid., 92–93.

22. Ibid., 111.

23. Bloy, *Celle qui pleure,* 221.

24. The original is worth quoting in full, as the intensity is hard to capture in English: "Il ne reste plus que l'Art. Un art proscrit, il est vrai, méprisé, subalternisé, famélique, fugitif, guenilleux et catacombal. Mais, quand même, c'est l'unique refuge pour quelques âmes altissimes condamnées à traîner leur souffrante carcasse dans les charogneux carrefours du monde." Bloy, *Désespéré,* 20.

25. R. Maritain, *Journal de Raïssa, OCJRM* 15:239–40.

26. "Crainte des règles établies? Vieille rudesse masculine? Il ne paraîtra que sous mon nom. J'aurais dû exiger que Raïssa le signe avec moi." J. Maritain, *Carnet de notes, OCJRM* 12:217.

27. My thanks to René Mougel of JRMA for showing me these various versions of *Art and Scholasticism.*

28. Jacques Maritain, *Art and Scholasticism,* translated by J. F. Scanlan (New York: Scribner's, 1930), 150.

29. Ibid., 37. For an excellent discussion of Jacques's influence on European artists affiliated with the modernist movement, see the essays in Rajesh Heynickx and Jan De Maeyer, eds., *The Maritain Factor: Taking Religion into Interwar Modernism* (Leuven: Leuven University Press, 2010).

30. R. Maritain, *Journal de Raïssa, OCJRM* 15:241.

31. One Jewish convert remembers the overlaps between André Breton and other surrealists and the Maritains' salon: "Only years later did I realize how similar those two milieus were. In their discussions of poetry, both the Maritains and Breton would allude to Aloysius Bertrand and the dark Nerval, especially from his blackest period. Both admired Max Jacob, who was also a convert, and treated Lautréamont's youthful ravings reverentially and with deadly seriousness. . . . There were more similarities than differences between the 'convulsive beauty' that Breton advocated and the 'transcendental beauty' that is the *form* of being. There were differences in language

and in metaphysics, but the saliva and earthy nourishment were the same. Neither the demonic Breton, who practiced training the imagination, nor the mystical Raïssa, nor the last of the great scholastics, Maritain, had any confidence in nature. Neither art nor morality was supposed to serve nature or imitate it. Rather they were to conquer it, to subvert it, to irradiate it, or at least to shake loose everything that is simply natural." Kott, *Still Alive,* 20.

32. R. Maritain, "Sens et non-sens," *OCJRM* 15:680.

33. R. Maritain, "Magie, poésie, et mystique," *OCJRM* 15:689.

34. Raïssa Maritain, "De la poésie," *OCJRM* 15:711–12.

35. Ibid., 710.

36. Jan Kott, "Raised and Written in Contradictions: The Final Interview," interview by Allen J. Kuharski, *New Theater Quarterly* 18, no. 70 (May 2002): 104.

37. Raïssa Maritain to Catherine Pozzi, 1930, in Pozzi et al., *Élégance et le chaos,* 57.

38. Ibid.

39. R. Maritain, "Prière et poésie," *OCJRM* 15:847.

40. R. Maritain, *Journal de Raïssa, OCJRM* 15:373.

41. Ibid., 374.

42. Printed in ibid., 410–12.

43. Ibid., 407.

44. Henri de Lubac discusses this in his appended commentary to Étienne Gilson, "Annexes," in *Lettres de M. Étienne Gilson adressées au P. Henri de Lubac et commentées par celui-ci,* ed. Henri de Lubac (Paris: Éditions du Cerf, 1986), 195–96.

45. Ibid.

46. Lawrence Shook, *Étienne Gilson* (Toronto: Pontifical Institute of Medieval Studies, 1984), 346.

47. R. Maritain, *Journal de Raïssa, OCJRM* 15:399.

48. R. Maritain, "Message aux poètes," *OCJRM* 14:1136–37. "Ceux qui sont capables de ce silence dans tout le mystère de sa hauteur, de sa largeur et de sa profondeur, ils ont aussi mission de lui prêter leur voix."

49. Ibid., 1137.

50. Ibid.

51. R. Maritain, *Journal de Raïssa, OCJRM* 15:398.

52. Ibid., 410.

53. Schloesser, *Jazz Age Catholicism,* 119. See Stephen Schloesser, "'Not Behind but Within': *Sacramentum et Res,*" *Renascence: Essays on Values in Literature* 58, no. 1 (Fall 2005): 17–39.

54. Raïssa Maritain, *Journal de Raïssa, OCJRM* 15:397.

55. Raïssa Maritain, "Méditation," *OCJRM* 15:750; English translation by Raïssa Maritain. For a second translation, see the volume of her poetry translated by an anonymous Benedictine monk, collected in *Patriarch Tree / Arbre Patriarche* (Worcester: Stanbrook Abbey Press, 1965). For a wonderful introduction to Maritain's poetry as well as a powerful English-language analysis of her poetic corpus, see chs. 5 and 6 in Suther, *Raïssa Maritain*.

56. Raïssa Maritain, "De profundis," *OCJRM* 15:759; English translation by Raïssa Maritain.

57. Raïssa Maritain, "Tout est lumière," *OCJRM* 15:534; English translation in *Patriarch Tree*.

58. Raïssa Maritain, "Chagall," *OCJRM* 15:551–52; English translation by Thomas Merton, *Jubilee,* April 1963, 26.

59. Ibid.

60. Ziva Amishai-Maisels, "Chagall's *White Crucifixion,*" *Art Institute of Chicago Museum Studies* 17, no. 2 (1991): 138–53.

61. Ibid.

62. Raïssa Maritain, "Chagall ou l'orage enchanté," *OCJRM* 15:29.

63. R. Maritain, *Journal de Raïssa, OCJRM* 15:414–16.

64. Ibid., 414.

65. Ibid., 379.

66. R. Maritain, *Journal de Raïssa, OCJRM* 15:402.

67. Ibid.

68. Raïssa Maritain, "De quelques musiciens," *OCJRM* 14:1117.

69. Catherine Pozzi to Raïssa Maritain, July 18, 1931, in Pozzi et al., *Élégance et le chaos,* 94.

70. For my thinking on devotional practice and history, I am indebted to Michel de Certeau's *Possession at Loudun;* Orsi's *Between Heaven and Earth,* 3–5, 169–70; and Amy Hollywood's "Gender, Agency, and the Divine in Religious Historiography," *Journal of Religion* 84, no. 4 (October 2004): 514–24.

71. R. Maritain, *Journal de Raïssa, OCJRM* 15:413.

72. Raïssa Maritain, "Aux morts désespérés," *OCJRM* 15:546; English translation in *Patriarch Tree*.

73. Raïssa Maritain, "Pietà," *OCJRM* 15:542.

74. Ibid.

75. Carolyn Forché, *Against Forgetting: Twentieth-Century Poetry of Witness* (New York: Norton, 1993), 31.

76. R. Maritain, *Journal de Raïssa, OCJRM* 15:150.

77. Certeau, *Writing of History,* 119.

78. This language comes from Certeau's analysis in *Possession at Loudon,* 51.

79. Suther, *Raïssa Maritain,* 106; Marget, "Too Much Ado."

Chapter 5. Holy Suffering, Memory, and the Irredeemable Present ·

1. R. Maritain, *Grandes amitiés, OCJRM* 14:625–26.

2. René Mougel, "Les années de New York, 1940–1945," *Cahiers Jacques Maritain* 16–17 (April 1988): 9–11.

3. After the publication of the first volume in 1941, *Les grandes amitiés* (New York: Éditions de la Maison Française, 1941), which was translated into English by Julie Kernan as *We Have Been Friends Together* (New York: Longmans Press, 1942), the second volume was published along with the first volume in the French edition, *Les grandes amitiés, Les aventures de la grâce* (New York: Éditions de la Maison Française, 1944), but was issued separately in an English translation by Julie Kernan as *Adventures in Grace (Sequel to We Have Been Friends Together)* (New York: Longmans Press, 1945).

4. See Julie Kernan, *Our Friend Jacques Maritain: A Personal Memoir* (Garden City, NY: Doubleday, 1975), ch. 2.

5. In addition to the two volumes of *Les grandes amitiés,* Maritain's other memoirs during and immediately following the war include "Quelques souvenirs sur Ève Lavallière," *La Rotonde* 8, no. 4 (February 20, 1940): 4; "Henri Bergson," *Commonweal* 33, no. 13 (January 17, 1941): 317–19; "Notre maître perdu et retrouvé," *Revue Dominicaine* 47 (February 1941): 61–68; "Léon Bloy as We Knew Him," *Commonweal* 34, no. 16 (August 15, 1941): 390–94; "Bergson," *Commonweal* 34, no. 19 (August 29, 1941): 446–47; "Rouault," *Art News* 40, no. 17 (December 15, 1941): 14, 27–28; "Léon Bloy's Columbus," *Commonweal* 36, no. 26 (October 16, 1942): 606–10; *Marc Chagall* (New York: Éditions de la Maison Française, 1943); *De ordinatione angelorum,* musical arrangement by Arthur Lourié to texts of Thomas Aquinas chosen by Raïssa Maritain, *Thomist* 5 (January 1943): 319–44; "Jours de soleil en France: Souvenirs," in *Les oeuvres nouvelles III* (New York: Éditions de la Maison Française, 1943), 47–76; "My First Reading of the *Summa Theologica,*" *Commonweal* 39, no. 10 (December 24, 1943): 246–47; "Souvenirs," *Gants du Ciel* 2 (December 1943): 61–79; "Souvenirs de sa filleule," *Cahiers du Rhône* 11 (1943): 127–38; "De quelques-uns qui étaient jeunes en 1912," *Nova et Vetera* 19, no. 4 (October–December 1944): 380–401; "André Gide," *Revue Dominicaine* 51 (February 1945): 120–23; "Rouault: Remembering a Friendship," *Art News* 44, no. 5 (April 15–30, 1945): 17–18, 30; "Ernest Psichari: 1911–1912,"

Commonweal 42, no. 1 (April 20, 1945): 10, 12, 14; "Léon Bloy: Souvenirs inédits," *Témoignage Chrétien* 123 (October 4, 1946): 4; her edition of Bloy's writings entitled *Pilgrim of the Absolute;* "Henri Ghéon: Raïssa Maritain ci parla del suo grande amico," *Filodrammatica* 3 (March 1947): 4–5; "Léon Bloy et Israël," *Confluences* 7, nos. 15–17 (1947): 305–16; "Léon Bloy: Master of Paradox," *Commonweal* 54, no. 7 (May 25, 1951): 161–65.

6. Walter Benjamin, "Theses on the Philosophy of History," in *Illuminations,* ed. Hannah Arendt, trans. Harry Zohn (New York: Shocken Books, 1968), 255.

7. Ibid., 256.

8. For the notion of French exiles in New York as aristocratic intellectuals, see Jeffrey Mehlman, *Émigré New York: French Intellectuals in Wartime Manhattan, 1940–1944* (Baltimore: Johns Hopkins University Press, 2000). For a discussion of Benjamin's suicide, see Hannah Arendt's introduction to *Illuminations,* 11–13.

9. R. Maritain, *Grandes amitiés, OCJRM* 14:808.

10. In thinking about how various genres of writing, including memoirs, can relate to the political imagination, I have been aided by the work of Dipesh Chakrabarty, particularly "Nation and Imagination," in *Provincializing Europe,* 149–79, as well as his later essay "Memories of Displacement: The Poetry and Prejudice of Dwelling," in *Habitations of Modernity,* 115–37.

11. R. Maritain, *Grandes amitiés, OCJRM* 14:626.

12. This phrase is taken from a letter she wrote to her friend and goddaughter Achsa Belkind on December 24, 1945, reprinted in R. Maritain, *Journal de Raïssa, OCJRM* 15:436.

13. R. Maritain, "Deus excelsus terribilis," *Commonweal* 40, no. 24 (September 29, 1944), 563–66 (for a revised, slightly condensed version of this poem, see *OCJRM* 15:625–31).

14. To help me think about the need for less teleological and progressivist language to deal with historical subjects like the one I treat here, see Chakrabarty, *Provincializing Europe,* and his "Subaltern Histories and Post-Enlightenment Rationalism," in *Habitations of Modernity,* 20–37.

15. I have relied on the following for background historical information for this chapter: Michel Fourcade, "Jacques Maritain et l'Europe en exil," *Cahiers Jacques Maritain* 28 (June 1994), 5–38; Emmanuelle Loyer, *Paris à New York: Intellectuels et artistes français en exil 1940–1947* (Paris: Grasset, 2005); Mougel, "Années de New York"; Mehlman, *Émigré New York.*

16. Raïssa Maritain to Charles Journet, January 24, 1940, in Journet and Maritain, *Correspondance,* 3:42.

17. R. Maritain, *Journal de Raïssa, OCJRM* 15:428.

18. Ibid., 425.

19. R. Maritain, *Journal de Raïssa, OCJRM* 15:432.

20. Jacques Maritain to Charles Journet, May 6, 1940, in Journet and Maritain, *Correspondance,* 3:68.

21. Jacques Maritain, private note, published for the first time in Mougel, "Années de New York," 10–12.

22. Ibid.

23. *Devant la crise mondiale: Manifeste de catholiques européens séjournant en Amérique* (New York: Éditions de la Maison Française, 1942).

24. For Jacques's extensive political activity as an exile, see Mougel, "Années de New York"; Fourcade, "Jacques Maritain." For a helpful overview of history of the founding of the École libre, see Aristide R. Zolberg, "The École Libre at the New School, 1941–1946," *Social Research* 65 (Winter 1998): 921–51. For an excellent overview of how the events of the Shoah in 1940–44 prompted shifts in Jacques's thinking on Judaism, see Crane, *Passion of Israel,* ch. 3.

25. One of the most interesting activities at the school during Jacques's presidency was the Entretiens (symposia) de Pontigny held at Mount Holyoke College from 1942 to 1944. These symposia were modeled on the ten-day discussion meetings founded in Paris in 1910 and held in the Abbey Pontigny in Burgundy, France, until World War II. For three consecutive summers at Mount Holyoke, European and American intellectuals, musicians, artists, and writers attended and presented at these conferences, including Jacques, Gustave Cohen, Marc Chagall, Claude Lévi-Strauss, and Hannah Arendt. After the liberation of France in 1944, the Entretiens de Pontigny resumed in Burgundy. The Entretiens de Pontigny at Mount Holyoke were recently recreated at Mount Holyoke the summer of 2003 in a conference entitled "Artists, Intellectuals, and World War II: The Pontigny Encounters at Mount Holyoke College, 1942–1944." See the book under that same title, *Artists, Intellectuals, and World War II: The Pontigny Encounters at Mount Holyoke College, 1942–1944,* ed. Christopher E. Benfey and Karen Remmler (Amherst: University of Massachusetts Press, 2006).

26. Jean-Luc Barré, *Jacques and Raïssa Maritain: Beggars for Heaven,* trans. Bernard Doering (Notre Dame: University of Notre Dame Press, 1999), 361. Czeslaw Milosz's original preface is reprinted in *Cahiers Jacques Maritain* 16–17 (April 1988): 25–40.

27. For the reception history of *Les grandes amitiés,* see Élodie Chapelle, "La réception des *Grandes Amitiés*," *Cahiers Jacques Maritain* 48 (June 2004): 38–67, and "La réception des *Grandes Amitiés* de Raïssa Maritain," PhD diss., Université de Paris IV Sorbonne, 2002–3.

28. Éditions de la Maison Française was a New York publisher that specialized in the publication of the works of the numerous French writers who had recently arrived as war exiles to the United States.

29. For publication information on the various translations of *Les grandes amitiés*, see "Bibliographie générale," in *OCJRM* 15:876–77, 884–86. René Mougel's "Relire *Les grandes amitiés*," *Cahiers Jacques Maritain* 48 (June 2004): 27–37, helpfully traces the new editions in various languages throughout the 1950s, '60s, and '70s.

30. For an overview of the American responses and reception of the news of the Holocaust, see the report by Walther Laqueur, *The First News of the Holocaust* (New York: Leo Beck Institute, 1979). See also Martin Gilbert, *The Holocaust: A History of the Jews in Europe during the Second World War* (New York: Henry Holt, 2005), 43.

31. Johannes Oesterreicher, *Racisme, antisémitisme et antichristianisme* (New York: Éditions de la Maison Française, 1943). Johannes Oesterreicher was an Austrian Jew who converted to Roman Catholicism and became a priest and an ardent Nazi resister. Later a theologian, Oesterreicher became a leading advocate of Jewish-Catholic reconciliation. He was one of the architects of *Nostra Aetate*. On Oesterreicher's work in Europe in the 1930s and throughout the Holocaust, see *Christian Responses to the Holocaust*, ed. Donald Dietrich (Syracuse: Syracuse University Press, 2003), 138–49.

32. On the refusal of many to publicly acknowledge what was happening, Jacques was always much more biting than Raïssa. In 1940, he wrote in *Commonweal* how shocking it was that people closed their eyes to the persecution. In 1941 he added, this time more sardonically, in Reinhold Niebuhr's *Christianity and Crisis*, "People think that, after all, the concentration camps are more comfortable for their neighbors than the Jews say, and finally they will find themselves perfectly able to look at or contribute to the destruction of their friends, with the smile of a clear conscience (life must go on!)." Jacques Maritain, "Ten Months Later," *Commonweal* 32, no. 9 (June 1940): 180–84; J. Maritain, "On Anti-Semitism," 2.

33. For an overview of Catholic responses to these facts as they emerged, both in the United States and in Europe, see Phayer, *Catholic Church*.

34. Letter reprinted in R. Maritain, *Journal de Raïssa, OCJRM* 15:436.

35. Charles Journet to Raïssa Maritain, September 10, 1940, in Journet and Maritain, *Correspondance*, 3:60. Journet's characteristic encouragement of Raïssa's writing bolstered his advice: "Oh que c'est bien cette idée des *Souvenirs!* J'ai toujours pensé que vous deviez avoir un Journal, Raïssa, pour

dire tant des choses qui n'ont pas été sues, ou que nous oublions. Et qui apporteraient une lumière si chère sur ce passé."

36. J. M. Cameron, "Frank Sheed and Catholicism," *Review of Politics* 37, no. 3 (July 1975): 275–85.

37. R. Maritain, *Journal de Raïssa, OCJRM* 15:253.

38. R. Maritain, *Grandes amitiés, OCJRM* 14:807–8.

39. Jay Winter, *Sites of Memory, Sites of Mourning: The Great War in European Cultural History* (Cambridge: Cambridge University Press, 1995), 222.

40. R. Maritain, *Journal de Raïssa, OCJRM* 15:407.

41. R. Maritain, *Grandes amitiés, OCJRM* 14:636–37.

42. Ibid., 637.

43. Ibid., 628.

44. Ibid., 630–31.

45. Rev. James Gilles, "Sursum Corda: What's Right with the World," *Catholic News,* May 24, 1943, JRMA.

46. Graham Greene, "The Maritains," *New Statesman and Nation,* September 9, 1944, JRMA.

47. R. Maritain, *Grandes amitiés, OCJRM* 14:736–38.

48. Ibid., 736.

49. Ibid., 741.

50. Ibid., 1057.

51. Ibid., 1058.

52. Ibid.

53. Ibid.

54. Ibid., 1059.

55. Quoted in Jean Wahl, "Concerning Bergson's Relation to the Catholic Church," *Review of Religion* 9, no. 1 (November 1944): 45–50.

56. R. Maritain, *Aventures de la grâce, OCJRM* 14:899.

57. Ibid., 1060.

58. R. Maritain, *Grandes amitiés, OCJRM* 14:791.

59. Ibid., 745.

60. R. Maritain, *Aventures de la grâce, OCJRM* 14:1077.

61. Ibid., 1074.

62. Ibid., 627.

63. Ibid., 639.

64. Ibid.

65. These are unpublished letters written to Raïssa and currently catalogued in JRMA. I thank the initial work of Élodie Chapelle, whose excellent unpublished dissertation, "Réception des *Grandes Amitiés*," provided me with an essential map into many of the archived letters I examined and cite here.

66. J. Wilberforce to Raïssa Maritain, November 17, 1941, JRMA.

67. Matisia Maroni to Raïssa Maritain, n.d., JRMA.

68. Rev. Maurice Pierquin, Canada, to Raïssa Maritain, December 13, 1941, JRMA.

69. Père Pressoir to Raïssa Maritain, May 4, 1947, JRMA.

70. Ibid.

71. Robert Leclercq to Raïssa Maritain, February 10, 1956, JRMA.

72. R. Maritain, *Marc Chagall.*

73. Ibid., 21.

74. Daniel Catton Rich, Director of Fine Arts at the Chicago Art Institute, to Monroe Wheeler, MoMA, November 27, 1944, reprinted in Benjamin Harshav, *Chagall and His Times: A Documentary Narrative* (Palo Alto: Stanford University Press, 2004), 548–50.

75. See Harold Rosenberg's review of *Marc Chagall* and the published exchange of letters between Maritain and Rosenberg in *Contemporary Jewish Record* (American Jewish Committee) 7, no. 1 (1945): 190–91. As for Chagall himself, he seems to have appreciated Maritain's book and they became very close friends. Chagall admitted to Raïssa in a letter that he was often misunderstood and expected controversy around issues of his religion. See Chagall to Raïssa Maritain, April 15, 1955, in JRMA: "Ce dont je ne doute pas, c'est que j'aurai des critiques de tous côtés et surtout du côté des juifs qui veulent découvrir autre chose, ce qu'il y a dans mon âme et qui se permettent le luxe de douter, de toutes manières. . . . Il est vrai que je doute et que je m'ignore moi-même, la seule chose que je sache: c'est que je suis fidèle à quelque chose; fidèle bien sûr, à ma manière." He felt the critiques from the Jewish community acutely, but he also refused some of the Maritains' efforts to make Catholic-Jewish links through his art. After the Holocaust, he refused Jacques's requests to donate one of his paintings to the Vatican Museum of Modern Art. Harshav, *Chagall and His Times,* 704.

76. R. Maritain, *Grandes amitiés, OCJRM* 14:631.

77. R. Maritain, "Deus excelsus terribilis."

78. Because issues of translation are more difficult in relation to her poetry, I quote the original: "Quand nous avons reçu votre Parole / Nous avons souffert il est vrai / Dans le corps et dans l'âme—les sens et l'esprit / Et nous avons connu l'angoisse // Mais toujours nous avons pu situer notre souffrance / Et connaître qu'ailleurs le bonheur existait. / Toujours nous avons pu trouver quelque réponse / De la terre ou du ciel / L'apaisement que répand la lumière / Le rafraîchissement des larmes— la prière / Le souvenir au moins de l'espérance / Et l'amitié égale à la douleur // Tout cela est aboli / Tout cela que fut avant / Nous cheminons

parmi les morts / Et pleurons amèrement. / Le Dieu de notre foi nous a abandonnés / Il nous laisse à nous-mêmes. // Tout cela est englouti dans l'éternel passé / Tout cela que fut avant. / Avant que Dieu se soit entouré de terreurs / Avant qu'Il ait laissé aller son bras pesant / Et qu'Il ait fait paraître sa Justice / En noir soleil de ses décrets mystérieux." "Deus excelsus terribilis," *OCJRM* 15:563. English translation by Emily Scarborough with the assistance of Jacques Maritain.

79. It was read as a prayer dedicated (according to the terms of Raïssa): "To the memory of those / whom Hell wanted to exterminate / whom Hitler murdered / whom the world let perish / but whose painful and humiliated heart is with God / with Him in the eternal life." This epigraph is quoted in R. Maritain, "Bibliographie générale," *OCJRM* 15:924.

80. "Avant le martyre des Nations, / La France—en croix entre ses larrons— / La Pologne et leurs sœurs de misère. // Avant le massacre innombrable des Juifs, / La pitié d'Israël immolé par des esclaves / Salus es Judaeis! // Avant que Dieu ait voilé son visage / De ce voile de sang / Avant qu'Il se soit détourné de l'innocence."

81. "Si nous crions Abba! Pater! / Vous n'accueillez pas notre cri / Il nous revient comme une flèche / Qui a frappé la cible impénétrable, / Vous nous replongez dans la nuit. // C'est comme si nous avions perdu Notre Père / Qui est aux Cieux / Un abîme s'est ouvert entre la Miséricorde et la Misère / Et vous ne voulez pas le franchir."

82. "Nous n'oublierons jamais notre agonie / Nous nous en souviendrons dans la vie éternelle. / Ce que l'âme ne peut soutenir / Ce que ne peut ni s'imaginer ni se dire, / Ce que nous souffrons, ce que nous aurons souffert, / Nous en garderons éternellement le souvenir."

83. "La France brisée, souillée, ravagé, / La famine, là-bas, qui amenuise les corps, / Les enfants qui ne grandiront pas, / Les adolescents qui sont en esclavage, / En prison en captivité / Les jeunes françaises, / Les femmes aux travaux forcés / Et les otages de la haine / Mis à mort par milliers. / Ce qui ne peut se dire / Ce que l'esprit se refuse à porter."

84. "Quatre millions de Juifs—et davantage—ont subi la mort / sans consolation, / Ceux qui restent sont promis au carnage. / . . . / C'est Votre lignée—Seigneur—que l'on extermine! / Israël a été conduit à la boucherie / Troupeau sans pasteur sans bergerie. / Il a été traqué comme du gibier / Dans les rues des villes et des villages, / Les Jardins de la France. / Des femmes se sont jetées par les fenêtres / Avec leurs enfants pour ne pas livrer / Et d'autres se sont donné la mort pour fuir l'ignominie. / Des vieillards ont abrégé leurs jours / Parce qu'ils ont vu leur espérance condamnée."

85. "Laissez-moi donc parler selon la folie que saisit mon âme. / Nos jours sont mauvais, infestés par l'enfer, / Le désespoir tend ses pièges. / Nul ne sera sauvé si vous n'abrégez les jours / Livrés au Prince de ce monde. / La foi nous assure que tout est bien de votre côté, / Vous qui gouvernez l'Univers par la Sagesse. / Mais nous portons notre foi dans des ténèbres de sang / Parce que la cruauté et la haine ont inondé la terre / De leurs torrents irréprimés."

86. "C'est parce que Vous-même notre Dieu / Vous nous avez abandonnés. / Et l'Ange de la Vérité se tait / Miroir de votre indifférence, / Parce que vous nous avez abandonnés à nous-mêmes."

87. "Il en est temps, réveillez-vous Seigneur Jésus, venez! / O Vous qui avez pris un cœur semblable au nôtre / Pour compatir à nos souffrances. / Envoyez-nous une parole de lumière et de paix / Donnez-nous de comprendre selon votre sagesse / De parler selon votre intelligence / De consoler selon votre miséricorde. / Faites cesser les crimes. / Souvenez-vous de l'innocence. / Ayez pitié de votre peuple, / Le peuple de la misère et de la peine / Des humiliés et des opprimés de toutes les Nations, / Et des Juifs, les opprimés du monde. / Envoyez les Apôtres qui enchanteront notre douleur / Selon l'efficacité de votre amour / Et la douceur du Saint-Esprit, / Comme jadis vous avez suscité vos psalmistes / Et donné l'enthousiasme et la connaissance / Aux Prophètes / Pour notre salut."

88. Raïssa Maritain, "Portes de l'horizon," *OCJRM* 15:621. English translation by Raïssa, *OCJRM* 15:760. "Portes de l'horizon chancelant dans l'ombre / Écroulement sans fin aux confins des cieux / Épaves des mondes brisés—décombres / Âmes tombées aux labyrinthes infernaux / De la démence Ô désespoir où courir / Dans l'orage universel où tout brûle / Sous la poussée des meurtriers désirs / Tout périt du bonheur de la vie / Plus rien ne sera où vivrait l'espérance / Le feu prend ce que l'homme a trahi / Et le ciel embrasé enfante des astres nouveaux / Luminaires orgueilleux pour éclairer le désastre / Et la mort."

89. Raïssa Maritain, "Le prisonnier," *OCJRM* 15:586–87, translated as "The Prisoner" by Thomas Merton in *Jubilée*, April 1963, 26. "Votre serviteur est dans les fers / À l'ombre de la mort / Délivrez-le Seigneur / Je vois son visage derrière la grille / Comme celui d'un saint sur les images de piété / Son large visage et ses yeux proéminents / Et la frange de ses cheveux noirs sur le front / Avec quelques traits de laine blanche / Il ressemble au Christ / De Quentin Matsys / Il regarde droit devant lui / Étonné du malheur / Il voit le ciel de Dieu / Et que tout sera bien // Mais non il n'est pas encore peint sur les images / Il est assis sur son grabat / Sa tête est pliée dans ses bras / Il pleure / Il est seul au milieu d'ennemis / Qui

haïssent tout ce qu'il aime / À qui sa bonté son esprit / Ne sont rien qu'objet de mépris / Il est prisonnier de son innocence / Il garde patience / Comme son Maître Jésus-Christ / Et il est triste jusqu'à la mort / comme lui / Il a tant aimé la justice / Il ressemble au Christ de Quentin Matsys / Il apprend la langue du ciel."

90. Raïssa Maritain to Achsa Belkind, December 24, 1945, in *Journal de Raïssa, OCJRM* 15:436.

91. Raïssa Maritain, "La poésie de notre temps," *OCJRM* 15:717.

92. R. Maritain, "De la poésie," *OCJRM* 15:711.

93. Bloy, *Pilgrim of the Absolute,* 130.

94. R. Maritain, *Grandes amitiés, OCJRM* 14:721.

95. Chakrabarty, "Modernity and the Past: A Critical Tribute to Ashis Nandy," in *Habitations of Modernity,* 45–46.

96. Henry Bergson, *Matter and Memory,* trans. Nancy Paul (London: Allan, 1912), 70.

97. Ibid., 93.

98. Bloy, *Woman Who Was Poor,* 85–86.

99. Augustine, *Confessions* 10.8, trans. R. S. Pine-Coffin (New York: Penguin Books, 1961).

100. R. Maritain, "Léon Bloy: Master of Paradox," 161.

101. Ibid., 161–65.

102. For the classic discussions of memory and Christianity, see Elizabeth Castelli, *Martyrdom and Memory: Early Christian Culture-Making* (New York: Columbia University Press, 2004), and Mary Carruthers, *The Book of Memory,* 2nd ed. (Cambridge: Cambridge University Press, 2008).

103. A. S. Wolfers to Raïssa Maritain, October 15, 1941, JRMA.

104. George Shuster, *New York Herald Tribune,* April 5, 1942, JRMA.

105. Chakrabarty, "Nation and Imagination," in *Habitations of Modernity,* 149.

106. Jacques Maritain, *Le mystère d'Israël et autres essais* (Paris: Desclée de Brouwer, 1965). Raïssa Maritain, "Le nom d'Israël," *OCJRM* 15:650.

Conclusion

1. "Raïssa Maritain, Bibliographie générale," *OCJRM* 15:876–77, 884–86. See also Mougel's "Relire *Les grandes amitiés.*"

2. This scrapbook is available for viewing at the Maritain archives.

3. J. Maritain, "Avertissement," *OCJRM* 15:156.

4. C. G. Paulding, speech published in *Commonweal,* April 13, 1945, 333.

5. Ibid.

6. See Richard Crane's excellent article, "A Heart-Rending Ambivalence: Jacques Maritain and the Complexity of Postwar Catholic Philosemitism," *Studies in Christian-Jewish Relations* 6, no. 1 (2011), http://ejournals.bc.edu/ojs/index.php/scjr/article/view/1820.

7. This story is recounted by Elizabeth Fourest, friend of the Maritains, in the documentary film *Jacques Maritain's Farewell to America,* dir. Elizabeth Fourest, 1996.

8. Raïssa Maritain, "Comme on meurt" [As One Dies], English translation by Raïssa Maritain, *OCJRM* 15:761. "Comme on meurt / O douloureux repos ô pure inconnaissance / Dieu présent mais voile / Du voile éblouissant de Vos Mystères de Votre essence // Aimant de toute creature / Et l'âme de Votre Espirit attire / Vous meme êtes présent et seul en elle / Vous Dieu cache / Que nul de Son vrai Nom n'appelle // Elle n'a pour Vous parler que son souffle et sa plainte / Elle éprouve d'une crainte sacrée / L'ouevre que Vous accomplissez dans les profondeurs / Où elle s'ignore / Elle gémit comme l'arbe qui va tomber."

9. R. Maritain, "Deus excelsus terribilis," *OCJRM* 15:625.

10. Jean Cocteau to Jacques Maritain, December 11, 1960, in Cocteau and Maritain, *Correspondance,* 238–40.

11. J. Maritain, "Avertissement," *OCJRM* 15:159.

12. Ibid., 160–61.

13. Jacques Maritain to Joseph Cunneen, November 21, 1966, Thomas Merton Center, www.merton.org.

14. Thomas Merton to Joseph Cunneen, November 21, 1966, Thomas Merton Center, www. merton.org.

15. Jacques Maritain to Charles Journet, June 1967, in Journet and Maritain, *Correspondance,* 6:478.

16. Ibid.

17. Jacques Maritain, *Peasant of the Garonne: An Old Layman Questions Himself about the Present Time* (New York: Holt, Rinehart and Winston, 1968), 251.

18. J. Maritain, *Carnet de notes, OCJRM* 12:172–86.

19. R. Maritain, *Journal de Raïssa, OCJRM* 15:150.

20. Ibid., 325.

21. Recounted in ibid., 190.

22. R. Maritain, *Histoire d'Abraham, OCJRM* 14:597.

23. J. Maritain, *Peasant of the Garonne,* 251.

24. Philip Nord, "Catholic Culture in Interwar France," *French Politics, Culture, and Society* 21, no. 33 (Fall 2003): 1.

25. R. Maritain, "Récit de ma conversion," *OCJRM* 15:837.

26. Simone de Beauvoir, *Memoirs of a Dutiful Daughter* (New York: Harper, 2005), 195.

27. J. Maritain, "Ten Months Later," 180.

28. Ibid.

29. J. Maritain, "On Anti-Semitism," 2.

30. R. Maritain, *Aventures de la grâce, OCJRM* 14:1070.

31. R. Maritain, *Journal de Raïssa, OCJRM* 15:436.

32. My thinking on religious writing as (sometimes) occupying an imaginative space at a step removed from the historical and political is indebted to Marshall, *Shattering of the Self*, and Hollywood, "Gender, Agency."

33. Jonas, *France and the Cult*. Kenneth Silver adds to this conversation by exploring the transition in the interwar avant-garde art scene from images of sacrifice and suffering to images of a pure classical past that could animate notions of a more pure, whole, harmonious French nation in *Esprit de Corps: The Art of the Parisian Avant-Garde and the First World War, 1914–1925* (Princeton: Princeton University Press, 1989).

34. R. Maritain, *Aventures de la grâce, OCJRM* 14:1072.

35. Bynum, *Fragmentation and Redemption*, 27–52.

36. Orsi, *Between Heaven and Earth*, 144–45.

37. Ibid.

38. Suther, *Raïssa Maritain*, 106; Lubac, "Annexes," 195–96.

39. On how gender ideology influences women's own scholarly and amateur writing, I have been aided by Bonnie Smith, *The Gender of History: Men, Women, and Historical Practice* (Cambridge, MA: Harvard University Press, 1998).

40. Jacques records this conversation in a footnote in R. Maritain, *Journal de Raïssa, OCJRM* 15:347.

41. Sachs, *Witches' Sabbath*, 33.

42. J. Maritain, "Avertissement," *OCJRM* 15:160.

43. Jean Cocteau to Jacques Maritain, December 11, 1960, in Cocteau and Maritain, *Correspondance*, 238–40.

44. Hollywood, "Inside Out," 79.

45. Certeau, *Possession at Loudun*, 225.

46. Bloy, *Pilgrim of the Absolute*, 301.

47. Moyn, "Antisemitism, Philosemitism," 3.

48. Robert Jay Lifton, "An Interview with Robert Jay Lifton," in *Trauma: Explorations in Memory*, ed. Cathy Caruth (Baltimore: Johns Hopkins University Press, 1995), 139.

49. Ibid.

50. Weingrad, "Jews (in Theory)."

51. Ibid.

52. Hammerschlag also discusses this issue (including Lyotard in particular and Weingrad's assessment of him) in *Figural Jew*, 9–10, 198.

53. Judt, "Problem of Evil," 35; see also Judt, "From the House of the Dead."

BIBLIOGRAPHY

Primary Sources (Raïssa Maritain)

Maritain, Raïssa. *Oeuvres complètes de Jacques et Raïssa Maritain.* 17 vols. Frieburg: Éditions Universitaires, 1982–2000. Vols. 14 and 15.

———. Unpublished manuscripts, notes, and correspondence. Maritain Archives, Cercle d'Études Jacques et Raïssa Maritain, Kolbsheim, France.

Note: Although Raïssa Maritain's complete works are found in volumes 14 and 15 of *Oeuvres complètes de Jacques et Raïssa Maritain,* and I have primarily cited this edition in the notes, the following list provides as well details of her significant publications at their original appearance. English translations are listed directly after the French when available. For a complete, detailed bibliography of Maritain's works, see *OCJRM* 15:855–930.

Maritain, Raïssa. "André Gide." *Revue Dominicaine* 51 (February 1945): 120–23.

———. *L'ange de l'école: Vie de Saint Thomas d'Aquin racontée aux enfants. OCJRM* 14:333–413. Originally published by Desclée de Brouwer (Paris, 1934). Translated by Julie Kernan as *St. Thomas Aquinas, the Angel of the Schools* (New York: Sheed and Ward, 1935).

———. "À propos du Christianisme de Henri Bergson." *OCJRM* 14:1146. Originally published in *Commonweal* 33, no. 13 (January 17, 1941): 317–19.

———. *Au creux du rocher: Poèmes.* Paris: Alsatia, 1954.

————. "Aux morts désespérés." *OCJRM* 15:546.

————. *Les aventures de la grâce. OCJRM* 14:818–1083. Originally published in *Les grandes amitiés. Les aventures de la grâce: Souvenirs* (New York: Éditions de la Maison Française, 1944). Translated by Julie Kernan as *Adventures in Grace (Sequel to We Have Been Friends Together)* (New York: Longmans, 1945).

————. "Bergson." *OCJRM* 14:1138–50. Originally published in *Commonweal* 34, no. 19 (August 29, 1941): 446–47.

————. "Chagall." *OCJRM* 15:551–52.

————. *Chagall ou l'orage enchanté. OCJRM* 15:12–44. Originally published by Éditions des Trois Collines (Geneva, 1948). Updated and revised version of Raïssa Maritain, *Marc Chagall* (Éditions de la Maison Française, 1943). An excerpt translated by Judith Suther as "Marc Chagall" in *French-American Review* 1, no. 1 (Winter 1976): 54–64.

————. "Comme on meurt." *OCJRM* 15:621. Originally published in *Portes d'horizon* (Bethlehem, CT: Regina Laudis, 1952).

————. "Concerning Henri Bergson: A Letter from Dr. A. S. Oko and a Reply from Raïssa Maritain." *OCJRM* 14:1138–50. Originally published in *Commonweal* 33, no. 20 (March 7, 1941): 492–94.

————. "La couronne d'épines." *OCJRM* 15:544–45. Originally published in *Vigile* 1 (1931): 97–101.

————. "De la poésie comme expérience spirituelle." *OCJRM* 15:710–15. Originally published as "La poésie comme expérience spirituelle" in *Fontaine* 19, no. 20 (March–April 1942): 22–25. Translated by Julie Kernan as "Poetry as Spiritual Experience" in *Spirit: A Magazine of Poetry* 9, no. 6 (January 1943): 181–83.

————. *De ordinatione angelorum.* Musical arrangement by Arthur Lourié to texts of Thomas Aquinas chosen by Raïssa Maritain. *Thomist* 5 (January 1943): 319–44.

————. "De profundis." *OCJRM* 15:759.

————. "De quelques musiciens." *OCJRM* 14:1117.

————. "De quelques-uns qui étaient jeunes en 1912." *Nova et Vetera* 19, no. 4 (October–December 1944): 380–401.

———— [R.M., pseud.], trans. *Des moeurs divines: Opuscule attribué à Saint Thomas d'Aquin. OCJRM* 14:177–203. Originally published by Pouart (Paris, 1921).

————. "Deus excelsus terribilis." *OCJRM* 15:625–31. Originally published in both French and English (translation by Emily Scarborough) in *Commonweal* 40, no. 24 (September 29, 1944): 563–66.

———— [R.M., pseud.], trans. *Les dons du Saint-Esprit: Traité de Jean de Saint-Thomas. OCJRM* 14:215–482. Translated from Latin to French with a preface by Réginald Garrigou-Lagrange, O.P. Juvisy: Éditions du Cerf. Originally published as a series of articles in 1926–29.

———. "Du recueillement poétique." *OCJRM* 14:1117. Originally published in *Études Carmélitaines* 22 (October–December 1937): 46–49.

———. "Ernest Psichari: 1911–1912." *Commonweal* 42, no. 1 (April 20, 1945): 10, 12, 14.

——— [R.M., pseud.], ed. and trans. "Est-il pour nous 'De la plus grand utilité de connaître les grâces dont nous sommes favorisés?'" *OCJRM* 14:1087–97. Originally published in *La Vie Spirituelle* 65, no. 11 (February 5, 1925).

———. *Les grandes amitiés: Souvenirs. OCJRM* 14:625–1085. Originally published by Éditions de la Maison Française (New York, 1941). Translated by Julie Kernan as *We Have Been Friends Together* (New York: Longmans, Green, 1942).

———. "Henri Bergson." *Commonweal* 33, no. 13 (January 17, 1941): 317–19.

———. "Henri Ghéon: Raïssa Maritain ci parla del suo grande amico." *Filodrammatica* 3 (March 1947): 4–5.

———. *Histoire d'Abraham, ou La sainteté dans l'état de nature. OCJRM* 14:568–617. Originally published in *Revue Catholique pour la Suisse Romande* 3 (1935).

———. *Journal de Raïssa.* Edited by Jacques Maritain. *OCJRM* 15:143–507. Originally published by Desclée de Brouwer (Paris, 1963). Translated by Antonia White as *Raïssa's Journal* (Albany, NY: Magi Books, 1975).

———. "Jours de soleil en France: Souvenirs." *OCJRM* 14:1117–26. Originally published in *Les oeuvres nouvelles III* (New York: Éditions de la Maison Française, 1943), 47–76. Translated as "A Handful of Musicians: Auric, Vines, Poulenc, Milhaud, Satie, Ravel, Falla, Stravinsky, Lourié," in *Commonweal* 39, no. 2 (October 29, 1943): 32–35.

———. "Léon Bloy as We Knew Him." *OCJRM* 15:793–804. Originally published in *Commonweal* 34, no. 16 (August 15, 1941): 390–94.

———. "Léon Bloy et Israël." *Confluences* 7, nos. 15–17 (1947): 305–16.

———. "Léon Bloy et le Révélateur du Globe." *OCJRM* 14:1097–1110.

———. "Léon Bloy: Master of Paradox." *Commonweal* 54, no. 7 (May 25, 1951): 161–65.

———. "Léon Bloy's Columbus." *OCJRM* 14:1097–1110. Originally published in *Commonweal* 36, no. 26 (October 16, 1942): 606–10.

———. "Léon Bloy: Souvenirs inédits." *Témoignage Chrétien* 123 (October 4, 1946): 4.

———. *Lettre de nuit; La vie donnée. OCJRM* 15:521–78. Originally published by Desclée de Brouwer (Bruges, 1939).

————. "Life of Jesus: The Only Book by Mauriac Which Is Free from Bitterness." *OCJRM* 15:809–16. Originally published in *Books on Trial* 10 (October 1951).

————. "Magie, poésie, et mystique." *OCJRM* 15:683–98. Originally published in *La Vie Intellectuelle* 10, no. 3 (June 25, 1938): 442–55.

————. *Marc Chagall.* New York: Éditions de la Maison Française, 1943.

————. "Méditation." *OCJRM* 15:750.

————. "Message aux poètes qui sont à la guerre." *OCJRM* 14:1136–37. Originally published in *Fontaine* 1, no. 6 (November–December 1939): 99.

————. "My First Reading of the *Summa Theologica.*" *Commonweal* 39, no. 10 (December 24, 1943): 246–47.

————. "Le nom d'Israël." *OCJRM* 15:650.

————. *Notes sur le Pater. OCJRM* 15:53–142. Originally published by Desclée de Brouwer (Paris, 1962). Translated by Julie Kernan as *Notes on the Lord's Prayer* (New York: P. J. Kenedy, 1964).

————. "Notre maître perdu et retrouvé." *Revue Dominicaine* 47 (February 1941): 61–68.

————. *Patriarch Tree / Arbre Patriarche.* Worcester: Stanbrook Abbey Press, 1965. English translation of a selection of Maritain's poems.

————. "Pietà." *OCJRM* 15:542.

————, ed. *Pilgrim of the Absolute,* by Léon Bloy. Translated by John Coleman. New York: Pantheon Books, 1947.

————. "Le poème en prose." *OCJRM* 14:1133–35. Originally published in *Le Journal des Poètes* 5, no. 6 (July 25, 1935): 4.

————. "La poésie de notre temps." *OCJRM* 15:717–19.

————. "La poésie est-elle un mensonge?" *OCJRM* 14:1135–37. Originally published in *Les Cahiers du Journal des Poètes* 70 (November 15, 1939): 30–31.

————. "Le poète et son temps." *OCJRM* 15:699–700. Originally published in *Les Cahiers du Journal des Poètes* 16 (July 10, 1936): 46–47.

————. "Portes de l'horizon." *OCJRM* 15:621. Originally published in *Portes de l'horizon* (Bethlehem, CT: Regina Laudis, 1952).

————. "Prière et poésie." *OCJRM* 15:841–50. Originally presented as a lecture to the Second American Congress for Aesthetics, April 24, 1942.

————. *Le prince de ce monde. OCJRM* 14:207–18. Paris: Desclée de Brouwer, 1929. Translated by Gerald B. Phelan as *The Prince of This World* (Toronto: Pontifical Institute of Medieval Studies, 1933).

————. "Le prisonnier." *OCJRM* 15:586–87. Translated by Thomas Merton as "The Prisoner" in *Jubilee,* April 1963, 26.

———. "Quelques souvenirs sur Ève Lavallière." *La Rotonde* 8, no. 4 (February 20, 1940): 4.

———. "Récit de ma conversion." *OCJRM* 15:827–34. Originally published in *Cahiers Jacques Maritain* 7–8 (1983): 77–84.

———. "Rouault." *Art News* 40, no. 17 (December 15, 1941): 14, 27–28.

———. "Rouault: Remembering a Friendship." *Art News* 44, no. 5 (April 15–30, 1945): 17–18, 30.

———. "Saint Thomas d'Aquin ou la sainteté de l'intelligence." *Temps Présent* 3, no. 69 (March 10, 1939): 7.

———. "Sens et non-sens en poésie." *OCJRM* 15:659–82. Originally published in *Deuxième Congrès International d'Esthétique et de Science de l'Art*, 171–74 (Paris: Félix Alcan, 1937).

———. "Souvenirs." *Gants du Ciel* 2 (December 1943): 61–79.

———. "Souvenirs de sa filleule." *Cahiers du Rhône* 11 (1943): 127–38.

———. "Three Poems from *Portes de l'horizon*." *Yale French Studies* 12 (1953): 4–7.

———. "Tout est lumière." *OCJRM* 15:534.

———. "Trois lettres de Raïssa." *Cahiers Jacques Maritain* 7–8 (September 1983).

———. *La vie donnée*. Paris: Raphaël Labergerie, 1935.

Primary Sources (Raïssa and Jacques Maritain)

Maritain, Jacques, and Raïssa Maritain. *De la vie d'oraison. OCJRM* 14:12–80. Originally published by L'Art Catholique (Paris, 1924). Translated by Algar Thorold as *Prayer and Intelligence: La Vie d'Oraison* (London: Sheed and Ward, 1938).

———. *Exiles and Fugitives: The Letters of Jacques and Raïssa Maritain, Allen Tate, and Caroline Gordon*. Baton Rouge: Louisiana State University Press, 1992.

———. *Liturgie et contemplation. OCJRM* 14:83–154. Originally published by Desclée de Brouwer (Bruges, 1959). Translated by Joseph Evans as *Liturgy and Contemplation* (New York: P. J. Kenedy, 1960).

———. "Notre maître perdu et retrouvé." *OCJRM* 14:159–65. Originally published in *Revue Dominicaine* 47 (1941): 61–68.

———. "Ode to the Confederate Dead" / "Ode aux morts confédérés." *Sewanee Review* 60 (Autumn–Winter 1952): 512–21.

———. *Situation de la poésie. OCJRM* 15:658–98. Originally published by Desclée de Brouwer (Paris, 1938). Translated by Marshall Suther as *The*

Situation of Poetry: Four Essays on the Relations between Poetry, Mysticism, Magic, and Knowledge (New York: Philosophical Library, 1955).

Additional Sources

Adorno, Theodor. "Commitment." In *Aesthetics and Politics: Key Texts of the Classic Debate within German Marxism,* edited by Ernst Bloch, 177–95. London: Verso, 2002.

Albert, Phyllis Cohen. *The Modernization of French Jewry.* Hanover: University Press of New England, 2007.

Allard, Jean-Louis. "Raïssa Maritain (1883–1960), une contemplative dans le monde." *Notes et Documents de l'Institut International Jacques et Raïssa Maritain* 4 (October–December 1983): 77–80.

Amishai-Maisels, Ziva. "Chagall's *White Crucifixion.*" *Art Institute of Chicago Museum Studies* 17, no. 2 (1991): 138–53.

Anderson, Amanda. "The Temptations of Aggrandized Agency: Feminist Histories and the Horizon of Modernity." *Victorian Studies* 43, no. 1 (Autumn 2000): 43–65.

Andral, Jean-Louis, and Sophie Krebs. *L'école de Paris, 1904–1929: La part de l'autre.* Paris: Gallimard, 2000.

Angelier, François. "Les écrivains et La Salette: Huysmans, Bloy, Claudel." *Communio: Revue Catholique Internationale* 22, no. 4 (1997): 49–56.

Angelier, François, and Claude Langlois, eds. *La Salette: Apocalypse, pèlerinage et littérature (1856–1996).* Grenoble: Éditions Jérôme Millon, 2000.

Antliff, Mark. *Avant-Garde Fascism: The Mobilization of Myth, Art, and Culture in France, 1909–1939.* Durham: Duke University Press, 2007.

Arendt, Hannah. *Between Past and Future.* New York: Penguin, 1968.

———. "Christianity and Revolution." *Nation,* September 22, 1945.

Aronowicz, Arnette. *Jews and Christians on Time and Eternity: Charles Péguy's Portrait of Bernard-Lazare.* Palo Alto: Stanford University Press, 1998.

Asad, Talal. "Trying to Understand French Secularism." In *Political Theologies: Public Religions in a Postsecular World,* edited by Hent de Vries and Lawrence E. Sullivan, 494–526. New York: Fordham University Press, 2006.

Atkin, Nicholas. *Priests, Prelates, People: A History of European Catholicism since 1750.* Cambridge: Oxford University Press, 2004.

Aubert, Roger. *La théologie catholique au milieu du XXe siècle.* Tournai: Casterman, 1954.

Augustine. *Confessions.* Translated by R. S. Pine-Coffin. New York: Penguin Books, 1961.

Avon, Dominique. *Les frères prêcheurs en Orient: Les dominicains du Caire (années 1910–années 1960)*. Paris: Éditions du Cerf, 2005.

Barré, Jean-Luc. *Jacques and Raïssa Maritain: Beggars for Heaven*. Translated by Bernard Doering. Notre Dame: University of Notre Dame Press, 1999. Originally published as *Jacques et Raïssa Maritain: Les mendicants du ciel: Biographies croisées* (Paris: Stock, 1995).

Baudelaire, Charles. "The Widows." In *The Poems and Prose of Charles Baudelaire*, edited by James Huneker, 125. New York: Bretanos, 1919.

Bazin, René. *Charles de Foucauld: Explorateur du Maroc, ermite au Sahara*. Paris: Plon, 1921.

Beauvoir, Simone de. *Memoirs of a Dutiful Daughter*. New York: Harper, 2005.

Becker, Annette. *War and Faith: The Religious Imagination in France, 1914–1930*. Translated by Catherine Temerson. New York: Berg, 1998.

Bédarida, Renée. *Les armes de l'esprit: Témoignage chrétien*. Paris: Ouvrières, 1977.

Benbassa, Esther. *The Jews of France: A History from Antiquity to the Present*. Translated by M. B. DeBevoise. Princeton: Princeton University Press, 1999.

Benfy, Christopher E., and Karen Remmler, eds. *Artists, Intellectuals, and World War II: The Pontigny Encounters at Mount Holyoke College, 1942–1944*. Amherst: University of Massachusetts Press, 2006.

Benjamin, Walter. *The Correspondence of Walter Benjamin (1910–1940)*. Edited by Gershom Scholem and Theodor Adorno. Translated by Manfred R. Jacobson. Chicago: University of Chicago Press, 1994.

———. "Theses on the Philosophy of History." In *Illuminations*, edited by Hannah Arendt, translated by Harry Zohn. New York: Shocken Books, 1968.

Berg, Christian. "Théodicées victimales au dix-neuviéme siècle en France de Joseph de Maistre à J. K. Huysmans." In *Victims and Victimization in French and Francophone Literature*, edited by Buford Norman, 87–100. New York: Rodopi, 2005.

Bergson, Henri. *Creative Evolution*. Translated by Arthur Mitchell. New York: H. Holt, 1911.

———. *Matter and Memory*. Translated by Nancy Paul. London: Allan, 1912.

———. *Time and Free Will: An Essay on the Data of Immediate Consciousness*. Translated by F. L. Pogson. New York: Dover, 2001.

Berlinerblau, Jacques. "On Philo-Semitism." In *Occasional Papers on Jewish Civilization, Jewish Thought and Philosophy*, 8–19. Washington, DC: Georgetown University, Program for Jewish Civilization, Winter 2007.

Bernard-Donals, Michael F., and Richard R. Glejzer. *Between Witness and Testimony: The Holocaust and the Limits of Representation*. New York: SUNY Press, 2001.

Bernauer, James. "The Holocaust and the Catholic Church's Search for Forgiveness." Paper presented at the Boisi Center for Religion and American Public Life, Boston College, October 30, 2002, www.bc.edu/dam/files/research_sites/cjl/texts/cjrelations/resources/articles/bernauer.htm.

Blackbourn, David. *Marpingen: Apparitions of the Virgin Mary in a Nineteenth-Century German Village*. New York: Knopf, 1994.

Blanc de Saint-Bonnet, Antoine. *De la douleur*. Lyon: Giberton et Brun, 1849.

Bliss, Michael. *The Making of Modern Medicine: Turning Points in the Treatment of Disease*. Chicago: University of Chicago Press, 2011.

Bloy, Léon. *Celle qui pleure: Notre Dame de La Salette*. Paris: Société du Mercure de France, 1908.

———. *Dans les ténèbres*. Paris: Mercure de France, 1918.

———. *Le désespéré*. Paris: A. Soirat, 1886.

———. *La femme pauvre*. 1897. Reprint, Paris: Mercure de France, 1932.

———. *Letters to His Fiancée*. Translated by Barbara Wall. New York: Sheed and Ward, 1937.

———. *Lettres à sa fiancée*. Paris: Stock, 1922.

———. *Lettres à ses filleuls, Jacques Maritain et Pierre van der Meer de Walcheren*. Paris: Librairie Stock, 1928.

———. *Mon journal*. Vol. 2. *1905–1907*. Paris: Mercure de France, 1956.

———. *Pilgrim of the Absolute*. Edited by Raïssa Maritain. Translated by John Coleman and Henry Lorin Binsse. New York: Pantheon Books, 1947.

———. *Le salut par les juifs*. 1892. Reprinted in *Le salut par les juifs: suivi de Le sang du pauvre; Sur la tombe de Huysmans; La résurrection de Villiers de l'Isle-Adam*. Paris: Union générale d'éditions, 1983.

———. *Le sang du pauvre*. 1922. Reprint, Paris: Librairie Stock, 1932.

———. *Le vieux de la montagne*. In *Le mendiant ingrat; Le vieux de la montagne*, vol. 7 of *L'oeuvre complète de Léon Bloy*. Paris: François Bernouard, 1948.

———. *The Woman Who Was Poor*. Translated by I. J. Collins. New York: Sheed and Ward, 1947.

Bosco, Mark. *Graham Greene's Catholic Imagination*. New York: Oxford University Press, 2005.

Boym, Svetlana. *The Future of Nostalgia*. New York: Basic Books, 2001.

Brady, Mary Rosalie. *Thought and Style in the Works of Léon Bloy*. Washington, DC: Catholic University of America Press, 1945.

Bremond, Henri. *Histoire littéraire du sentiment religieux en France depuis la fin des guerres de religion jusqu'à nos jours*. Paris: Bloud et Gay, 1916–36.

Bressolette, Michel. Preface to *Correspondance: Maurice Sachs / Jacques et Raïssa Maritain, 1925–1938*. Paris: Éditions Gallimard, 2004.

Brusco, Elizabeth. *The Reformation of Machismo: Evangelical Conversion and Gender in Colombia.* Austin: University of Texas Press, 1995.

Burton, Richard D. E. *Holy Tears, Holy Blood: Women, Catholicism, and the Culture of Suffering in France, 1840–1970.* Ithaca: Cornell University Press, 2004.

Bush, William. *Georges Bernanos.* New York: Twayne, 1969.

————. "Raïssa, Jacques and the Abyss of Christian Orthodoxy: The True Face of God, or Love and the Law." In *Jacques Maritain: The Man and His Metaphysics,* edited by John Knasas. Notre Dame, IN: American Maritain Association, 1988.

Bynum, Caroline Walker. *Fragmentation and Redemption: Essays on Gender and the Human Body in Medieval Religion.* New York: Zone Books, 2002.

————. "Introduction: The Complexity of Symbols." In *Gender and Religion: On the Complexity of Symbols,* edited by Caroline Walker Bynum, Stevan Harrell, and Paula Richman, 1–20. Boston: Beacon Press, 1986.

————. *Wonderful Blood: Theology and Practice in Later Medieval Northern Germany and Beyond.* Philadelphia: University of Pennsylvania Press, 2006.

Bynum, Caroline Walker, Stevan Harrell, and Paula Richman, eds. *Gender and Religion: On the Complexity of Symbols.* Boston: Beacon Press, 1986.

Byrnes, Joseph. *Catholic and French Forever: Religious and National Identity in Modern France.* University Park: Pennsylvania State Press, 2005.

Cameron, J. M. "Frank Sheed and Catholicism." *Review of Politics* 37, no. 3 (July 1975): 275–85.

Carruthers, Mary. *The Book of Memory.* 2nd ed. Cambridge: Cambridge University Press, 2008.

Caruth, Cathy, ed. *Trauma: Explorations in Memory.* Baltimore: Johns Hopkins University Press, 1995.

Castelli, Elizabeth. *Martyrdom and Memory: Early Christian Culture-Making.* New York: Columbia University Press, 2004.

Cattaui, Georges. "Raïssa Maritain." *Preuves,* January 1961, 68–69.

"Le Centenaire de Raïssa." Special issue, *Cahiers Jacques Maritain* 7–8 (September 1983).

Certeau, Michel de. *Heterologies: Discourse on the Other.* Translated by Tom Conley. Minneapolis: University of Minnesota Press, 1986.

————. "History and Mysticism." In *Histories: French Constructions of the Past,* edited by Jacques Revel and Lynn Hunt. 1973. Reprint, New York: New Press, 1998.

————. *The Mystic Fable.* Translated by Michael B. Smith. Chicago: University of Chicago Press, 1992.

———. *The Possession at Loudun*. Chicago: University of Chicago Press, 1996.

———. *The Writing of History*. Translated by Tom Conley. New York: Columbia University Press, 1988.

Chadwick, Kay, ed. *Catholicism, Politics and Society in Twentieth-Century France*. Liverpool: Liverpool University Press, 2000.

Chadwick, Owen. *The Secularization of the European Mind in the Nineteenth Century*. New York: Cambridge University Press, 1990.

Chaine, Joseph. "La Révélation de Dieu en Israël." In *Israël et la foi chrétienne*, by Henri de Lubac, Joseph Chaine, Louis Richard, and Joseph Bonsirven. Fribourg: Éditions de la Librairie de l'Université, 1942.

Chakrabarty, Dipesh. *Habitations of Modernity: Essays in the Wake of Subaltern Studies*. Chicago: University of Chicago Press, 2002.

———. *Provincializing Europe: Postcolonial Thought and Historical Difference*. Princeton: Princeton University Press, 2000.

Chapelle, Élodie. "La réception des *Grandes amitiés*." *Cahiers Jacques Maritain* 48 (June 2004): 38–67.

———. "La réception des *Grandes amitiés* de Raïssa Maritain." PhD diss., Université de Paris IV Sorbonne, 2002–3.

Chenaux, Philippe. *Entre Maurras et Maritain: Une génération intellectuelle catholique (1920–1930)*. Paris: Éditions du Cerf, 1999.

———. "Fumet éditeur." In *Stanislas Fumet ou La présence au temps,* edited by E. Germain. Paris: Cerf, 1999.

———. "Léon Bloy et sa postérité." In *Juifs et chrétiens: Entre ignorance, hostilité et rapprochement, 1898–1998,* edited by Annette Becker, Danielle Delmaire, and Frédéric Gugelot. Lille: Université Charles-de-Gaulle-Lille, 2002.

———. "Maritain et La Salette." In *La Salette: Apocalypse, pèlerinage et littérature, 1856–1996,* edited by François Angelier and Claude Langlois, 107–19. Grenoble: Editions Jérôme Millon, 2000.

Chenu, M.-D. "A conversation with Père Chenu." *Dominicana* 50 (1965): 141–45.

Coakley, John W. *Women, Men, and Spiritual Power: Female Saints and Their Male Collaborators*. New York: Columbia University Press, 2006.

Cocteau, Jean, and Jacques Maritain. *Correspondance, 1923–1963*. Edited by Michel Bressolette and Pierre Glaudes. Paris: Gallimard, 1998.

———. *Lettre à Jacques Maritain et la Réponse à Jean Cocteau*. Paris: Delamain, 1926.

Cohen, Paul M. *Piety and Politics: Catholic Revival and the Generation of 1905–1914 in France*. New York: Garland, 1987.

Comfort, Kathleen Ann. "Divine Images of Hysteria in Emile Zola's Lourdes." *Nineteenth-Century French Studies* 30, nos. 3 and 4 (Spring–Summer 2002): 330–46.

Comte, August. *The Positivist Philosophy of August Comte.* Translated by Harriet Martineau. Bristol: Themmes, 2001.

Congar, Yves. *The Meaning of Tradition.* Translated by A. Woodrow. San Francisco: Ignatius Press, 2004.

Connor, Peter Tracey. *Georges Bataille and the Mysticism of Sin.* Baltimore: Johns Hopkins University Press, 2000.

Coppa, Frank. *The Papacy, the Jews, and the Holocaust.* Washington, DC: Catholic University of America Press, 2006.

Courtine-Denamy, Sylvie. "Rejet identitaire et quête de 'spiritualité': Raïssa Maritain, Edith Stein, Simone Weil." In *L'Europe et les juifs,* edited by Esther Benbassa and Pierre Gisel, 141–66. Geneva: Labor et Fides, 2002.

———. *Three Women in Dark Times: Edith Stein, Hannah Arendt, Simone Weil.* Ithaca: Cornell University Press, 2001.

Crane, Richard. "A Heart-Rending Ambivalence: Jacques Maritain and the Complexity of Postwar Catholic Philosemitism." *Studies in Christian-Jewish Relations* 6, no. 1 (2011), http://ejournals.bc.edu/ojs/index.php /scjr/article/view/1820.

———. "Jacques Maritain, the Mystery of Israel, and the Holocaust." *Catholic Historical Review* 95 (January 2009): 25–56.

———. *The Passion of Israel: Jacques Maritain, Catholic Conscience, and the Holocaust.* Scranton: University of Scranton Press, 2010.

Daley, Brian. "The *Nouvelle Théologie* and the Patristic Revival: Sources, Symbols, and the Science of Theology." *International Journal of Systematic Theology* 7, no. 4 (October 2005).

Day, Dorothy. "There Is No Time with God." *Catholic Worker,* November 1953, 1, 7.

Delmarie, Danielle. "Antisémitisme des catholiques au vingtième: De la revendication au refus." In *Catholicism, Politics and Society in France,* edited by Kay Chadwick. Liverpool: Liverpool University Press, 2000.

Denis, Marcel. *La spiritualité victimale en France.* Rome: Centre Générale d'Études, 1981.

Devant la crise mondiale: Manifest de catholiques Européens séjournant en Amérique. New York: Éditions de la Maison Française, 1942.

Diébolt, Évelyne. "Les femmes catholiques: Entre église et société." In *Catholicism, Politics, and Society in Twentieth-Century France,* edited by Kay Chadwick, 219–43. Liverpool: Liverpool University Press, 2000.

Dietrich, Donald, ed. *Christian Responses to the Holocaust.* Syracuse: Syracuse University Press, 2003.

Doering, Bernard E. "The Jewish Question." In *Jacques Maritain and the French Catholic Intellectuals,* 126–67. Notre Dame: University of Notre Dame Press, 1983.

————. "Loneliness and the Existent: The Dark Nights of Raïssa Maritain and Pierre Reverdy." In *Jacques Maritain: The Man and His Metaphysics,* edited by John Knasas. Notre Dame, IN: American Maritain Association, 1988.

Dotoli, Giovanni. *Autobiographie de la douleur: Léon Bloy, écrivain et critique.* Paris: Klincksieck, 1998.

Dunn, Dennis. *The Catholic Church in Russia: Popes, Patriarchs, Tsars and Commissars.* Burlington, VT: Ashgate, 2004.

Durkheim, Emile. *Suicide: A Study in Sociology.* Translated by John Spaulding. New York: Free Press, 1961.

Eagleton, Terry. *Sweet Violence: The Idea of the Tragic.* Malden, MA: Blackwell, 2002.

Elliott, Dyan. "The Physiology of Rapture and Female Spirituality." In *Medieval Theology and the Natural Body,* edited by Peter Biller and A. J. Minnis. Woodbridge, Suffolk: York Medieval, 1997.

Emery, Elizabeth Nicole, and Laura Morowitz. *Consuming the Past: The Medieval Revival in fin-de-siècle France.* Burlington, VT: Ashgate, 2003.

Evans, David, and Kate Griffiths, eds. *Pleasure and Pain in Nineteenth-Century French Literature and Culture.* London: Whitford and Hughes, 2009.

Ezra, Elizabeth. *The Colonial Unconscious: Race and Culture in Interwar France.* Ithaca: Cornell University Press, 2000.

Fackenheim, Emil L. *To Mend the World: Foundations of Post-Holocaust Jewish Thought.* Bloomington: Indiana University Press, 1994.

Felski, Rita. *The Gender of Modernity.* Cambridge, MA: Harvard University Press, 1995.

Fiorenza, Francis Schüssler. "Neo-Scholasticism: Its Distinctive Characteristics." In *Systematic Theology: Roman Catholic Perspectives,* vol. 1, edited by Francis Schüssler Fiorenza and John Galvin. Minneapolis: Fortress Press, 1991.

Fitzer, Joseph, ed. *Romance and the Rock: Nineteenth-Century Catholics on Faith and Reason.* Minneapolis: Fortress Press, 1989.

Forché, Carolyn. *Against Forgetting: Twentieth-Century Poetry of Witness.* New York: Norton Press, 1993.

Ford, Caroline. *Divided Houses: Religion and Gender in Modern France.* Ithaca: Cornell University Press, 2005.

Foucault, Michel. "Truth, Power, Self: An Interview with Michel Foucault, October 25, 1982." In *Technologies of the Self: A Seminar with Michel Foucault,* edited by Luther H. Martin, Huck Gutman, and Patrick H. Hutton. Amherst: University of Massachusetts Press, 1988.

———. *The Uses of Pleasure.* Vol. 2 of *The History of Sexuality.* London: Penguin Books, 1991.

Foucault, Michel, and Paul Rabinow. *Ethics: Subjectivity and Truth.* Vol. 1 of *Essential Works of Foucault, 1954–1984.* London: Penguin Books, 2000.

Fouilloux, Étienne. *Les chrétiens français entre crise et libération, 1937–1947.* Paris: Seuil, 1997.

———. "Dialogue théologique? 1946–1948." In *Saint Thomas au XXe siècle,* edited by S.-T. Bonino, O.P., 153–95. Paris: Saint-Paul, 1995.

———. *Une église en quête de liberté: La pensée catholique française entre modernisme et Vatican II, 1914–1962.* Paris: Desclée de Brouwer, 1998.

Fourcade, Michel. "Jacques Maritain et l'Europe en exil." *Cahiers Jacques Maritain* 28 (June 1994): 5–38.

———. "Maritain face au réveil de l'antisémitisme (1933–1939)." *Cahiers Jacques Maritain* 41 (2001): 3–51.

Furey, Constance. "Body, Society, and Subjectivity in Religious Studies." *Journal of the American Academy of Religion* 80, no. 1 (2012): 7–33.

———. *Erasmus, Contarini, and the Religious Republic of Letters.* Cambridge: Cambridge University Press, 2006.

———. "'Intellects Inflamed in Christ': Women and Spiritualized Scholarship in Renaissance Christianity." *Journal of Religion* 84, no. 1 (January 2004): 1–22.

Gallagher, Donald Arthur, and Idella Gallagher. *The Achievement of Jacques and Raïssa Maritain: A Bibliography, 1906–1961.* Garden City, NY: Doubleday, 1962.

Garrigou-Lagrange, Réginald. *Le judaïsme avant Jésus-Christ.* Paris: Gabalda et fils, 1931.

Geroulanos, Stefanos. *An Atheism That Is Not Humanist Emerges in French Thought.* Stanford: Stanford University Press, 2010.

Gignoux, P., and A. Tafazzoli, eds. *Mémorial Jean de Menasce.* Louvain: Fondation culturelle iranienne, 1974.

Gilbert, Martin. *The Holocaust: A History of the Jews in Europe during the Second World War.* New York: Henry Holt, 2005.

Gilles, Rev. James. "Sursum Corda: What's Right with the World." *Catholic News,* May 24, 1943.

Giraud, Sylvain-Marie. *De l'esprit et de la vie de sacrifice dans l'état religieux.* Paris: Beauchesne, 1929.

————. *De l'union à Notre Seigneur Jésus dans sa vie de victime*. Paris: V. Sarlit, 1877.

————. *The Spirit of Sacrifice and the Life of Sacrifice in the Religious State*. Translated by Herbert Thurston. New York: Benziger, 1905.

Glotin, Édouard. "Réparation." In *Dictionnaire de spiritualité*, 13:369–413. Paris: Beauchesne et ses fils, 1932–95.

Glucklich, Ariel. *Sacred Pain: Hurting the Body for the Sake of the Soul*. New York: Oxford University Press, 2001.

Golan, Romy. *Modernity and Nostalgia: Art and Politics in France between the Wars*. New Haven: Yale University Press, 1995.

Gordon, Sarah. "Flannery O'Connor and the French Catholic Renaissance." In *Flannery O'Connor's Radical Reality*, edited by J. Gretland. Columbia: University of South Carolina Press, 2006.

Greene, Graham. "The Maritains." *New Statesman and Nation,* September 9, 1944.

Griffin, John Howard. *Jacques Maritain: Homage in Words and Pictures*. New York: Magi Books, 1974.

Griffiths, Richard. *The Reactionary Revolution: The Catholic Revival in French Literature*. London: Constable, 1966.

————. *The Use of Abuse: The Polemics of the Dreyfus Affair and Its Aftermath*. New York: Berg, 1991.

Grogin, R. C. *The Bergsonian Controversy in France, 1900–1914*. Calgary: University of Calgary Press, 1988.

Guéranger, Dom Prosper. *L'année liturgique*. Paris: H. Oudin, 1868.

Gugelot, Frédéric. *La conversion des intellectuels au catholicisme en France (1885–1935)*. Paris: CNRS, 1998.

————. "De Ratisbonne à Lustiger: Les convertis à l'époque contemporaine." *Les Belles Lettres: Archives Juives* 1, no. 35 (2002): 8–26.

————. "Le temps des convertis: Signe et trace de la modernité religieuse au début du XXe siècle." *Archives de Sciences Sociales des Religions* 47, no. 119 (2002): 45–64.

Hadot, Pierre, and Arnold Ira Davidson. *Philosophy as a Way of Life: Spiritual Exercises from Socrates to Foucault*. Translated by Michael Chase. Oxford: Blackwell, 1995.

Halévy, Daniel. *Charles Péguy and Les Cahiers de la Quinzaine*. Translated by Ruth Bethell. New York: Longmans, 1947.

Hammerschlag, Sarah. *The Figural Jew: Politics and Identity in French Postwar Thought*. Chicago: University of Chicago Press, 2010.

Hannah, Martha. *The Mobilization of Intellect: French Scholars and Writers during the Great War*. Cambridge, MA: Harvard University Press, 1996.

Hannah, Thomas, ed. *The Bergsonian Heritage*. New York: Columbia University Press, 1962.

Hanson, Ellis. *Decadence and Catholicism*. Cambridge, MA: Harvard University Press, 1997.

Harris, Ruth. *Dreyfus: Politics, Emotion, and the Scandal of the Century*. New York: Henry Holt, 2010.

———. "How the Dreyfus Affair Explains Sarkozy's Burqua Ban." *Foreign Policy*, May 12, 2010.

———. "Letters to Lucie: Spirituality, Friendship, and Politics during the Dreyfus Affair." *French Historical Studies* 28, no. 4 (Fall 2005): 601–27.

———. *Lourdes: Body and Spirit in the Secular Age*. New York: Viking, 1999.

Harshav, Benjamin. *Chagall and His Times: A Documentary Narrative*. Stanford: Stanford University Press, 2004.

Hellman, John. "Bernanos, Drumont, and the Rise of French Fascism." *Review of Politics* 52, no. 3 (Summer 1990): 441–59.

———. *Emmanuel Mounier and the New Catholic Left, 1930–1950*. Toronto: Toronto University Press, 1981.

———. "French Left-Catholics and Communism in the Nineteen-Thirties." *Church History* 45 (1976): 507–23.

———. "The Humanism of Jacques Maritain." In *Understanding Maritain: Philosopher and Friend*, edited by Deal W. Hudson and Matthew J. Mancini, 117–32. Macon, GA: Mercer University Press, 1987.

Hello, Ernest. *Le livre des visions et instructions de la bienheureuse Angèle de Foligno*. Paris: Poussielgue frères, 1868.

Heynickx, Rajesh, and Jan De Maeyer, eds. *The Maritain Factor: Taking Religion into Interwar Modernism*. Leuven: Leuven University Press, 2010.

Hill, Harvey. "Henri Bergson and Alfred Loisy: On Mysticism and the Religious Life." In *Modernists and Mystics*, edited by C. J. T. Talar, 104–36. Washington, DC: Catholic University of America Press, 2009.

Hirschkind, Charles. "The Ethics of Listening: Cassette-Sermon Audition in Contemporary Egypt." *American Ethnologist* 28, no. 3 (2001): 623–49.

Hofmann, Michael. Introduction to *Report from a Parisian Paradise: Essays from France, 1925–1939*, by Joseph Roth, translated by Michael Hofmann. New York: Norton, 2004.

Hollywood, Amy. "Acute Melancholia." *Harvard Theological Review* 99, no. 4 (2006): 381–406.

———. "Gender, Agency, and the Divine in Religious Historiography." *Journal of Religion* 84, no. 4 (October 2004): 514–24.

————. "Inside Out: Beatrice of Nazareth and Her Hagiographer." In *Gendered Voices: Medieval Saints and Their Interpreters,* edited by Catherine Mooney, 79–81. Philadelphia: University of Pennsylvania Press, 1999.

————. *Sensible Ecstasy: Mysticism, Sexual Difference, and the Demands of History.* Chicago: University of Chicago Press, 2002.

————. *The Soul as Virgin Wife: Mechthild of Magdeburg, Marguerite Porete, and Meister Eckhart.* Notre Dame: University of Notre Dame Press, 1995.

Holsinger, Bruce W. *The Premodern Condition: Medievalism and the Making of Theory.* Chicago: University of Chicago Press, 2005.

Hudson, Deal, ed. *Understanding Maritain, Philosopher and Friend.* Macon, GA: Mercer University Press, 1988.

Hufton, Olwin. "The Reconstruction of a Church." In *Beyond the Terror: Essays in French Regional and Social History, 1794–1814,* edited by G. Lewis. Cambridge: Cambridge University Press, 1983.

————. "Women in Revolution, 1789–1796." *Past and Present* 53 (1971): 90–108.

Hughes, H. Stuart. *Consciousness and Society: The Reorientation of European Social Thought, 1890–1930.* New York: Knopf, 1961.

Huysmans, Joris-Karl. *Là-haut or Notre-Dame de La Salette.* Edited by Michéle Barriére. Nancy: Presses Universitaires de Nancy, 1988.

————. *Trois églises et trois primitifs.* Paris: Plon-Nourri, 1908.

Hyman, Paula E. *The Jews of Modern France.* Berkeley: University of California Press, 1998.

Irwin, Alexander. *Saints of the Impossible: Bataille, Weil, and the Politics of the Sacred.* Minneapolis: University of Minnesota Press, 2002.

Iswolsky, Hélène. *Light before Dusk: A Russian Catholic in France, 1923–1941.* New York: Longmans, Green, 1942.

Jacobson, David J. "Jews for Genius: The Unholy Disorders of Maurice Sachs." *Yale French Studies* 85 (1994): 181–200.

Jonas, Raymond. *France and the Cult of the Sacred Heart.* Berkeley: University of California Press, 2000.

Journet, Charles, and Jacques Maritain. *Correspondance.* Vols. 2, 3, and 6. Edited by René Mougel. Fribourg: Éditions Universitaires, 1996–2008.

Judt, Tony. "From the House of the Dead: An Essay on European Memory." In *Postwar: A History of Europe since 1945,* 803–34. New York: Penguin Books, 2005.

————. "The Problem of Evil in Postwar Europe." *New York Review of Books,* February 14, 2008, 33–35.

Kalman, Julie. *Rethinking Anti-Semitism in Nineteenth-Century France.* Cambridge: Cambridge University Press, 2010.

Kane, Paula M. "'She Offered Herself Up': The Victim Soul and Victim Spirituality in Catholicism." *Church History* 71, no. 1 (2002): 80–119.

Kernan, Julie. *Our Friend Jacques Maritain: A Personal Memoir*. Garden City, NY: Doubleday, 1975.

Kerr, Donal. *Jean-Claude Colin, Marist: A Founder in an Era of Revolution and Restoration: The Early Years, 1790–1836*. Blackrock: Columba Press, 2000.

Kienzle, Beverly, and Nancy Nienhuis. "Battered Women and the Construction of Sanctity." *Journal of Feminist Studies in Religion* 17 (Spring 2001): 33–62.

Knasas, John, ed. *Jacques Maritain: The Man and His Metaphysics*. Notre Dame, IN: American Maritain Association, 1988.

Komonchak, Joseph A. "Modernity and the Construction of Roman Catholicism." *Cristianesimo nella Storia* 18 (1997): 353–85.

———. "Returning from Exile: Catholic Theology in the 1930s." In *The Twentieth Century: A Theological Overview*, edited by Gregory Baum, 35–48. Maryknoll, NY: Orbis Books, 1999.

———. "Theology and Culture at Mid-Century: The Example of Henri de Lubac." *Theological Studies* 51 (1990): 579–602.

Kott, Jan. "Raised and Written in Contradictions: The Final Interview." Interview by Allen J. Kuharski. *New Theater Quarterly* 18, no. 70 (May 2002): 103–20.

———. *Still Alive: An Autobiographical Essay*. Translated by Jadwiga Kosicka. New Haven: Yale University Press, 1994.

Kristeva, Julia. *Black Sun: Depression and Melancholia*. New York: Columbia University Press, 1989.

Kselman, Thomas. "The Bautain Circle and Catholic-Jewish Relations in Modern France." *Catholic Historical Review* 92, no. 3 (July 2006): 177–96.

———. "Challenging Dechristianization: The Historiography of Religion in Modern France." *Church History* 75 (2006): 130–39.

LaCapra, Dominic. *History and Reading: Tocqueville, Foucault, French Studies*. Toronto: University of Toronto Press, 2000.

Langlois, Claude. *Le catholicisme au féminin: Les congrégations françaises à supérieure générale au XIXe siècle*. Paris: Éditions du Cerf, 1994.

Laqueur, Walther. *The First News of the Holocaust*. New York: Leo Beck Institute, 1979.

La Rocca, Sandra. "Le Petit Roi d'Amour: Entre dévotion privée et politique." *Archives de Sciences Sociales des Religions* 113 (January–March 2001): 5–26.

Levinas, Emmanuel. "Fraterniser sans convertir." *Paix et Droit* 16, no. 8 (October 1936): 12.

———. "From Existence to Ethics." In *The Levinas Reader,* edited by Sean Hand. Oxford: Blackwell, 1989.

Levy, Richard, ed. *Antisemitism: An Encyclopedia History.* Santa Barbara, CA: ABC Clio, 2005.

Lifton, Robert Jay. "An Interview with Robert Jay Lifton." In *Trauma: Explorations in Memory,* edited by Cathy Caruth, 128–50. Baltimore: Johns Hopkins University Press, 1995.

Lesniak, Valerie A. "'Suffering the Divine': An Interpretation of the 'Journal' of Raïssa Maritain." PhD diss., Graduate Theological Union, 1992.

Livingston, James C., and Francis Schüssler Fiorenza. *Modern Christian Thought.* Vol. 2. Minneapolis: Fortress Press, 2001.

Loyer, Emmanuelle. *Paris à New York: Intellectuels et artistes français en exile, 1940–1947.* Paris: Grasset, 2005.

Lubac, Henri de. "Annexes." In *Lettres de M. Étienne Gilson adressées au P. Henri de Lubac et commentées par celui-ci,* edited by Henri de Lubac. Paris: Éditions du Cerf, 1986.

———. *Catholicism: Christ and the Common Destiny of Man.* Translated by Lancelot Sheppard and Elizabeth Englund, O.C.D. San Francisco: Ignatius Press, 1988. Originally published as *Catholicisme: Les aspects sociaux du dogme* (Paris, 1938).

———. *The Drama of Atheist Humanism.* Translated by Edith Riley. San Francisco: Ignatius Press, 1983.

———. *Le fondement théologique des missions.* Paris: Éditions de Seuil, 1946.

———. *Memoire sur l'occasion de mes écrits.* Namur: Culture et verité, 1989.

———. "A New Religious 'Front.'" In *Theology in History,* translated by Anne Englund Nash, 457–87. San Francisco: Ignatius Press, 1996.

———. *Résistance chrétienne à l'antisémitisme: Souvenirs, 1940–1944.* Paris: Fayard, 1988.

———. *Théologie dans l'histoire.* Paris: Desclée, 1990.

———. *Theology in History.* Translated by Anne Englund Nash. San Francisco: Ignatius Press, 1996.

Lubac, Henri de, Joseph Chaine, Louis Richard, and Joseph Bonsirven. *Israël et la foi chrétienne.* Fribourg: Éditions de la Librairie de l'Université, 1942.

Mahmood, Saba. *Politics of Piety: The Islamic Revival and the Feminist Subject.* Princeton: Princeton University Press, 2005.

Maître, Jacques. *Mystique et féminité: Essai de psychanalyse sociohistorique.* Paris: Éditions du Cerf, 1997.

Manguel, Alberto. *Black Water: The Book of Fantastic Literature.* New York: Three Rivers Press, 1984.

Manzoni, Giuseppe. "Victimale (spiritualité)." In *Dictionnaire de spiritualité,* 16:531–45. Paris: Beauchesne et ses fils, 1932–95.

Marget, Madeline. "Too Much Ado about Raïssa." *Commonweal* 117, no. 17 (October 12, 1991): 586–87.

Maritain, Jacques. *Art and Scholasticism.* Translated by J. F. Scanlan. New York: Scribner's, 1930.

———. *Art et scholastique.* Paris: L. Rouart, 1927.

———. "Avertissement." Introduction to *Journal de Raïssa,* by Raïssa Maritain. *OCJRM* 15:155–68.

———. *Carnet de notes. OCJRM* 12:126–312. Originally published by Desclée de Brouwer (Paris, 1965).

———. *Existence and the Existent: An Essay on Christian Existentialism.* Translated by Lewis Galantiére. New York: Pantheon, 1948.

———. *L'impossible antisémitisme.* In *L'impossible antisémitisme, précédé de Jacques Maritain et les juifs, par Pierre Vidal-Naquet.* Paris: Desclée de Brouwer, 2003.

———. *Le mystère d'Israël et autres essais.* Paris: Desclée de Brouwer, 1965.

———. *Notebooks.* Translated by Joseph Evans. Albany, NY: Magi Books, 1984.

———. "On Anti-Semitism." Originally published in *Christianity and Crisis* 1, no. 17 (1941): 2–5.

———. *Peasant of the Garonne: An Old Layman Questions Himself about the Present Time.* New York: Holt, Rinehart and Winston, 1968.

———. "Ten Months Later." *Commonweal* 32, no. 9 (June 21, 1940): 180–84.

Marshall, Cynthia. *The Shattering of the Self: Violence, Subjectivity, and Early Modern Texts.* Baltimore: Johns Hopkins University Press, 2002.

Martin, Rux. "Truth, Power, Self: An Interview with Michel Foucault, October 25, 1982." In *Technologies of the Self: A Seminar with Michel Foucault,* edited by Luther H. Martin, Huck Gutman, and Patrick H. Hutton, 9–15. Amherst: University of Massachusetts Press, 1988.

Massis, Henri. *Evocations.* Paris: Plon, 1931.

Massis, Henri, and Alfred de Tarde. *L'esprit de la nouvelle Sorbonne: La crise de la culture classique, la crise du français.* Paris: Mercure de France, 1911.

Mazzoni, Cristina. *Saint Hysteria: Neurosis, Mysticism, and Gender in European Culture.* Ithaca: Cornell University Press, 1996.

McGinn, Bernard. "God as Eros: Metaphysical Foundations of Christian Mysticism." In *New Perspectives on Historical Theology,* edited by Bradley Nassif. Grand Rapids, MI: Eerdmans, 1996.

McGreevy, John T. *Catholicism and American Freedom: A History.* New York: W. W. Norton, 2003.

McLeod, Hugh. "New Perspectives on the Religious History of Western and Northern Europe, 1850–1960." *Kyrkohistorisk årsskrift* 100, no. 1 (2000): 135–45.

McMahon, Darrin. *Enemies of the Enlightenment: The French Counter-Enlightenment and the Making of Modernity, 1778–1830.* Oxford: Oxford University Press, 2001.

Meer de Walcheren, Pieter van der. *Journal d'un converti.* Paris: Téqui, 1921.

———. *Rencontres: Léon Bloy, Raïssa Maritain, Christine et Pieterke.* Paris: Desclée de Brouwer, 1961.

Mehlman, Jeffrey. *Émigré New York: French Intellectuals in Wartime Manhattan, 1940–1944.* Baltimore: Johns Hopkins University Press, 2000.

———. *Legacies of Anti-Semitism in France.* Minneapolis: University of Minnesota Press, 1983.

Merton, Thomas. *Literary Essays of Thomas Merton.* Edited by Patrick Hart. New York: New Directions, 1984.

———. *The Seven Storey Mountain.* New York: Doubleday, 1989.

Mettepenningen, Jürgen. *Nouvelle Théologie—New Theology: Inheritor of Modernism, Precursor of Vatican II.* New York: T & T Clark, 2010.

Milosz, Czeslaw. *The Witness of Poetry.* Cambridge, MA: Harvard University Press, 1983.

Mitterand, Henri. "Jouir/souffrir: Le sensible et la fiction." In *Pleasure and Pain in Nineteenth-Century French Literature and Culture,* edited by David Evans and Kate Griffiths, 31–44. London: Whitford and Hughes, 2009.

Moi, Toril. *Simone de Beauvoir: The Making of an Intellectual Woman.* Oxford: Oxford University Press, 2008.

Montrevaud, Florence. "Raïssa Maritain." *Le XXe siècle des femmes.* Paris: Nathan, 1989.

Mooney, Catherine, ed. *Gendered Voices: Medieval Saints and Their Interpreters.* Philadelphia: University of Pennsylvania Press, 1999.

Mougel, René. "Les années de New York: 1940–1945." *Cahiers Jacques Maritain* 16–17 (April 1988): 7–28.

———. "À propos du mariage des Maritain: Leur voeu de 1912 et leurs témoignages." *Cahiers Jacques Maritain* 22 (June 1991): 5–44.

———. *Expérience philosophique, spiritualité et poésie chez Raïssa Maritain.* Naples: Institut Universitaire oriental de Naples / Casa Editrice, 1993.

———. "Les Maritain et La Salette." *Cahiers Jacques Maritain* 52 (June 2006): 53–76.

———. "Relire *Les grandes amitiés.*" *Cahiers Jacques Maritain* 48 (June 2004): 27–37.

Moyn, Samuel. "Antisemitism, Philosemitism, and the Rise of Holocaust Memory." *Patterns of Prejudice* 43, no. 1 (2009): 1–16.

Munro, Thomas, and Leo Balet. "Detailed Communications." *Journal of Aesthetics and Art Criticism* 1, no. 4 (Winter 1941–42): 73–81.

Nord, Philip. "Catholic Culture in Interwar France." *French Politics, Culture, and Society* 21, no. 33 (2003): 1–20.

———. *The Republican Moment: Struggles for Democracy in Nineteenth-Century France.* Cambridge, MA: Harvard University Press, 1998.

Oesterreicher, Johannes. *Racisme, antisémitisme et antichristianisme.* New York: Éditions de la Maison Française, 1943.

Orsi, Robert. *Between Heaven and Earth: The Religious Worlds People Make and the Scholars Who Study Them.* Princeton: Princeton University Press, 2005.

———. *Thank You, St. Jude: Women's Devotion to the Patron Saint of Hopeless Causes.* New Haven: Yale University Press, 1998.

———. "When 2 + 2 = 5." *American Scholar* 76, no. 2 (Spring 2007): 34–43.

Owen, Alex. *The Place of Enchantment: British Occultism and the Culture of Modernism.* Chicago: University of Chicago Press, 2004.

Paul, Harry W. *The Second Ralliement: The Rapprochment between Church and State in France in the Twentieth Century.* Washington, DC: Catholic University of America Press, 1967.

Péguy, Charles. *Notre jeunesse* [1910]. In *Oeuvres en prose, 1909–1914.* Paris: Gallimard, 1957.

———. Preface to *Cahiers de la Quinzaine,* March 1, 1904.

———. "Les suppliants parallèles" [1905]. In *Oeuvres en prose complètes,* vol. 2. Paris: Gallimard, 1988.

Pelletier, Denis. Review of *La conversion des intellectuels au catholicisme en France,* by Frédéric Gugelot. *Vingtième Siècle: Revue d'Histoire* 63 (July 1999): 167–69.

Phayer, Michael. *The Catholic Church and the Holocaust, 1930–1965.* Bloomington: Indiana University Press, 2000.

Pierrard, Pierre. *Juifs et catholiques français, d'Édouard Drumont à Jacob Kaplan, 1886–1994.* Paris: Cerf, 1997.

Pincikowski, Scott E. *Bodies in Pain: Suffering in the Works of Hartman von Aue.* New York: Routledge, 2002.

Pope, Barbara Corrado. "Immaculate and Powerful: The Marian Revival in the Nineteenth Century." In *Immaculate and Powerful: The Female in Sacred Image and Social Reality,* edited by Clarissa W. Atkinson, Constance H. Buchanan, and Margaret R. Miles. Boston: Aquarian Press, 1986.

Possenti, Nora. "Au foyer de Meudon." *Cahiers Jacques Maritain* 51 (December 2005): 11–31.

————. *Les trois Maritain: La présence de Véra dans le monde de Jacques et Raïssa Maritain.* Translated by René Mougel. Paris: Parole et Silence, 2006.

Poulain, Auguste. *Des grâces d'oraison: Traité de théologie mystique.* Paris: V. Retaux, 1901.

Poulat, Emilie. *L'église, c'est un monde.* Paris: Cerf, 1986.

————. "La *laïcité* en France au vingtième siècle." In *Catholicism, Politics, and Society in Twentieth-Century France,* edited by Kay Chadwick, 18–25. Liverpool: Liverpool University Press, 2000.

Pozzi, Catherine, Raïssa Maritain, Jacques Maritain, Hélène Kiener, and Audrey Deacon. *L'élégance et le chaos: Correspondance de Catherine Pozzi avec Raïssa et Jacques Maritain, Hélène Kiener et Audrey Deacon.* Edited by Nicolas Cavaillès. Paris: Editions Non Lieu, 2011.

Prajs, Lazare. *Péguy et Israël.* Paris: Nizet, 1970.

Raczymow, Henri. *Maurice Sachs ou Les travaux forcés de la frivolité.* Paris: Gallimard, 1988.

Raeff, Marc. *Russia Abroad: A Cultural History of the Russian Immigration, 1919–1939.* New York: Oxford University Press, 1990.

Rayez, André. "France: 19e siècle." In *Dictionnaire de spiritualité,* 5:970–94. Paris: Beauchesne et ses fils, 1932–95.

Rémond, René. *La droite en France de 1815 à nos jours: Continuité et diversité d'une tradition politique.* Paris: Aubier, 1954.

Le repentir: Déclaration de l'Église de France. Paris: Desclée de Brouwer, 1997.

"A 'Revival' in France." *Nation,* October 3, 1872, 215–16.

Riley, Denise. *The Words of Selves: Identification, Solidarity, Irony.* Stanford: Stanford University Press, 2000.

Robert, Mary Louise. *Civilization without Sexes: Reconstructing Gender in Postwar France.* Chicago: University of Chicago Press, 1994.

Roberts, Tyler. "Between the Lines: Exceeding Historicism in the Study of Religion." *Journal of the American Academy of Religion* 74, no. 3 (September 2006): 697–719.

Rodwell, Rosemary. "Mysticism and Sexuality in the Writings of Léon Bloy." *Journal of European Studies* 24 (1994): 23–40.

Roth, Joseph. "The Leviathan." In *The German-Jewish Dialogue: An Anthology of Literary Texts, 1794–1993,* edited by Richie Robertson, 264–93. Oxford: Oxford University Press, 1999.

————. *Report from a Parisian Paradise: Essays from France, 1925–1939.* Translated by Michael Hofmann. New York: Norton, 2004.

Royal, Robert. *Jacques Maritain and the Jews.* Notre Dame: University of Notre Dame Press, 1994.

Ryan, Thomas, S.M. "Revisiting Affective Knowing and Connaturality in Aquinas." *Theological Studies* 66, no. 1 (March 2005): 49–68.

Sachs, Maurice. *Decade of Illusion, Paris, 1918–1928*. Translated by Gwladys Sachs. New York: Alfred A. Knopf, 1933.

———. *Witches' Sabbath*. Translated by Richard Howard. New York: Stein and Day, 1964.

Sachs, Maurice, Jacques Maritain, and Raïssa Maritain. *Correspondance: Maurice Sachs, Jacques et Raïssa Maritain, 1925–1939*. Edited by Maurice Sachs. Paris: Éditions Gallimard, 2004.

Saler, Michael. "Modernity and Enchantment: A Historiographic Review." *American Historical Review* 111, no. 3 (September 2006): 692–716.

Sánchez, José M. *The Spanish Civil War as a Religious Tragedy*. Notre Dame: University of Notre Dame Press, 1987.

Sanders, Mathijs. "Maritain in the Netherlands: Pieter van der Meer de Walcheren and the Cult of Youth." In *The Maritain Factor: Taking Religion into Interwar Modernism*, edited by Rajesh Heynickx and Jan De Maeyer, 84–99. Leuven: Leuven University Press, 2010.

Santon, Susan. *Great Women of Faith*. Mahweh, NJ: Paulist Press, 2003.

Scarry, Elaine. *The Body in Pain: The Making and Unmaking of the World*. New York: Oxford University Press, 1985.

Schloesser, Stephen. "From 'Spiritual Naturalism' to 'Psychical Naturalism': Catholic Decadence, Lutheran Munch, *Madone Mysterique*." In *Edvard Munch: Psyche, Symbol, and Expression*, edited by Jeffrey Howe, 75–110. Boston: Boston College, McMullen Museum of Art, 2001.

———. *Jazz Age Catholicism: Mystic Modernity in Postwar Paris, 1919–1933*. Toronto: University of Toronto Press, 2005.

———. "Maritain on Music: His Debt to Cocteau." In *Beauty, Art, and the Polis*, edited by Alice Ramos. Washington, DC: Catholic University Press, 2000.

———. "Mounier and Maritain: A French Catholic Understanding of the Modern World." *Theological Studies* 65 (2004): 676–77.

———. "No Pain, No Gain." *Commonweal* 131, no. 16 (September 24, 2004): 24–27.

———. "'Not Behind but Within': *Sacramentum et Res*." *Renascence: Essays on Values in Literature* 58, no. 1 (Fall 2005): 17–39.

———. "'What of That Curious Craving?' Catholicism, Conversion, and Inversion *au Temps du Boeuf sur le Toit*." *Historical Reflections / Réflexions Historiques* 30, no. 2 (2004): 221–53.

Schneider, Judith Morganroth. "Max Jacob juif." *French Review* 63, no. 1 (October 1989): 78–87.

Schoof, Mark T. *A Survey of Catholic Theology, 1800–1970*. Translated by N. D. Smith. Paramus, NJ: Paulist Press, 1970.

Schor, Ralph. *L'antisémitisme en France pendant les années trente*. Bruxelles: Éditions Complexe, 1992.

Scott, Joan Wallach. *The Fantasies of Feminist History*. Durham: Duke University Press, 2011.

Sebban, Joël. "Être juif et chrétien: La question juive et les intellectuels catholiques français issus du judaïsme (1898–1940)." *Archives Juives* 44, no. 1 (2011): 102–22.

"Sensitive Plants." Review of *Les grandes amitiés*, by Raïssa Maritain. *Church Times*, February 1, 1946.

Serry, Harvé. "Les écrivains catholiques dans les années 20." *Actes de Recherche en Sciences Sociales* 124 (September 1998): 80–87.

Shook, Lawrence. *Étienne Gilson*. Toronto: Pontifical Institute of Medieval Studies, 1984.

Silver, Kenneth. *Esprit de Corps: The Art of the Parisian Avant-Garde and the First World War, 1914–1925*. Princeton: Princeton University Press, 1989.

Smith, Bonnie. *The Gender of History: Men, Women, and Historical Practice*. Cambridge, MA: Harvard University Press, 1998.

Smith, Brooke Williams. *Jacques Maritain: Antimodern or Ultramodern? A Historical Analysis of His Critics, His Thought, and His Life*. New York: Oxford University Press, 1976.

Soucy, Robert. *French Fascism: The First Wave, 1924–33*. New Haven: Yale University Press, 1986.

———. *French Fascism: The Second Wave, 1933–1939*. New Haven: Yale University Press, 1995.

Sterhnhell, Zeev. *Neither Right nor Left: Fascist Ideology in France*. Translated by David Maisel. Princeton: Princeton University Press, 1986.

Stock, Phyllis. "Students versus the University in Pre–World War Paris." *French Historical Studies* 7, no. 1 (1971): 93–101.

Strenski, Ivan. *Contesting Sacrifice: Religion, Nationalism, and Social Thought in France*. Chicago: University of Chicago Press, 2002.

Surkis, Judith. *Sexing the Citizen: Morality and Masculinity in France, 1870–1920*. Ithaca: Cornell University Press, 2006.

Suther, Judith D. *Raïssa Maritain: Pilgrim, Poet, Exile*. New York: Fordham University Press, 1990.

Sweets, John F. "Hold That Pendulum! Redefining Fascism, Collaborationism, and Resistance in France." *French Historical Studies* 15 (1988): 731–58.

Talar, C. J. T., ed. *Modernists and Mystics.* Washington, DC: Catholic University of America Press, 2009.

Taylor, Charles. *Modern Social Imaginaries.* Durham, NC: Duke University Press, 2004.

———. *A Secular Age.* Cambridge, MA: Harvard University Press, 2007.

Thompson, William M. Introduction to *Bérulle and the French School: Selected Writings,* edited by William M. Thompson, translated by Lowell M. Glendon, 32–76. Mahweh, NJ: Paulist Press, 1989.

Torres, Tereska. *Le choix.* Paris: Desclée de Brouwer, 2002.

———. *The Converts.* New York: Knopf, 1970.

Toupin-Guyot, Claire. *Les intellectuels catholiques dans la société française.* Rennes: Presses Universitaires de Rennes, 2002.

Turin, Yvonne. *Femmes et religieuses au XIXe siècle: Le féminisme "en religion."* Paris: Nouvelle Cité, 1989.

Valman, Nadia. "Bad Jew/Good Jewess." In *Philosemitism in History,* edited by Jonathan Karp, 149–69. Cambridge: Cambridge University Press, 2011.

Vidal-Naquet, Pierre. "Jacques Maritain et les juifs: Réflections sur un parcours." In *L'impossible antisémitisme* [by Jacques Maritain]*, précédé de Jacques Maritain et les juifs, par Pierre Vidal-Naquet.* Paris: Desclée de Brouwer, 2003.

Viswanathan, Guari. *Outside the Fold: Conversion, Modernity, and Belief.* Princeton: Princeton University Press, 1998.

Von Arx, Jeffrey, ed. *Varieties of Ultramontanism.* Washington, DC: Catholic University of America Press, 1998.

Wahl, Jean. "Concerning Bergson's Relation to the Catholic Church." *Review of Religion* 9, no. 1 (November 1944): 45–50.

Weber, Eugene. *The Hollow Years.* New York: W. W. Norton, 1994.

Weil, Simone. "L'amour de Dieu et le malheur." In *Simone Weil: Oeuvres complètes.* Paris: Gallimard, 1989–2006.

———. *Gravity and Grace.* Translated by Arthur Will. New York: Putnum, 1952.

———. "The Love of God and Affliction." In *Waiting for God,* translated by Emma Craufurd, 67–82. London: Fount, 1977.

Weingrad, Michael. "Jews (in Theory): Representations of Judaism, Anti-Semitism, and the Holocaust in Postmodern French Thought." *Judaism* 45 (Winter 1996): 79–98.

———. "Juifs imaginaires." *Prooftexts: A Journal of Jewish Literary History* 21, no. 2 (Spring 2001): 255–76.

———. "Parisian Messianism: Catholicism, Decadence, and the Transgressions of Georges Bataille." *History and Memory* 13, no. 2 (Fall/Winter 2001): 113–33.

Welch, Edward. *François Mauriac: The Making of an Intellectual.* New York: Editions Rodopi, 2006.

Williams, Rowan. *Grace and Necessity: Reflections on Art and Love.* London: Continuum, 2005.

Winter, Jay. *Sites of Memory, Sites of Mourning: The Great War in European Cultural History.* Cambridge: Cambridge University Press, 1995.

Wiser, William. *The Crazy Years: Paris in the Twenties.* New York, 1983.

Wright, Gordon. *France in Modern Times: From the Enlightenment to the Present.* New York: Norton, 1995.

Ypersele, Laurence van, and Anne-Dolorès Marcélis. *Rêves de chrétienté, réalités du monde: Imaginaires catholique.* Louvain: Actes du Colloque, 1999.

Zimdars-Swartz, Sandra L. *Encountering Mary: From La Salette to Medjugorje.* Princeton: Princeton University Press, 1991.

Zolberg, Aristide R. "The École Libre at the New School, 1941–1946." *Social Research* 65 (Winter 1998): 921–51.

Zuccotti, Susan. *Under His Very Windows: The Vatican and the Holocaust in Italy.* New Haven: Yale University Press, 2005.

INDEX

In this index the following abbreviations are used: JM for Jacques Maritain, RM for Raïssa Maritain, and VO for Véra Oumançoff.

BRENNA MOORE

is assistant professor of theology at Fordham University.